Was Mao Really a Monster?

Mao: The Unknown Story by Jung Chang and Jon Halliday was published in 2005 to a great fanfare. The book portrays Mao as a monster – equal to or worse than Hitler and Stalin – and a fool who won power by native cunning and ruled by terror. It received a rapturous welcome from reviewers in the popular press and rocketed to the top of the worldwide bestseller list. Few works on China by writers in the West have achieved its impact.

Reviews by serious China scholars, however, tended to take a different view. Most were sharply critical, questioning its authority and the authors' methods, arguing that Chang and Halliday's book is not a work of balanced scholarship, as it purports to be, but a highly selective and even polemical study that sets out to demonise Mao.

This book brings together 14 reviews of *Mao: The Unknown Story* – all by internationally well-regarded specialists in modern Chinese history, and mostly published in relatively specialised scholarly journals. Taken together they demonstrate that Chang and Halliday's portrayal of Mao is in many places woefully inaccurate. While agreeing that Mao had many faults and was responsible for some disastrous policies, they conclude that a more balanced picture is needed.

Gregor Benton is Professor of Chinese History at Cardiff University. His book *Mountain Fires: The Red Army's Three-Year War in South China, 1934–1938* won several awards, including the Association of Asian Studies' best book on modern China. Recent work includes *Chinese Migrants and Internationalism: Forgotten Histories, 1917–1945* and *Mao Zedong and the Chinese Revolution* (also published by Routledge).

Lin Chun is Senior Lecturer in Comparative Politics at the London School of Economics. She is the author of a number of books, of which the most recent is *The Transformation of Chinese Socialism*.

Was Mao Really a Monster?

The academic response to Chang and
Halliday's *Mao: The Unknown Story*

Edited by Gregor Benton and Lin Chun

Routledge
Taylor & Francis Group

LONDON AND NEW YORK

First published 2010
by Routledge
2 Park Square, Milton Park, Abingdon, Oxon, OX14 4RN

Simultaneously published in the USA and Canada
by Routledge
270 Madison Avenue, New York, NY 10016

Routledge is an imprint of the Taylor & Francis Group, an informa business

© 2010 Gregor Benton and Lin Chun for selection and editorial matter;
individual contributors their contribution

Typeset in Times New Roman by Pindar NZ, Auckland, New Zealand

British Library Cataloguing in Publication Data
A catalogue record for this book is available from the British Library

Library of Congress Cataloging-in-Publication Data
Was Mao really a monster?: the academic response to Chang and
Halliday's Mao, the unknown story / edited by Gregor Benton and Lin Chun.
   p. cm.
"Simultaneously published in the USA and Canada" — T.p. verso.
Includes bibliographical references and index.
   1. Chang, Jung, 1952- Mao. 2. Mao, Zedong, 1893–1976. 3. Heads of
state—China—Biography. I. Benton, Gregor. II. Lin, Chun, 1952-
   DS778.M3C3839 2009
   951.05092—dc22   2008055407

ISBN 10: 0-415-49329-3 (hbk)
ISBN 10: 0-415-49330-7 (pbk)

ISBN 13: 978-0-415-49329-1 (hbk)
ISBN 13: 978-0-415-49330-7 (pbk)

Contents

Acknowledgements   vii

Introduction   1
GREGOR BENTON AND LIN CHUN

PART I
Reviews in non-specialist academic publications   13

 1 Dark tales of Mao the Merciless   15
    DELIA DAVIN

 2 Jade and plastic   21
    ANDREW J. NATHAN

 3 Portrait of a monster   30
    JONATHAN D. SPENCE

PART II
Reviews in *The China Journal*   41

 4 The portrayal of opportunism, betrayal and
    manipulation in Mao's rise to power   43
    GREGOR BENTON AND STEVE TSANG

 5 The new number one counter-revolutionary inside the
    party: academic biography as mass criticism   55
    TIMOTHY CHEEK

 6 Pitfalls of charisma   64
    LOWELL DITTMER

7 'I'm So Ronree'   73
   GEREMIE R. BARMÉ

PART III
Reviews in other specialist academic journals   85

8 Mao and *The Da Vinci Code*: conspiracy, narrative
   and history   87
   DAVID S. G. GOODMAN

9 Mao: a super monster?   99
   ALFRED CHAN

PART IV
Chinese reviews   109

10 Jung Chang and Jon Halliday, *Mao: The Unknown
    Story*: a review   111
    CHEN YUNG-FA

11 *Mao: The Unknown Story*: an intellectual scandal   119
    MOBO GAO

12 A critique of Jung Chang and Jon Halliday, *Mao:
    The Unknown Story*   135
    JIN XIAODING

PART V
Other reviews   163

13 Mao lives   165
    ARTHUR WALDRON

14 From *Wild Swans* to *Mao: The Unknown Story*   176
    BILL WILLMOTT

    Notes   187
    Index   197

Acknowledgements

The Publishers and the Editors would like to thank the following for permission to reprint their material:

Delia Davin for kind permission to reprint her 'Dark Tales of Mao the Merciless', first published in *The Times Higher Educational Supplement*, 12 August 2005, p. 22.

London Review of Books and Andrew J. Nathan for permission to reprint Andrew J. Nathan, 'Jade and Plastic', originally published in *London Review of Books*, vol. 27, no. 22 (17 November 2005) pp. 10–13. This article first appeared in the *London Review of Books*. www.lrb.co.uk

The New York Review of Books and Jonathan Spence for kind permission to reprint Jonathan Spence, 'Portrait of a Monster', NYRB, vol. 52, no. 17, 3 November 2005.

The China Journal and the authors for permission to reprint 'The Portrayal of Opportunism, Betrayal, and Manipulation in Mao's Rise to Power' by Gregor Benton and Steve Tsang, *The China Journal*, vol. 55, January 2006, pp. 95–106.

The China Journal and Timothy Cheek for kind permission to reprint Timothy Cheek, 'The New Number One Counter-Revolutionary inside the Party: Academic Biography as Mass Criticism', *The China Journal*, vol. 55, January 2006, pp. 109–18.

The China Journal and Lowell Dittmer for kind permission to reprint Lowell Dittmer, 'Pitfalls of Charisma', *The China Journal*, vol. 55, January 2006, pp. 119–28.

The China Journal and Geremie R. Barmé for kind permission to reprint Geremie R. Barmé, 'I'm So Ronree', *The China Journal*, vol. 55, January 2006, pp. 128–39.

David Goodman for kind permission to reprint David Goodman, 'Mao and *The Da Vinci Code*: Conspiracy, Narrative and History', *The Pacific Review*, vol. 19, no. 3, September 2006, pp. 359–84.

Pacific Affairs and Alfred Chan for kind permission to reprint 'Mao: A Super Monster?' originally published in *Pacific Affairs*, vol. 79, no. 1, 2006, pp. 91–103.

Twentieth-Century China and Chen Yung-fa for kind permission to reprint 'Jung Chang and Jon Halliday, *Mao: The Unknown Story*, A Review', translated by Wenjuan Bi with Christopher A. Reed, published by *Twentieth-Century China*, vol. 33, no. 1 (November 2007) pp. 104–13. With thanks also to the translators Christopher A. Reed and Wenjuan Bi for their permission. This review first appeared in Chinese in the *Bulletin of the Institute of Modern History*, no. 2 (2006), pp. 211–19.

Pluto Press for permission to reprint Mobo Gao, '*Mao: The Unknown Story*: An Intellectual Scandal', originally published in *The Battle for China's Past: Mao and the Cultural Revolution* by Mobo Gao, London: Pluto Press, 2008.

Commentary Magazine and Arthur Waldron for kind permission to reprint Arthur Waldron, 'Mao Lives', first published in *Commentary Magazine*, October 2005, pp. 31–8. 'Reprinted from *Commentary*, October 2005, by permission; copyright © 2005 by Commentary, Inc.' (http://www.commentarymagazine.com/searcharchive. cfm?authorKeywords=Arthur%252520%252520Waldron)

Bill Wilmott for kind permission to reprint Bill Willmott, 'From *Wild Swans* to *Mao: The Unknown Story*'. Originally published online: http://www.nzchinasociety.org. nz/news.html

Disclaimer

The publishers have made every effort to contact authors/copyright holders of works reprinted in *Was Mao Really a Monster? The Academic Response to Chang and Halliday's 'Mao: The Unknown Story'*. This has not been possible in every case, however, and we would welcome correspondence from those individuals/ companies whom we have been unable to trace.

Introduction

Gregor Benton and Lin Chun

In 2005, the British publisher Jonathan Cape launched Jung Chang and Jon Halliday's *Mao: The Unknown Story*, to great fanfare. The book pictures Mao as a liar, ignoramus, fool, philistine, vandal, lecher, glutton, hedonist, drug-peddler, ghoul, bully, thug, coward, posturer, manipulator, psychopath, sadist, torturer, despot, megalomaniac and the greatest mass murderer of the twentieth century – in short, a monster, equal to or worse than Hitler and Stalin. He cared nothing about the fate of the Chinese people and his fellow human beings, or even his close friends and relatives. He was driven by bloodlust and the craving for power and sex. He ruled by terror, led by native cunning, and defeated Chiang Kai-shek by leaning towards Stalin and treacherously insinuating moles and sleepers into the Guomindang.

The book rocketed to the top of the best-seller list in the UK and elsewhere and was hailed as a bombshell, triumph and irrefutable authority. Its success was due in part to the popularity of *Wild Swans* (1991), a family biography of Chang herself, her mother, and her grandmother, which sold 12 million copies and made her an international celebrity; but also due to the rapturous welcome press reviewers gave the expertly marketed *Mao*. The media ferment was in turn part of the larger political context of selective China-bashing in the long aftermath of the Cold War, with Mao still haunting the intellectual debates beyond China's borders about the legitimacy of its post-Mao order. Non-specialist commentators marvelled at the 'authenticity' of the book's scholarship and its 139 pages of references. In *The Guardian*, Lisa Allardice predicted that it would 'shake the world'.[1] In *The New York Times Book Review*, Nicholas Kristof wrote: 'Based on a decade of meticulous interviews and archival research, this magnificent biography methodically demolishes every pillar of Mao's claim to sympathy or legitimacy.'[2] In *The Sunday Times*, Simon Sebag Montefiore called the book 'a triumph ... a barrage of revisionist bombshells, and a superb piece of research' and concluded that 'Mao is the greatest monster of them all – the Red Emperor of China'.[3] For Donald Morrison in *Time* magazine, the book had the power of an 'atom bomb'.[4] In *The New York Times*, Michiko Kakutani wrote that it makes 'an impassioned case for Mao as the most monstrous tyrant of all times'.[5] Media commentators, establishment politicians and representatives of the publishers lined up to say the book would completely change the way in which people think of Mao, and indeed change history. George Walden went so far as to call it 'the most powerful, compelling, and revealing political biography of modern times'. 'Few books are destined to change history', he concluded, 'but this one will'.[6] Some, including Chang herself, voiced the hope it would change even China.

A Chinese translation was issued by Kaifang Publishers in Hong Kong in September 2006, after tortuous negotiations. In Taiwan, the Yuanliu Publishing Company cancelled the contract for another translation because of unrelenting protests by the family and former subordinates of the Nationalist general Hu Zongnan (described in the book as a communist mole) and experts' objections to some of its assertions.[7] In mainland China, the book remains banned – which is ironic given that the authors' general line could be said to support the current official position of abandoning Mao and his revolutions.

Few works on the Chinese Revolution by writers based in the West have ever achieved anything like the impact of *Mao: The Unknown Story*. Its sole competitor in sales terms is Edgar Snow's *Red Star over China*, which was reprinted five times within a month of its publication in London in 1937 (by Gollancz) and led to China taking over from the Spanish Civil War as the international focus of European and American antifascism. Keen (like Chang) to change opinion about the Chinese communists not just in the West but in China, Snow relinquished his copyright on the book and encouraged its translation into Chinese and its underground publication in China, where it also went through many reprints and helped persuade hundreds of patriots to join Mao in Yan'an.[8] But here the likeness ends. The politics and content of the two books contrast starkly. Whereas Snow's helped create Mao's image, in China and the world, Chang and Halliday's seeks to destroy it, from the minutest details of his character and personal life to his grandest schemes, including the very idea of a revolution.

Another difference is in the books' reception. *Red Star Over China* set Snow at odds with political establishments both in the West (where he was blackballed and blacklisted) and in China, while Chang and Halliday's endeared them to mainstream media and the powers that be everywhere except in China (at least for now). The Chinese authorities banned *Mao* not because it comprehensively contradicts the official position but because that position is itself ideologically and politically ambivalent. A comprehensive repudiation of Mao is difficult, because of important historical continuities between his regime and theirs as well as widespread social discontent with some of the post-Mao changes. The party's Propaganda Department knows demonizing Mao would be unpopular and could backfire, given that the legacies of the revolution are still a source of regime legitimacy. Mao is inseparable from China's national and social progress, with which most Chinese identify, and with China's delivery from semicolonialism and backwardness. This is why even many Chinese highly critical of Mao as an individual despise the book.

In the West, the same considerations do not apply. Admirers of the book on the right included George W. Bush Jr, who 'thrilled' Chang by recommending it as 'a good book' that showed Mao to be 'a bad man'. On the centre-left, Labour's Roy Hattersley and *The Guardian*'s Will Hutton also wrote praising it. In China, the picture is more complicated. An indirect rebuff by Pang Xianzhi, Director of the Party Documents Research Office, appeared in the official media.[9] Although the book is not available to the general public, many Chinese have criticized it on unofficial websites. Some welcomed it. On the right, Xu Youyu, an influential thinker in the Chinese Academy of Social Sciences, saw the book as 'the truest of all the Mao biographies ever written' and 'a huge, historic contribution'.[10] On the left, however, Huang Jisu, a well-known commentator and playwright, called it 'a trash heap of old news and senseless rumours ... lacking minimal maturity in its presentation, understanding and perspective'.[11] Chinese students abroad also denounced it.[12]

Because the book has sold so many copies, was so widely and favourably reviewed in the commercial press, and has such ambitious political goals, we thought it would be a good idea to bring out a collection of commentary on it by experts and thus give its many readers the chance to view its subject from other angles. The collection is also intended as a resource for use in classroom discussions. Chang and Halliday's findings and conclusions have begun to figure increasingly in essays by students on China courses, impressed by its apparent solidity and authority. Some teachers and scholars who distrust the authors' methods and approach see this development as a disaster for modern China studies. To them, we offer this work as an antidote.

Most writing about Mao is of three general sorts: standard academic studies of his life and career, personal memoirs (published mainly in China), and political screeds – either demonographies (usually by Chinese exiles) or hagiographies (also published mainly in China). Chang and Halliday's book has characteristics of all three genres. Its chief author, Chang, drew some of her material from her own interpretation of events she lived through. She makes no secret of her loathing for Mao – she incessantly demonizes him. Yet the book has the trappings of massive scholarship, citing more than a thousand sources and interviews with hundreds of people ranging from George Bush Sr to the Dalai Lama, Wang Guangmei (Liu Shaoqi's widow), and various non-Chinese ex-Maoists. The authors are, of course, entitled to their opinion and memory. Where critics can legitimately take issue with them is in their methods and judgement.[13]

It would be interesting to know how people interviewed in China react to the words Chang and Halliday attribute to them. Would they approve of the book's message? In many cases, probably not. Wang Guangmei, for example, herself a victim of the Cultural Revolution, showed respect for Mao before she died in 2006. In 2004, with the help of Mao's and her own children and grandchildren, she organized a gathering at which the two families celebrated their shared feelings about Mao and Liu and the extraordinary experiences of China's first communist generation.[14] It is hard to imagine she would have agreed with Chang and Halliday's portrayal of Mao.

Nearly all the essays in this volume are by internationally known scholars in the China field, most of them specialists in Chinese communist history. Geremie R. Barmé, Professor at the Australian National University, works on Chinese culture and intellectual history and published a book on Mao's posthumous cult. Gregor Benton, Professor of Chinese History at Cardiff University, has published books on Chinese communist history, Chinese Trotskyism, Chinese dissent, and Mao.

Alfred Chan, Associate Professor of Political Science at the University of Western Ontario, has published studies on Mao and the Great Leap Forward. Timothy Cheek, Research Professor at the University of British Columbia, has published books on China's intellectuals and Chinese Communist Party (CCP) history, including documentary studies on Mao. Chen Yung-fa, Distinguished Research Professor in the Institute of Modern History at Taiwan's Academia Sinica, is the author of major studies on Chinese communism. Delia Davin, Emeritus Professor of Chinese Studies at the University of Leeds, has written a pioneering study on women in the Chinese Revolution and books on migration and on Mao. Lowell Dittmer, Professor of Political Science at the University of California at Berkeley, has published studies on Chinese politics, including a book on Liu Shaoqi. Mobo Gao, Professor of Chinese Studies at the University of Adelaide, is best known for his books on rural life and on the Cultural Revolution. David S. G. Goodman, Professor of Chinese Politics and Director of the Institute of Social Sciences, University of Sydney, is the author of books on Deng Xiaoping and on provincial politics and local social and political change in China. Lin Chun, Senior Lecturer in Comparative Politics at the London School of Economics, has published books and articles on Chinese socialism and development. Andrew J. Nathan, a Professor at Columbia University, publishes in the fields of Chinese politics and foreign policy, the comparative study of political participation and political culture, and human rights. He co-edited *The Tiananmen Papers* and is the author, with Bruce Gilley, of *China's New Rulers*. Jonathan Spence, Sterling Professor of History at Yale University and former President of the American Historical Association, is an authority on Chinese civilization and the rise of modern China. Steve Tsang, Reader in Politics at Oxford University, is a widely published author and expert on China's foreign and security policy and its governance. Arthur Waldron, Professor of International Relations in the Department of History at the University of Pennsylvania and vice president of the International Assessment and Strategy Center in Washington DC, co-edited the Civil War volumes of *Mao's Road to Power* together with Stuart Schram.

Only Jin Xiaoding and Bill Willmott, Emeritus Professor in Sociology at the University of Canterbury, New Zealand, are not directly engaged in academic study on the Chinese Revolution, but both are deeply familiar with the issues Chang and Halliday raise and well qualified to comment. Jin is a freelance journalist. Willmott, born in Sichuan, is an expert on the Chinese communities in the Pacific Islands and a long-standing observer of Chinese politics.

Most of the essays are largely critical. The two exceptions are those by Dittmer and Waldron. Dittmer finds the 'cumulative picture' of Chang and Halliday's chapters on the People's Republic of China (PRC) before the Cultural Revolution convincing and even devastating. However, he criticizes their 'incessant imputation of evil motives' and their 'vacuum-cleaner' approach to every titbit conceivably damaging to Mao's reputation. Apart from these two, the rest are generally quite damning. One condemns its 'histrionic tone and unwavering certainty'.[15] Another calls it a Maoist-style denunciation 'done in the florid style of the Cultural Revolution denunciations ... a Chinese version of a TV soap opera'.[16]

It must be said that Chang and Halliday reciprocate the disesteem. A barely suppressed theme of the biography is that established Mao scholarship is incompetent and uncritical. 'Bits of the information were around', said Chang, 'but they were like pieces of a jigsaw that didn't make any sense. Nobody has put them together into this coherent picture of Mao. People looked but they didn't see'.[17] David Goodman, writing in this volume, classes *Mao* with good reason among a clutch of recent 'revisionist' China books that imply 'a conspiracy of academics and scholars who have chosen not to reveal the truth'. He likens this view to the conspiracy theory in the *Da Vinci Code* (adding that the 'facts' in the thriller are about as reliable as Chang and Halliday's). The implication that China scholars have failed to maintain a strict critical distance from Mao and his regime is regrettable, not least in the case of contributors to this volume. Far from acting as Mao's apologists, they have criticized his views and actions, often savagely, and consistently defended his victims. Some were even prevented for a while from doing research in China as a result of their criticisms – at a time when Halliday was among those praising Mao.

Jeffrey Wasserstrom (Director of East Asian Studies at Indiana University) also found that the book crossed the divide between biography and fiction and compared it to Elizabeth Kostova's novel about Vlad the Impaler. Like a thriller, it presents Mao 'in a sensationalist manner', moves at a brisk pace, and reads as if written by an omniscient narrator with direct access to his or her character's innermost thoughts and feelings. But Wasserstrom thinks Chang and Halliday's *Mao* lacks the complexity and multidimensionality of Kostova's Dracula, whose motivations appear more plausible.[18] Frank McLynn, a well-regarded biographer of Pancho Villa, Emiliano Zapata, Carl Jung, and Napoleon, commented that it is 'axiomatic that a good biography (never mind a great one) of a towering political figure cannot be written from a stance of pure hatred'. Thus *Mao* 'has a certain entertainment value. But it is neither serious history nor serious biography'.[19]

Reviews of the book fall into two broad categories: substantial responses by China scholars writing from a position of expertise; and lighter commentary by China scholars specializing in fields other than the Chinese Revolution, writers generally knowledgeable about China, and journalists, commentators and publicists. The non-experts tend to welcome or denounce the book in line with their general views on the Chinese Revolution. Those hostile to Mao find their prejudices confirmed and praise it as a 'triumph' of scholarship. Those friendly or less hostile to him question its methods and findings. On the other hand, China scholars of the sort represented here are less divided. Although a minority praise it, most find little to redeem it and much to censure in it. This goes both for political opponents of Mao's revolution, either mild or outright, and for its supporters, equivocal or enthusiastic. This selection includes the Chinese Revolution's critical supporters and its relentless adversaries, as well as others who take an intermediate stance. Most wince at the authors' methods and repudiate many of their findings.

There is no point in rehearsing or summarizing the reviews, which better speak for themselves. Two champion the book's findings. The rest, taken together, form a comprehensive indictment of it. The critical studies argue that Chang and

Halliday distort small details of history to 'prove' their point. The studies charge that evidence is used selectively, where it serves the authors' purpose, and otherwise ignored. Slurs and innuendos are made to look like hard fact. Judgements seemingly based on strong evidence cited in footnotes collapse on closer scrutiny of the sources. Citations are garbled. Sources are inadequately referenced or uncheckable. Speculation is presented as certainty. Sweeping generalizations are found to rest on flimsy evidence, or no evidence. 'Myths' the authors 'bust' turn out not to be myths, in the cold light of facts. 'Sensational' findings turn out to be old hat, revealed years ago by others. (Even the idea of Mao as monster is not new but was around all along, perhaps most notably in the controversial portrait of Mao published by Li Zhisui, one of his doctors, in 1994.[20])

On the whole, Chang and Halliday are disinclined to tackle and sometimes even to reference the work of others, preferring to present their conclusions as original even where they are not. Most scholarly books engage with 'the field', but Chang and Halliday ignore established work – except, occasionally, when it coincides with their own preconceived ideas. Many academic studies in English or Chinese that deal with Mao's character and career are absent from their bibliography. Where they do cite existing work, they sometimes bend its meaning and draw unfair and untrue inferences. Where expert opinion is irreconcilable with their prejudices, they apparently dismiss it. This approach is unacceptable in a book promoted as serious scholarship, especially one as contentious as this. Despite Chang and Halliday's academic pretensions, they show little inclination to follow basic scholarly procedure. Scholars' duty to engage with one another's work is not just a professional formality but a necessary step in the testing of their findings. They must be able to show that their own arguments are either truer and more authoritative than those of others working on the same subject or at least equally legitimate. Chang and Halliday do not do this.

For the most part, the reviewers in this volume confine themselves to questioning Chang and Halliday's methods and approaches, their treatment of specific issues and events, and their judgement. On the whole, they do not tackle the wider question of whether the Chinese Revolution was, on balance, good or bad for China. Chang and Halliday's answer is, of course, that it was irredeemably bad. The Chinese Revolution was not only unnecessary and undesirable but a disaster. This theory is comforting for opponents of radical change everywhere and explains why Western conservative establishments hailed the book with such glee and deference. In what remains of this introduction, we make a counterargument in the revolution's critical defence at a time when revisionist histories of the great social revolutions are in the ascendancy.

Chang and Halliday explain the Chinese Revolution as the evil product of one man at the head of a conspiracy of dupes and slaves. Their book is essentially the story of a court intrigue, what Barmé calls 'despot-centred history'. They erase the active contribution of men and women other than Mao from the events they describe – even major leaders like Zhou Enlai are discounted, as Mao's servile tools. Mao is shown to win out over his fellow conspirators by exercising greater viciousness and cunning. The authors talk almost exclusively about conspiracy and manipulation. They say practically nothing about the revolution's social, economic, political and cultural setting. The intellectual context that shaped Mao's and his fellow leaders' ideas vanishes almost entirely from sight in their view of it. In contrast, serious studies treat the Chinese Revolution as a complex, creative process in which millions of ordinary Chinese pursued their transforming visions in interaction with the party and its leaders.[21] When others' agency and the historical context are restored to view in this way, the revolution appears in a quite different light.

At the time of its founding in 1921, the CCP was inspired by noble aims. Its founders had stepped out of the New Culture Movement of the late 1910s, which campaigned for enlightenment, democracy, women's liberation, social justice, internationalism and the resolution of China's crisis of sovereignty. Its first General Secretary, Chen Duxiu, pioneered China's democracy movement in the early twentieth century. In the 1920s, the humanist and universalist values for which he stood continued to inspire the party. In 1929, however, he was expelled as a Trotskyist. At the time of his expulsion, he reminded the other party leaders that 'democracy is a necessary instrument for any class that seeks to win the majority to its side' and warned against the suppression of dissident viewpoints.[22] Although his former comrades dismissed these ideas as 'bourgeois', the party carried on its struggle for a 'new democratic revolution' with the support not only of the rural and urban poor but also of many educated Chinese. Li Dazhao, another founder of the CCP who died a martyr in 1927, also championed the idea of national, social and individual liberation and insisted on the necessary coherence of individualism, socialism and liberalism in a democratic system of 'commoners' politics'.[23]

The party's drift towards bureaucratic centralism started in the mid 1920s with its 'Bolshevization' – the imposition of 'iron discipline' and extreme centralism of the sort promoted by the Communist International in Moscow, particularly under Stalin. Bolshevization of this sort was speeded by the communists' defeat in the cities in 1927 and their immersion in the countryside, where they switched to a strategy of armed struggle. Geared up for war, party leaders stressed the need for regimentation, secrecy and top-down command. In the villages, they came to see themselves as the sole source of decision and authority. The administration they formed in Beijing in 1949 reflected this experience of infallible command. It was run from above, along authoritarian lines, and based explicitly on a statist model, despite Mao's efforts to combat bureaucracy and Stalinist dogmatism.

However, it is important to contextualize these turns in the party's strategic thinking and organizational methods, for it faced powerful enemies on all fronts and constant white terror. To historicize the revolution is not to defend its weaknesses, mistakes and crimes. Although tragically deformed by its militarization, rustication, and Stalinization, the party continued to retain many of its founding goals and characteristics. After the Long March, when the Red Army battled its way north at the cost of enormous losses, the party spearheaded the resistance in the Sino-Japanese War of 1937–45. In the rural areas after 1945, it led the poor in transforming their local communities. In the villages in the revolutionary years and in the cities after 1949, it changed women's lives for the better – not completely, but nevertheless massively. Chiang Kai-shek, by comparison, failed to reform the agrarian economy, was an ineffectual leader against Japan, did little to improve women's status, ruled over an unjust society, and headed a brutal, corrupt and reactionary regime.

Chang and Halliday focus exclusively on the failures of the revolution, including the disastrous outcome of the Great Leap Forward and the excesses of the Cultural Revolution. The picture they give is thus distorted and incomplete. Rounded studies of the Mao years argue that the CCP's achievements outweighed its failures. Stuart Schram, the doyen of Mao studies, concluded in an essay published in 1994 on Mao's legacy that

> at other times during his years in power, impressive rates of growth and technological exploits … were recorded…. Though the Great Leap Forward brought the peasants widespread misery rather than the promised collective prosperity and happiness, the successive phases in agrarian policy from 1946 onward destroyed the old landlord economy and thus laid the foundations for the emergence of a system of peasant smallholdings in the 1980s.[24]

The historian Maurice Meisner, a rigorous critic of Mao, argued in a lecture in 1999 that the Chinese communist victory and China's subsequent socio-economic development 'must be seen as one of the greatest achievements of the twentieth century'. He concluded that despite 'all the horrors and crimes that accompanied the revolution, … few events in world history have done more to better the lives of more people'.[25]

A balanced view of China in the decades of reconstruction after 1949 would also give full weight to the international environment. Blockades and threats by foreign powers created a fear of subversion that degenerated for long periods into cruel hysteria. Political controls tightened even further. Barry Naughton pointed out that resources were massively diverted from production and welfare spending to defence.[26] As John Gittings noted in his review of *Mao*, 'we should ask how far western (effectively US) hostility encouraged Mao's radical turn from the mid-1950s onwards, fostering a climate of chauvinism from which China has not yet completely emerged'.[27]

Even some of Chang and Halliday's admirers question the polemical one-sidedness of their approach. Kristof, for example, felt obliged to remind his readers of Mao's successes:

> Land reform in China … helped lay the groundwork for prosperity today. The emancipation of women … moved China from one of the worst places in the world to be a girl to one where women have more equality than in, say, Japan or Korea. Indeed, Mao's assault on the old economic and social structure made it easier for China to emerge as the world's new economic dragon.

Other triumphs included the steep rise in life expectancy after 1949, despite the famines, and China's emergence as a strong and independent country. Even before the spectacular reform-induced growth, China was already leading much of the developing world in terms of life expectancy, infant mortality, educational attainment and gender equality.[28] Once 'the sick man of Asia', China awakened under Mao as a world power, a transformation inextricably tied in the minds of most Chinese to Mao's very person.

Because Mao's party never entirely turned its back on the ideals that gave birth to it, it continued to receive the support after 1949 of widely respected humanists like Liu Binyan, Wang Ruoshui and Su Shaozhi who used Marxism to criticize Deng Xiaoping and the post-Deng regime. Worker and peasant activists protested against some of the Deng-ite reforms by appealing to Mao's revolutionary tradition.[29] Among younger intellectuals, 'new left' thinking took off in the 1990s, disseminated by websites and other e-media.[30] These responses from below are worth noting, for commentators outside China often fail to distinguish sufficiently between the CCP before and after 1978. Despite denouncing Mao while praising Deng, many such commentators talk of the Chinese 'party', 'state', and 'regime' as if they had not undergone remarkable transformations. Yet inside China, the post-1978 regime is criticized by some for its institutional and other systemic continuities with the 1949 revolution, while others regret the abandoning of old ideological tenets and socio-economic policies. The legacies of Maoism are highly pertinent to these debates in Chinese critical discourse.

Chang and Halliday start their book with the claim that Mao 'was responsible for well over 70 million deaths in peacetime, more than any other twentieth century leader', principally during the Great Leap Forward, when they say 38 million died. They also say Mao was not only indifferent to the thought of mass deaths but positively welcomed and even celebrated them. On this point of relative despotism, brutality and vileness, we round off this introduction. Apologists for the CCP often seek to minimize the effects of its political crimes and the social disasters it caused by resorting to analogies or comparisons with supposedly worse crimes and disasters perpetrated elsewhere. On the other hand, some of its critics try, through what Barmé calls 'competitive body counting', to cast Mao as the world's greatest monster. But if it is dishonourable to use a comparative framework to disguise the extent of Chinese wrongdoing, it is also unacceptable to put Mao at the top of a league of modern atrocities without due regard for historical perspective, given that the twentieth century is littered with such tragedies and evils. This is especially true in China studies, where the claim that Mao outmonstered everyone risks chiming with the Sinophobic idea of a special 'oriental' despotism. As Bill Willmott points out, 'So many people are keen to believe the worst about China, and this book will reinforce their beliefs. Already prejudiced readers will see the Chinese Revolution as nothing more than megalomaniacs killing each other and millions of others'.

Scholars have offered widely differing estimates of the death toll in China between 1959 and 1962, many of them far lower than Chang and Halliday's. Wim Wertheim, emeritus professor at the University of Amsterdam, reported in his review of Chang's *Wild Swans* that Chinese scholars and demographers in the 1950s privately doubted the accuracy of the Census of 1953 upon which calculations of the scale of deaths are often based, on the grounds that it was carried out unscientifically and registered 'an unbelievable increase of some 30 percent in the period 1947–1953'. Wertheim concluded that 'the claim that in the 1960s a number between 17 and 29 million people was "missing" is worthless' if one cannot say for certain that the population in 1953 was 600 million.[31] Others, including Ping-ti Ho, an expert in Chinese demography, have pointed to many flaws in the 1953 'nationwide enumeration'. Further studies either sweepingly or partially at odds with Chang and Halliday's could be cited.[32] It is symptomatic of Chang and Halliday's approach that they largely ignore such counter-arguments, which raise serious questions about their findings. Few would deny that the Great Leap led to a catastrophe of unimaginable proportions. Even admirers of Mao who support the Great Leap's basic goals concede that it failed – because 'the hierarchical, authoritarian party system was totally inappropriate for the leadership of a campaign which could only flourish on popular support', according to Jack Gray.[33] However, many would doubt the assumptions that underlie Chang and Halliday's projections, and their lack of balance and perspective.

A closer look at modern death tolls suggests the record of the British Empire is at least as deplorable as China's. Under the Raj between 1896 and 1900, more than ten million people died in avoidable famines out of a population little more than one third the size of China's in 1960. In the Bengal famine of 1943, between three and seven million died, out of a population of 60 million. The 1943 famine was just one of a series of crises in colonial India that together resulted in millions of avoidable fatalities. Chang and Halliday might wish to object that the Bengal deaths were caused, at least in part, by the war, but Winston Churchill himself famously blamed them on the people's tendency to 'breed like rabbits'[34] and historians attribute the severity of the crisis to British indifference and incompetence (Churchill thought the Indians 'the beastliest people in the world, next to the Germans'). Needless to say, a proportionately far greater number died in Ireland under British rule in 1845–46. On an even larger scale, the Aboriginal population of Australia and the American Indian population were wiped out in many areas. In any case, the Great Leap deaths were unintended: any equation of them with colonial and racist genocides would be preposterous and indefensible.

We note these other tragedies and atrocities not to minimize the Chinese suffering between 1959 and 1962 but to provide the perspective Chang and Halliday ignore. Far from wishing to justify Mao's policies in those years, each of us has, in writings stretching back over many years, rigorously and consistently criticized the crimes and errors committed under his rule. However, we reject Chang and Halliday's indiscriminate approach to the catastrophe and their one-sided refusal to contextualize it or to consider accounts by other scholars and commentators that might undermine their own dogmatic certainty.

An extreme example of the authors' tendentiousness is their portrayal of Mao as a Chinese Hitler.[35] They liken the effects of the famine caused by the Great Leap to the extermination of the Jews at Auschwitz and draw a parallel between Mao's communes and Hitler's slave-labour camps. These analogies display a saddening lack of moral taste and historical judgement. Six million of Europe's eight million

Jews died in the Holocaust. Auschwitz was the chief instrument in Hitler's 'final solution' to the 'Jewish problem'. The Great Leap Forward, on the other hand, was designed to accelerate China's industrialization and farm production. Chang and Halliday show no understanding of the dilemma Chinese communists faced in the late 1950s, as a result of China's severe international isolation and the military blockade. In Chang and Halliday's view, the Great Leap was a crime perpetrated by a madman. Others, however, see it as a fundamentally rational scheme to mobilize surplus rural labour in order to create local industry, improve rural infrastructure, and achieve national self-sufficiency, as a way of resolving the crisis caused by China's quarantine. It also had a utopian dimension, rooted in a belief in the need for popular participation and self-government. That it went so catastrophically wrong was due to the manner of its implementation. No one ordered or desired the deaths. The Holocaust, in contrast, was a deliberate barbarity.

Readers will reach their own conclusions about whether *Mao: The Unknown Story* is good biography or caricature and propaganda, or a bit of both, or more the one than the other. We hope these essays help them make up their minds. Some may object that the selection is prejudiced against Chang and Halliday and therefore of little help in forming an opinion, yet there has been no bending of the stick. What might seem like bias reflects the weight of opinion in reviews by experts. Unlike the worldwide commercial media, which embraced the book with uncritical and even fawning adulation, most professional commentary has been disapproving. Such has been the avalanche of academic criticism that it is hard to fathom why the two authors apparently do not feel moved to answer it. Had they formulated a systematic defence against the many charges levelled at them, we would happily have published it here, but none has as yet transpired, three years after the criticisms first began appearing.[36]

We would like to thank Peter Sowden for supporting the publication of this book and Emma Davis for taking expert care of the manuscript. We greatly appreciated their valuable suggestions and admirable attention to detail.

Part I

Reviews in non-specialist academic publications

1   Dark tales of Mao the Merciless

Delia Davin

First published in *The Times Higher Education Supplement*, 12 August 2005.

Mao Zedong was indisputably one of the most important figures of the twentieth century. The revolution he led transformed the lives of hundreds of millions of Chinese and, as this study frequently reiterates, also took the lives of many millions. This new biography of Mao received unprecedented pre-publication publicity and media hype and has already spent weeks in the best-seller list. Ironically, the attention accorded to it may owe as much to the celebrity status of one its co-authors, Jung Chang, famous for her best-selling memoir *Wild Swans* (1991), as to the importance of its subject.

Chang and Jon Halliday, her co-author/husband, brought formidable resources to their work. They lavished time and money on their research for over a decade. Chang was able to use some Chinese archives and also trawled the voluminous published literature on Mao that has become available in Chinese in recent years. Halliday's command of Russian has given him access to Soviet archives and memoirs that offer a particular perspective on Chinese communist history. Chang's elite family connections and her international fame enabled them to secure interviews that might have been difficult for other scholars to obtain. Among the several hundred people to whom the authors spoke were Mao's close associates and family members, the relatives of some of his victims, and also non-Chinese ranging from big names such as Kissinger, Lee Kuan Yew and Mobutu to former members of Maoist movements in the West and in the third world.

The broad outlines of the life recounted in *Mao: The Unknown Story* are familiar. Born to a well-to-do peasant family, Mao had many conflicts with his authoritarian father and was deeply fond of his gentle mother. As he struggled to gain an education he began to seek the solutions to China's weakness in the world. Like other young nationalists of his time he believed he would find them in revolutionary politics. He was an early member of the Chinese Communist Party, and was involved in its internecine struggles in the 1920s and 1930s. He did not achieve absolute pre-eminence within its leadership until the 1940s. He led the People's Republic from its foundation in 1949 until his death in 1976. From the mid-1950s, his attempts to sustain and intensify the revolution frequently exercised a disruptive influence on China's economic progress and political stability. This was often the cause of policy splits between him and other senior party leaders. Mao demonstrated an increasing tendency to see any colleague who dared to disagree with his policies as challenging his leadership. Out of this grew tragedy. The Great Leap Forward, promoted by Mao to accelerate the pace of industrialization and to establish large scale collectivization, instead produced economic disaster. China's food production fell catastrophically, but the state continued to extract grain taxes from the peasants and for a time even increased the level of procurement. Demographers have shown that in the resultant famine (1959–61) there were up to 30 million excess deaths. Mao bears responsibility not only for the disaster but also for the government's tardy response to it. Even when the reports of the famine began to come in, he resisted any reversal of his projects. His last great social experiment, the Cultural Revolution, represented, in part, his effort to reassert his leadership and to depose those who had criticized the Great Leap. This led to the downfall of almost all Mao's potential rivals and produced a climate in which no one dared offer him an honest opinion.

True to their title, Chang and Halliday claim that astonishingly little is known about Mao and frequently assert that they are reporting previously unknown incidents or facts. These claims are overstated. Other recent biographies have also dealt with the many discreditable facts of Mao's political history: his role in the killing of the so-called 'anti-Bolshevik' elements in the 1930s, the opium trade that for a time sustained the economy of his revolutionary base area of Yan'an, his increasingly autocratic dealings even with colleagues, his responsibility for the post Great Leap famine of the 1960s. Other aspects of the man such as his unappealing personal hygiene, his imperial lifestyle in luxury villas and his licentious relationships with selected nurse/concubines were first revealed in memoirs published in China and abroad including one by a girlfriend and another by his doctor.

What is original in the Chang/Halliday biography is its unrelenting demonization of its subject. Whereas other biographers have given some credit to Mao's ideological commitment, to his role as a thinker, or to his achievement in the reassertion of China's national power, Chang and Halliday eschew any attempt to balance the good and bad in his legacy. Unfortunately, their determination to present Mao in a totally negative light leads to many problematic assertions. They use selective quotations from a commentary written by Mao as a 24-year-old student on Friedrich Paulsen's *System of Ethics*. Their claim is that these show that Mao 'shunned all constraints of responsibility and duty' and that 'absolute selfishness and irresponsibility lie at the heart of Mao's outlook'. A less unsympathetic reading of the naïve and rather idealistic notes would recognize that Mao was trying to arrive at a philosophical understanding of duty. In doing so he asserts that acts such as helping those in need and sacrificing oneself to save others are duty not to others, but to oneself, since only if one performs them will one's mind be at rest. This is hardly proof of 'absolute selfishness'.

A major thesis of the book is that Mao lacked any ideological commitment and was driven all his life only by the lust for power. Is this really credible? One can think of easier and more promising paths that an ambitious young man might have taken in Republican China than joining a tiny communist party that to most observers looked unlikely ever to attain power. Chang and Halliday also assert that, despite his own peasant origins, Mao voiced little interest in the peasants' lot before November 1925 and note that 'it was the Russians who first ordered the Chinese communist party to pay attention to the peasantry'. In fact, in one of his first substantial essays, written in 1919, Mao had identified landlordism, rents and taxes as problems for the 'tillers of the soil' and had envisaged the establishment of a peasants' union.

No one could argue that Mao was a good family man. His treatment of his wives was often callous or cruel and his children were certainly not lucky in their father. Some were left with peasants and disappeared during the revolutionary wars, others died, and two suffered mental breakdowns. But Chang and Halliday take the bleakest possible view in their depiction of Mao's family relations. They castigate him for having made no effort to save his second wife from execution in 1930. Yet contrary to their assertion, it is by no means clear that even had he known of her danger he could have helped her. (Had he attempted a rescue, one cannot but suspect that they would have blamed him for risking the lives of his soldiers for private ends.) Various accounts are available of Mao's reaction to the death of his son, Mao Anying, in the Korean War. Peng Dehuai, a Chinese general whom Chang and Halliday elsewhere treat as a reliable witness, recalled that when he spoke to Mao of the death, the chairman trembled so violently that he was unable to light his cigarette. After several minutes of silence he said that in revolutionary war there will be sacrifices, and that Anying was only one of many. Chang and Halliday ignore Peng's account, preferring to quote Mao's secretary's ambiguous comment that Mao had not really 'shown any great pain'. This is used to support their position that he was unfeeling in his reaction to the death of his son.

Chang and Halliday's hostility to Mao affects not only their interpretation of the man but also their historical narrative. They claim to explode the 'Long March myth created by Mao' by proving that the battle of Luding Bridge in 1935 had never taken place and by showing that Chiang Kai-shek deliberately allowed the communist armies to break out of their southern bases at the beginning of the March and failed to attack them at other points when they were vulnerable. They ignore substantial contrary evidence. Even Chang and Halliday's own account of the March confirms much of the orthodox history. It was indeed marked by physical endurance, suffering, fighting, privations, losses, arguments and near collapse. Their suggestion that Chiang Kai-shek was at this point soft on the communists because he was worried about the fate of his son, Jiang Jingguo, who was in the Soviet Union, is unconvincing. Jingguo had gone to study in the Soviet Union in 1925 (with his father's permission rather than as the near kidnap victim implied in this account). Concern for his son's well-being did not stop Chiang massacring communists in Shanghai in 1927.

One of many charges levelled against Mao by Chang and Halliday is that he was obsessed with building up China's military strength and obtaining a nuclear capacity at a time when standards of living were abysmal and even feeding the population remained difficult. Mao is well known for the observation that power grows out of the barrel of a gun. The background should be explained. His preoccupation with military development must be understood against both the humiliations and military defeat by the British, French, Russians and Japanese suffered by China in the nineteenth century and the vulnerability of the People's Republic in its early years to the hostility of the West, in particular the United States. China existed after all under a nuclear threat. Mao made the best of his diplomatic and economic isolation; he did not choose it, and he resented the dependence on the Soviet Union that it enforced. He saw greater military strength as the way out of this situation.

The Unknown Story contains various contradictions of the authors' earlier works. In *Wild Swans* Chang Jung shows warlord China in the 1920s to have been a chaotic, dangerous place where corrupt military men vied with each other for power, human life was cheap, and hunger common. The patriarchal family controlled the lives of its members and women were bought and sold at the whim of its head. *The Unknown Story* is less critical. We are told that 'the warlords always made sure that the social structure was preserved', and that 'life went on as usual for civilians as long as they were not caught in the crossfire'. It is the social revolution introduced by the nationalist and the communists that disrupts this stability. *Wild Swans* showed the communists as having offered the only effective opposition to the Japanese. In *The Unknown Story* we are assured that they avoided engagement with the Japanese whenever possible. The communist victory in the civil war is attributed in *Wild Swans* to the fact that the population welcomed both the social revolution it promised and the overthrow of Chiang Kai-shek's corrupt, oppressive and incompetent government. Returning to the scholarship of the early Cold War years, in *The Unknown Story* Chang and Halliday prefer to attribute the communist victory to mistakes by the Americans, help from the Soviets, betrayal by some of Chiang's generals and Mao's terror tactics.

There are other instances in which the authors of *The Unknown Story* appear to have changed their minds. Their first collaboration, published in 1986, was a book on Song Qingling, widow of Sun Yat-sen, sister-in-law of Chiang Kai-shek and later a vice-president of the People's Republic of China. In this almost hagiographic biography (*Mme Sun Yat-sen: Soong Ching-ling*, Penguin 1986) they refer to her 'unique eminence and unassailability'. In *The Unknown Story* they claim, on what seems to me thin evidence, that she was a Russian agent. Agnes Smedley, a left-wing feminist journalist whose writing they used as a source for the book on Song Qingling, is called a Comintern agent without any evidence being offered. This interesting American was a correspondent for the *Manchester Guardian* in China. She certainly sympathized with the Chinese communists but was a loose cannon who later fell into official disfavour with both the Soviet and the Chinese party authorities. Halliday is well-known as an expert on the Korean War and published extensively on the subject in the 1980s. The origins and course of the war receive a sharply different treatment in this study of Mao from that offered in his earlier work.

Of course scholars have the right to change their minds. Perspectives change, new evidence emerges. What is concerning in this case is that the whole tone of *The Unknown Story* is so absolute, so tendentious. Chang and Halliday are certainly aware that other interpretations are possible, but they rarely discuss the debates or give their reasons for preferring one view rather than another. They have obviously read all the available scholarship on Mao, but they do not choose to engage with versions of his life which differ from their own. Their methodology is always to choose the account least favourable to Mao. A related problem is that of sources. Their bibliography is impressive: what is lacking is any attempt to evaluate sources and their relative reliability. We are not made aware that different witnesses and participants all have their own axes to grind and are rarely reminded that much of the history of the CCP is contested.

A final technical quibble is with their treatment of Chinese names. Many different systems exist for the romanization of Chinese but Pinyin (the official mainland system) has gained general acceptance. Chang and Halliday's decision to spell Chinese names 'so as to make them as distinctive and easily recognizable as possible' – i.e. not to abide by any consistent system – in their text will cause confusion and is therefore to be deplored.

The treatment of other leading communist figures in the book seems often to be coloured by their relationship to Mao. Liu Shaoqi and Deng Xiaoping, persecuted by Mao in the Cultural Revolution, are presented in a sympathetic light (despite their association in earlier years with Maoist policies and movements that the authors condemn). Zhou Enlai, admired by most foreigners with whom he came in contact as a diplomat of brilliance, charm and intelligence and still revered by many Chinese, is portrayed here as Mao's cowardly henchman with a masochistic tendency to abase himself before the Chairman. Lin Biao (Mao's appointed successor before he plotted against the Chairman and died in plane crash when attempting to flee from China) appears mentally unbalanced, a sufferer from phobias and insomnia who had become totally dependent on sleeping pills.

Intriguingly the private lives of these figures seem to 'match' their political scores. Liu's marriage to Wang Guangmei is described as 'exceptionally happy' while the fact that Deng retained the companionship of his wife during his disgrace made the 'difference between life and death'. On the other hand Lin Biao's wife, Ye Qun, is described as 'a rather batty woman'. The authors assure us that she lived in a state of unremitting sexual frustration due to her husband's neglect (although they also claim that she took lovers). Zhou Enlai's family life is often held up elsewhere as ideal. Unlike other Chinese leaders (including Mao) who showed a tendency to swap the wives of their revolutionary days for younger models, Zhou remained with Deng Yingchao whom he married in his twenties until his death. They were childless but adopted various orphans. In conformity with their generally unsympathetic portrayal of the man, Chang and Halliday recount that Zhou entered a loveless marriage with Deng, a 'noticeably plain and ungainly ... zealot', because he needed a woman who would also devote herself to the revolution.

Mao emerges from this study as a posturing, brutal and deceitful tyrant, and as a lazy fool, an incompetent maniac who was unpopular and incapable of inspiring loyalty. His victories are all attributed to luck or to the mistakes of his many adversaries. In the end this is not a believable picture. We need a more complex, rounded account to understand Mao and his political legacy. A good biography would surely give more attention to evaluating his writing. This study also ignores or denies the practical successes of the People's Republic. No one relying on it for an understanding of Mao's China would have any idea that although he was responsible for millions of deaths, his regime also brought about huge improvements in the lives of his fellow countrymen. Of course these cannot cancel out the terrible famine toll of 1959–61, but they do need to be considered in any balanced assessment. The crude death rate was halved in the first eight years of the People's Republic and reduced to a quarter of its former level by the time of Mao's death. Over the Maoist period, there was real economic growth (although much less remarkable than under Deng), life expectancy doubled and illiteracy was reduced.

No honest person who has studied the Maoist record would wish to be cast as an apologist for him. His utopian dreams, his periodic refusal to engage with reality, his ruthlessness and his determination to win resulted in terrible human suffering. But his revolution reunified China and made the country a force to be reckoned with in the world. The Chinese still remember these achievements and so should we. It seems a pity that what is likely to be the most widely read biography of Mao should offer an entirely negative assessment of his life and an inadequate account of the historical background.

2 Jade and plastic

Andrew J. Nathan

First published in *London Review of Books*, vol. 27, no. 22 (17 November 2005).

Mao Zedong's long, wicked life has generated some lengthy biographies in English. Jung Chang and Jon Halliday's is the longest, having overtaken Philip Short's *Mao* (1999) and Li Zhisui's *The Private Life of Chairman Mao* (1995). It represents an extraordinary research effort. The authors have been working on the project since at least 1986, to judge by the date of the earliest interview cited, which – and this is typical of the access they gained to many highly placed and interesting people – was with Milovan Djilas. They have visited remote battle sites of the Long March, Mao's cave in Yan'an, 'over two dozen' of Mao's secret private villas around the country, the Russian presidential and foreign ministry archives, and other archives in Albania, Bulgaria, London and Washington DC. They even tried – and failed – to get access to the Chinese war memorial in Pyongyang.

The book cites by name 363 interviewees in 38 countries, including two former US presidents; Lee Kuan Yew, the first prime minister of Singapore; the Congolese dictator Mobutu Sese Seko; the Mao aide and later Chinese head of state Yang Shangkun; a former Japanese cabinet secretary who confided that Mao escorted his prime minister to the lavatory in Zhongnanhai; Mao's daughter and grandsons; and the Red Guard leader Kuai Dafu. Chang and Halliday also cite dozens of interviews with anonymous sources, including a laundry worker who describes the fine cotton used for Mao's underwear in Yan'an; a pharmacist who allegedly prescribed Lysol for one of Mao's political rivals in the 1940s; Mao's daughter's nanny in Yan'an; staff at Mao's villas; and 'multiple' Mao girlfriends. They have used about a thousand non-archival written sources, including published and unpublished works in Chinese, English, Russian, French and Italian. These include many that are unfamiliar to me and perhaps to many other specialists on Chinese communist history and politics.

As their subtitle proclaims, in virtually every chapter Chang and Halliday have turned up 'unknown stories' of Mao. Some, if true, will be big news for historians. Mao amassed a private fortune during the Jiangxi Soviet period; his troops fought only one real battle during the Long March; their break-out from Nationalist military encirclement was deliberately allowed by Chiang Kai-shek; the most famous battle of the Long March never took place; Mao attacked India in 1962 with the support of the Soviet Union.

Other scoops have important implications for Mao's character. He poisoned a rival during the Yan'an period. He would send his own soldiers to be massacred if it would help him to move up the ranks of the party. He took pleasure in the slow, agonizing death of Liu Shaoqi. We already knew that Mao was selfish and ruthless. Chang and Halliday add that he was a brutal, sadistic power-monger lacking in vision or ideals, comfort-loving and often lazy, riding the revolution to power to satisfy a lust for torture and sex.

It is hard to imagine a more panoramic subject in terms of time, geography and historical forces. Yet Chang and Halliday focus tightly on Mao. Around him we glimpse a communist party leadership of cowards and fools, either manipulated by Mao, as Zhou Enlai was, or killed by him. In the deeper background, we perceive a political-movement-turned-regime that engaged in fifty years of mass torture, killing and destruction for no good purpose, leaving its people impoverished and exhausted. Lost in the distance are the larger forces of history that some might think explain the violence and longevity of Mao's regime: sociological or institutional explanations, or explanations based on China's geostrategic position between two contending superpowers in the Cold War. Such theories would presumably be too impersonal for this intensely moralizing work. They might seem to exculpate Mao by suggesting that he did not always intend the disasters he presided over.

That Mao's story might still be to some extent unknown need not surprise us, given the secrecy that surrounds the Chinese archives, the regime's tight control over historiography and propaganda, and Deng Xiaoping's decision in 1981 to preserve the regime's continuity by committing the party to an official view of its former ruler as '70 per cent right, 30 per cent wrong'. Mao (or something resembling Mao) remains embalmed in the heart of Tiananmen Square, and his image remains branded on the official heart of the party. Deng's decision influences all officially sanctioned writing on the former dictator, and that means everything openly published on Mao in China. Few historians outside China in recent decades have clung to the older romantic image of Mao as a sage, visionary and humanist, but Chang and Halliday's Mao is a revelation even for today's demystified historiography.

There are problems, however: many of their discoveries come from sources that cannot be checked, others are openly speculative or are based on circumstantial evidence, and some are untrue.

The inaccessible sources are of two kinds: anonymous interviews and unpublished documents or books. The former include 'the wife of a Shanghai delegate', 'interview with a local Party historian', 'interview with an old underground worker', 'interviews with people who had been told', 'interview with a staff member who knew about Mao's account', 'interviews with Mao's girlfriends', 'interviews with Mao's personal staff', 'interview with a Russian insider' and 'interview with a family member'. The book contains dozens of citations like these. The inaccessible documents include the partially unpublished manuscript memoirs of Mao's second wife, Yang Kaihui (one of these manuscripts is quoted at length in words 'mostly recalled from memory after reading this document in an archive'); the 'records of interrogations of executioners in the 1960s, unpublished'; 'contemporary newspaper reports'; the 'unpublished manuscript of a person present'; the 'handwritten, unpublished' diaries of Mao's son Anying; 'medical documents that established the poisoning'; and many more.*

Basing their argument on such sources, Chang and Halliday claim that the most famous battle of the Long March, at the Dadu Bridge in 1935, never took place. Their key piece of evidence is an interview with a 'sprightly ... local woman ... who was 93 years old when we met her in 1997', supplemented by an interview in 1983 with the then curator of the museum at the bridge. Their related claim that Chiang Kai-shek had deliberately 'left the passage open for the Reds' is unsourced.

Chang and Halliday state that Mao's chief political rival in Yan'an, Wang Ming, was poisoned by a Dr Jin, acting at Mao's behest. They say that this was established by an official inquiry, whose 'findings, which we obtained, remain a well-kept secret'. They cite the document in the notes, but do not say where it can be seen. They assert that Mao blamed the Indonesian Communist Party for failing to seize power in Jakarta in 1965. Their evidence is a conversation Mao had with Japanese communists in 1966, in particular some remarks which, according to the source note, 'were withheld from the published version' of the talks and 'were made available to us by the Japanese Communist Party Central Committee'. How other scholars can consult these remarks isn't stated.

Chang and Halliday report that near the beginning of the Great Proletarian Cultural Revolution, Mao's ally Lin Biao warned the other members of the Politburo that Mao had been preparing to face a coup for years and had intensified these preparations in the previous few months. Their source is a three-volume work called 'Documents for Researching the Cultural Revolution' compiled by the People's Liberation Army Defence University, which they describe as unpublished. They do not say where they saw it.

They argue that Mao rejected a death sentence during the Cultural Revolution for the purged state president Liu Shaoqi because he preferred to have Liu suffer a slow, lingering death, that Mao was kept 'fully informed' of Liu's sufferings, that photographs of the dying Liu were taken and, by implication, that Mao saw them. The sources for this string of assertions are interviews with Liu's widow, Wang Guangmei, and with an unnamed member of Lin Biao's family.

---

* The structure of the book makes checking the sources more difficult than is usual for a work of serious scholarship. To identify a source, you have first to flip to a section of notes at the back, where source citations are arranged by the page numbers of the main text. Under each page number are several bold-face tag lines keyed to sentences on that page. After each tag line is a list of sources, often as many as five or six. These citations provide only the author's name and page numbers. You have to flip back and forth in the bibliography to identify the sources. The bibliography in turn is divided into two sections, one for Chinese sources and one for non-Chinese sources. Moreover, many of the source titles are abbreviated, so you have to check the two lists of abbreviations before going to the two bibliographies. When multiple sources are cited for a single assertion, it is often unclear which source is intended to support the controversial part of a passage in the text. If four sources fail to do so and the fifth is inaccessible, then the controversial assertion is impossible to check.

Of course, anonymous interviews and unpublished sources are often used in reputable China scholarship. They have to be, because of the secrecy imposed by the regime on its own history and workings. I have engaged in such research myself. What is troubling about *Mao: The Untold Story* (as the North American edition is subtitled) is the authors' failure to give readers any information to help them to evaluate their sources' reliability. A lengthy research project that denigrates Mao, involving access to many individuals and many remote and secret locations all over China, over a period of many years, and drawing on a significant number of sensitive unpublished sources, in a country where the keys to history are tightly held, legitimately raises questions that the authors should have anticipated and addressed.

How was it possible to gain access? Who gave authorization or protection, formal or informal, to this project, or if none was given, how was secrecy maintained as the research progressed? How were the interviewees found? In what settings were they interviewed? In what manner were they questioned? How were records of the interviews kept? What motivations did informants have for talking? What methods were used to confirm their identities and to corroborate their information? How were unpublished sources obtained? How were they authenticated? Where, if anywhere, may they be consulted by other scholars (and if they can't, why not)?

Such a methodological essay might have included some reflection by Chang and Halliday on the history of their project and their motives for taking it on. Chang is the author of the justly acclaimed *Wild Swans* (1991), which told the stories of her grandmother, her mother and herself, over the span of seven turbulent decades from 1909 to 1978. Chang was one of the millions of people damaged by Mao. Her anger, deeply justified, shapes this new book.

Halliday's name appears in smaller type on the spine and dust jacket, suggesting that his role in the project was secondary. He seems to have been responsible for the use of Russian, Bulgarian and Albanian archives and sources, and for interviews with Russian diplomats and Comintern officials. Not a China specialist, he is among other things the author of *A Political History of Japanese Colonialism*, the co-author of a revisionist history of the Korean War and the editor of the English-language edition of the memoirs of Enver Hoxha. In short, he appears to be a man of the left, whose disappointment with Mao may be political as well as personal.

It is clear that many of Chang and Halliday's claims are based on distorted, misleading or far-fetched use of evidence. They state, for example, that the Chinese Communist Party 'was founded in 1920', and not, as is usually said, in 1921 – a point they think important because Mao wasn't in Shanghai in 1920. The two sources they cite, however, merely confirm that early communist cells were founded a year before the First Party Congress met in Shanghai in 1921, something not contested by historians. They claim that the Kuomintang politician Wang Jingwei was the hidden 'patron' of Mao's early party career, which appears to be a misreading of the fact that Wang, who served briefly as head of the Nationalists, appointed Mao as well as other communists to KMT posts during the time of the KMT-communist united front.

Chang and Halliday cite four sources to support their statement that Mao amassed 'a private fortune' during the Jiangxi Soviet period of the early 1930s. One is an anonymous interview which cannot be checked. The second source is a book in Chinese by a writer called Shu Long, which says that Mao ordered his brother, Zemin, who was president of the communists' state bank, to disperse money from a 'secret treasury' to the various communist military units when a gathering enemy offensive threatened the money's security. The third is *The Long March* by Harrison Salisbury (1985), which says similarly that Zemin took part in hiding the Red Army's money and treasure in a mountain cave for two years until it was removed shortly before the Long March and divided among the communist armies that were about to set off on the March. The fourth source is a file in the Harrison Salisbury papers at Columbia University. However, the citation is garbled, so the file Chang and Halliday used cannot be located in Columbia's Rare Book and Manuscript Library (nor can the correct citation be reconstructed from the information given).

In the chapter subtitled 'Chiang Lets the Reds Go', Chang and Halliday say they have 'no doubt' that Chiang Kai-shek allowed Mao's army to escape from encirclement in 1934 so that it could threaten the warlords of Sichuan and Yunnan, who would then have to capitulate to Chiang to save themselves. It's true that the Red Army escaped, but most scholars attribute this to Chiang's incompetence. Chang and Halliday's clinching evidence is a published reminiscence that Chiang told his secretary: 'Now when the Communist army go into Guizhou, we can follow in. It is better than us starting a war to conquer Guizhou. Sichuan and Yunnan will have to welcome us, to save themselves.' Although the quote is accurate, it does not prove the existence of a strategy. The source – who is not the person to whom the remark was allegedly made, Chen Bulei, but a lower-ranking staff member, Yan Daogang – himself explains Chiang's remark by saying that he first made every effort to prevent the Red Army from entering Guizhou, and only after this failed decided to pursue the Reds there despite the opposition of the local warlord. In any case, one would expect a complex, long-term strategy of this kind to leave more than one fugitive piece of evidence.

They argue that the battle of Tucheng during the Long March was a huge defeat, not a victory as officially claimed, and that Mao engineered this disaster on purpose. This conclusion is reached by distorting what the sources say. The sources describe a protracted battle during which Mao refused to withdraw his troops and during which they suffered heavy casualties, but that nonetheless ended in a Red Army victory. Although the sources may be tendentious, Chang and Halliday do not explain why it is reasonable to use them in support of an opposite argument.

They believe that Chiang Kai-shek acceded to the communists' demands for a united front against Japan during the Xi'an Incident of 1936 because Stalin made this a condition for releasing Chiang's son, Jingguo, from Moscow. Chang and Halliday call this a 'Reds-for-son deal that Chiang had been working on for years' and that 'marked the end of the civil war between the CCP and the Nationalists'. Their sources for this argument, developed through several chapters, are all circumstantial; the key piece of evidence is that when Zhou Enlai met Chiang in

Xi'an, he told Chiang that Moscow would send his son home. Their source for this information is Han Suyin's biography of Zhou, in which it is claimed that a senior communist official overheard this remark while he was standing outside Chiang's door. Han – in any case an unreliable author – does report that Wang Bingnan overheard part of the conversation between Zhou and Chiang and that Zhou 'assured Chiang that his son would return, that he was patriotic and undoubtedly wished his father to resist the invaders'. But she does not frame this as part of a deal: rather, as evidence of Zhou Enlai's human touch. There is no direct evidence of a Stalin-Chiang deal and no good reason to think that Chiang would have altered his strategy for a personal reason.

The chapter entitled 'Red Mole Triggers China–Japan War' argues that the KMT general who in 1937 resisted Japanese encroachments in Shanghai against Chiang Kai-shek's orders, thus triggering an intense battle, was a communist agent acting on commands that 'almost certainly' came from Stalin. To support that interpretation, Chang and Halliday cite the general's memoirs, published years later, in which he states that as a military cadet at the Whampoa Academy more than a decade before the battle of Shanghai he had been sympathetic to the communists, who were then in their first united front with the KMT and formed part of the leadership of Whampoa. General Zhang says that Zhou Enlai told him at that time – 1925 – to 'wait for a while for the appropriate time' to join the party. 'But the CCP guarantees that from now on we will covertly support you and make your work go easily.' This becomes in Chang and Halliday's telling an instruction 'to stay in the Nationalists and collaborate "covertly" with the CCP' and – along with the fact that Russians in contact with Zhang were subsequently executed – shaky proof for the proposition that Zhang acted 12 years later on orders from Stalin.

Chang and Halliday say that Mao got Zhou Enlai to draw up a list of notable people to be exempted from persecution during the Cultural Revolution, and that Zhou does not deserve the credit that he later got for saving people. Neither of their sources backs this up. One is a compendium of Mao's memos and other documents, which includes a one-sentence directive from Mao to Zhou to protect one individual. The compilers' note says that Zhou did this and then also drew up a short list of other people who should be protected; it doesn't say that Mao told him to do this. The other source, an article by Michael Schoenhals, says that rather than intervening in persecutions managed by others, Zhou himself managed the main high-level persecutions of the Cultural Revolution. While this supports Chang and Halliday's point that Zhou was not blameless, it does nothing to clarify the issue of who drew up the lists of notables to be protected.

Some of Chang and Halliday's arguments go beyond the misuse of sources to make claims that are simply unsourced. Perhaps they think these are conclusions that flow self-evidently from the pattern of events. They include claims that Stalin deliberately kept his ambassador away from the Security Council meeting in June 1950 which authorized a UN response to North Korea's invasion of the South, because he wanted to draw US troops into Korea; that Mao helped cause Stalin's fatal stroke; that Mao's remarks to the East German leader Walter Ulbricht about the Great Wall had something to do with Ulbricht's decision some years later to erect the Berlin Wall; and that Mao started both the Taiwan Strait crises, in 1954 and 1958, in order to provoke an American nuclear threat to China that would in turn put pressure on the Soviet Union to give more help to China's own atomic bomb programme.

Chang and Halliday's false claims include the assertion that Mao had planned for some time what became in 1962 the Sino-Indian border war, and, as part of this, a 'hefty horse-trade' occurred in which Khrushchev told the outgoing Chinese ambassador that Moscow would take China's side if war broke out with India in return for Mao's support for the Russian position on missiles in Cuba. But according to their own source, Mao's ambassador reported these Russian protestations to Beijing as a hypocritical attempt to mask a growing alignment with India. Chang and Halliday further imply that Khrushchev's promise of support helped Mao decide to give 'the go-ahead for crack troops to storm Indian positions'; they fail to provide the important background information that, to quote an authoritative study by John Garver, Nehru had previously 'ordered Indian forces to advance into disputed areas and clear Chinese forces, though without firing first. India ignored Chinese warnings to halt this "forward policy"' and only then did the Red Army strike 'suddenly with overwhelming force'.

Chang and Halliday state that on the eve of the Cultural Revolution, Peng Zhen, the mayor of Beijing, flew to Sichuan for secret talks with the purged general Peng Dehuai. Their source confirms that this meeting took place. But they misreport what the source says, claiming that the meeting was conducted '*in secret*' (their italics), whereas it was arranged by the local party secretary, Li Jingquan, as indeed it would have had to have been under the bureaucratic system operating in China at that time, although Li and Peng Zhen agreed not to report the meeting to Beijing. 'What the two Pengs talked about has never been revealed', Chang and Halliday write, although the book they cite contains four pages of reconstructed dialogue. 'Judging from the timing and the colossal risk Mayor Peng took in visiting' Peng Dehuai, they say, 'it is highly likely that they discussed the feasibility of using the army to stop Mao'. Nothing of that sort is indicated in their source, which says that the two discussed an ideological campaign then unfolding in Beijing. It is unlikely that the two discussed military options, because neither of them – a civilian official and a purged general – had any access at all to troops.

Chang and Halliday report the case of a brigadier general called Cai Tiegen, who thought of organizing a guerrilla force to resist Mao during the Cultural Revolution and was shot for that crime. Their source, however, states that Cai was the victim of a frame-up by a political activist, who distorted some discussions between Cai and his friends about guerrilla warfare to create the false impression that Cai wanted to form guerrilla bands to oppose the regime.

These three kinds of flaw do not rule out the possibility that in some cases Chang and Halliday's findings may be true and represent a significant contribution to scholarship. The book makes the most thorough use to date of the many memoirs that have emerged since Mao's death, written by his colleagues, cadres, staff and victims, and shows special insight into the suffering of Mao's wives and children. It contains much information from Russian, Albanian and Bulgarian archives and publications, which so far as I know other scholars have not used. Among the new findings from these sources are that it was the Russians who first ordered the CCP to pay attention to the peasants; that Sun Yat-sen's widow, Soong Ching-ling, was a Soviet agent; that the Russians had dealings with a warlord rival of Chiang Kai-shek's in the 1930s, leading him to think they might sponsor him to replace Chiang as China's ruler; that Mao initiated a long-term collaboration with Japanese intelligence in 1939; that Mao had his own 'powerful intelligence network' within the American Communist Party, unavailable to the Russians; that, before the Korean War, Mao promised Kim Il-sung that China would send in Chinese troops; that at some unspecified date Mao plotted to depose Kim Il-sung; and that in the early 1950s Mao undertook unspecified 'conspiratorial operations' in the USSR. Such assertions must be examined in the future, but cannot yet be accepted as established conclusions.

Chang and Halliday are magpies: every bright piece of evidence goes in, no matter where it comes from or how reliable it is. Jade and plastic together, the pieces are arranged in a stark mosaic, which portrays a possible but not a plausible Mao. This Mao is lazy, uncommitted, driven by lust for power and comfort, lacking in original ideas, tactically smart but strategically stupid, disliked by everyone he works with, selfish and mindlessly cruel. 'Absolute selfishness and irresponsibility lay at the heart of Mao's outlook.' Mao was a 'lukewarm believer' in Marxism. 'Mao discovered in himself a love for bloodthirsty thuggery.' He 'demonstrated a penchant for slow killing'. He 'out-bandited the bandits'. He 'was addicted to comfort'. His 'most formidable weapon was pitilessness'. This was a man with many enemies, generated and regenerated by his persecutions and oppressions. 'Mao evinced no particular sympathy for peasants'; 'Mao was extremely unpopular'; 'Mao was disliked by the locals'.

How could a man like this win power? Chang and Halliday's answer is that he was more vicious than his rivals. Thanks to his possession of shameful secrets, his manipulation of slander, character assassination and actual murder, his withholding and falsifying of information, and his sheer skill at browbeating, he defeated the hardened revolutionaries who were his former comrades-in-arms, turning Zhou Enlai into 'a self-abasing slave', 'hyper-intimidating' Liu Shaoqi, forming a purely instrumental alliance with Lin Biao and then discarding him – and doing some matchmaking for Lo Fu, for Mao was 'shrewd about the ways of the heart, particularly in sexually inhibited men'. Mao ran rings around Chiang Kai-shek because 'Chiang ... let personal feelings dictate his political and military actions'. Mao 'had none of his weak spots'.

Chang and Halliday position themselves as near omniscient narrators, permitting themselves to say constantly what Mao and others really thought or really intended, when we seldom have any way of knowing. A cautious historian would avoid taking poems or speeches from Mao as a clear expression of what he felt or intended, understanding that poetry may express a state of feeling, and that a political speech or dialogue may contain rhetorical flourishes, humour or irony, or may be intended to mislead. Chang and Halliday take what Mao says literally, even his well-known outrageous statements that famine and nuclear warfare were no big deal. And they repeatedly impute feelings and intentions to him when they lack even a poem or a speech on which to base their interpretation.

Of course, Mao deserves harsh moral judgement. Too many previous accounts of his life, awed by his achievements, have overlooked their human cost. But this portrayal impedes serious moral judgement. A caricature Mao is too easy a solution to the puzzle of modern China's history. What we learn from this history is that there are some very bad people: it would have been more useful, as well as closer to the truth, had we been shown that there are some very bad institutions and some very bad situations, both of which can make bad people even worse, and give them the incentive and the opportunity to do terrible things.

Chang and Halliday's white-hot fury no doubt represents the unpublished and anonymous Chinese sources that they have used. More authentically than the officially licensed propaganda, these as yet subterranean opinions reflect the current evaluation of Mao within the party as well as outside. This book can thus be read as a report on the crumbling of the Mao myth, as well as a bombshell aimed at destroying that myth. That the Chinese are getting rid of their Mao myth is welcome. But more needs to take its place than a simple personalization of blame.

3   Portrait of a monster

Jonathan D. Spence

First published in *New York Review of Books*, vol. 52, no. 17 (3 November 2005).

1

It is close to seventy years since Edgar Snow, an ambitious, radical, and eager young American journalist, received word from contacts in the Chinese Communist Party that he would be welcome in the communists' northwest base area of Bao-an. Travelling there by train, by truck, on foot, and finally on horseback accompanied by a twenty-man escort of Chinese Red Army troops, Edgar Snow reached Bao-an, and was granted several long evening interviews by Mao in his lamp-lit cave. Mao's secretary served as Snow's interpreter, and Snow's 20,000-word English draft of the interview was then translated back into Chinese and transcribed by a young student named Huang Hua, for submission to Mao. Mao made corrections and cuts, and Huang thereupon translated that approved version back into English for Snow.[1] With Snow's extended commentaries and additions to supply historical context, the resulting book, *Red Star Over China*, was published in the United States and in Britain in 1938; an underground and abbreviated edition had already appeared in Chinese shortly after Snow returned to Beijing, and circulated widely in the communist base area. Snow later reflected on his book with these words:

> I had gone to the Northwest before any Westerner and at a dark moment in history for the Chinese Communists as well as for all China. I had found hope for the nation in that small band of survivors of the Long March, and formed a favorable impression of them ... and their policies. ... I admired their courage, their selflessness, their single-minded determination to save China (under their leadership) and the outstanding ability, the practical political sense, and personal honesty of their high Commanders.[2]

Snow's book was, indeed, highly flattering to both the Chinese communist leaders and their followers: the forty-three-year-old Mao, wrote Snow in *Red Star*, was 'a gaunt, rather Lincolnesque figure,' and his rank and file, whether at work or on the march, seemed to be always singing. Snow noted in his diary that the Chinese communists he met 'go about remaking the world like college boys to a football match,' and the Mao he portrayed was earthy, earnest, informal, jocular, and visionary.

Though sales of *Red Star* in the United States were disappointing – at 23,500 they were less than a quarter of the sales in Britain, where the book was published in Victor Gollancz's Left Book Club – the book had a profound influence on American thinking about China. Snow's detailed account of Mao's early life, education, first experiences as a revolutionary and on the Long March became staples of later biographical writings about Mao, and parts of them remain accepted to this day. In the period since *Red Star* first saw the light of day, this laudatory tradition was carried on by various writers who either travelled to the base area of Yan'an during World War II or watched with awe as the communists defeated Chiang Kai-shek in the civil war between 1945 and 1949, and then struggled to establish a new state on the wreckage. This sympathy died hard. But since his death in 1976, praise for the later Mao has pretty much dried up as irrefutable evidence has appeared on the tragedies of the Great Leap Forward, the ensuing famine between 1959 and 1962, and the Cultural Revolution between 1966 and 1976. Mao's youthful legacy, however, has not been totally erased.

In *Mao: The Unknown Story*, the co-authors Jung Chang and Jon Halliday launch a protracted assault on the entire concept of a favourable assessment of Mao's role in the rise and success of the Chinese communist movement, both before and after 1949. They come to their venture buoyed by the international best-seller status of Jung Chang's *Wild Swans: Three Daughters of China*, an absorbing account of her experiences growing up in the People's Republic, first published in 1991, and by Jon Halliday's knowledge of Russian and Eastern European languages and materials. The two authors provide readers with eighty-five pages of notes, an elaborately classified and extensive bibliography of the Chinese archival collections and other Chinese works they have consulted (twenty-six pages), twenty-three pages of Western-language materials (including Russian, Albanian, and Bulgarian) and English translations of Chinese sources, and fourteen pages containing the names of those they have interviewed in China, Russia, and the rest of the world. Their notes show that they conducted the first of these interviews in 1993, so we can assume they have worked for a decade on their book. And from this mountain they have constructed their Mao.

Their Mao has these main attributes: though 'born into a peasant family', he never spent much time seriously farming; at most, when still young, the authors argue, 'Mao did a little light farm work, gathering fodder for pigs and taking the buffaloes out for a stroll'. Later he gave up farm work for study at a local school (his teachers found him troublesome), and in 1911, the year of the revolution that toppled China's last dynasty, 'he said good-bye forever to the life of a peasant'. Nor did he draw any social lessons from such rural experience as he had: 'There is no sign that Mao derived from his peasant roots any social concerns, much less that he was motivated by a sense of injustice'. The sight of famine victims left him unmoved. He had not even absorbed the farmers' basic need for careful planning and calculation, so that 'all his life, he was vague about figures, and hopeless at economics'.

In the later teens of the twentieth century, Mao entered a teacher-training college; here, the authors tell us, Mao first mentioned 'one theme that was to typify his rule – the destruction of Chinese culture'. Here, too, he read in class a Chinese translation of the German philosopher Friedrich Paulsen's *A System of Ethics* published in 1899, from which he absorbed a personal feeling that the self dominated all, that destruction reigned supreme, and that 'morality does not have to be defined in relation to others'. Such thoughts were far from being just passages gleaned from an obscure volume, marking a phase in the awakening of a fledgling consciousness, as many readers today might assume. For the writers, these sentiments were the 'central elements' in Mao's character, which 'stayed consistent for the remaining six decades of his life and defined his rule'.

Out in the world, as in farming or in studying, another formative aspect of Mao's character lay in his laziness. The reason that Mao joined the Communist Party, which he did in either late 1920 or early 1921, the authors tell us, had nothing to do with his social conscience, for he felt no more sympathy for workers than he did for peasants. Being no good at languages, he could not go to Russia or France to study at the radical fonts, as many of his friends from Hunan chose to do at that time. So the simplest way Mao could find to survive – even at teaching he was inept – was to take the Comintern's proffered money and accept 'a comfortable berth as a subsidized professional revolutionary'. And being both an opportunist and 'ideologically woolly', Mao had little trouble adjusting to the tortuous world of the Comintern-ordered United Front, which brought the Communists into alliance with the bourgeois centrists or even right-wing militarists in the name of the protection of the Soviet Union and the future world revolution: 'Mao shifted with the prevailing wind'.

All that was now required was a setting in which Mao's latent sadistic side could develop to the full, and that chance, we are told, came in the bitter fighting that erupted in China in the mid-1920s, as the United Front disintegrated from its own fatal internal contradictions and political feuding. In the authors' reading, during the last months of 1926 and the first two of 1927 Mao followed the orders of his superiors to study (and/or foment) rural revolution through the peasant associations that had formed in various parts of China. Mao loved what he saw – the humiliations of the landlords, the pains of the prosperous, and the rough vengeance of the masses. Mao's celebrated report on these upheavals in his native province of Hunan, taken by many analysts to be a sign of his deepening awareness of the terrible problems that haunted the Chinese countryside, suggests something different to the authors:

> What really happened was that Mao discovered in himself a love for bloodthirsty thuggery. This gut enjoyment, which verged on sadism, meshed with, but preceded, his affinity for Leninist violence. Mao did not come to violence via theory. The propensity sprang from his character, and was to have a profound impact on his future methods of rule.

This new blood-lust accompanied Mao to his fugitive revolutionary base in the

Jinggang mountains in 1928. Mao, to the authors, now 'demonstrated a penchant for slow killing'. The authors add a gloss:

> Mao did not invent public execution, but he added to this ghastly tradition a modern dimension, organised rallies, and in this way made killing compulsory viewing for a large part of the population. To be dragooned into a crowd, powerless to walk away, forced to watch people put to death in this bloody and agonising way, hearing their screams, struck fear deep into those present.

With all this bleak analysis presented in the first fifty-four pages, the reader is attuned to the major themes of Mao's life that the authors unfold as they follow his activities during the Chinese communist domination of the Jiangxi region in the early 1930s, the subsequent establishment of the Yan'an base for anti-Japanese resistance, the civil war period when the Nationalists of Chiang Kai-shek were finally defeated, and the long painful years of the People's Republic, when millions of Chinese died from famine and the violence of the Cultural Revolution.

But the litany is by no means exhausted: among the themes introduced by the authors early in the work, which come to full blossoming only in their account of Mao's later years, one should include at least these: Mao's callousness to his wives (four in all) and to his children; his growing love of luxury, especially for large mansions with scenic views, but also for swimming pools and private trains; his paranoia and mania for security; his unclean personal habits; his lechery, deepening with each passing year; his personal avoidance of combat and his deep fear of violence directed at his person; his gluttony; his pandering to the sexual proclivities of chosen subordinates or foreign dignitaries; his dependence (from early in the revolution) on ever-increasing amounts of sleeping pills; his joy in humiliating others and in causing pain, often to leaders who had been close associates. During the Cultural Revolution, the authors write

> Mao made sure that much violence and humiliation was carried out in public, and he vastly increased the number of persecutors by getting his victims tormented and tortured by their own direct subordinates.

All of this culminated in his ambition, after conquering every corner of his own country, to dominate the world itself through the acquisition of nuclear bombs.

2

There are many passages in which the authors elaborate on the convergence of all these negative traits into one knowing and self-conscious whole, and this one, on the world of Mao in 1964, can stand both as their description of Mao at that time and for pretty much any period until his death in 1976:

> What Mao had in mind was a completely arid society, devoid of civilisation, deprived of representation of human feelings, inhabited by a herd with no

sensibility, which would automatically obey his orders. He wanted the nation to be brain-dead in order to carry out his big purge, and to live in this state permanently. In this he was more extreme than Hitler or Stalin, as Hitler allowed apolitical entertainment, and Stalin preserved the classics.

Around this portrait of a repulsive man, the authors construct a complexly patterned grid of national history, in which Mao seeks to turn every major confrontation to his own advantage, to fit in with his endless quest for dominance within the Communist Party of China, within the international communist movement, and in the world at large. There are, by my count, around twenty-two or more such crucial moments in the 631 pages of this book. Each one of them is designed by the authors to challenge some aspect of what they see as false received wisdom in the depictions of Mao's march to power that various historians and analysts have tried to develop over the last sixty years or so.

Their book is subdivided into fifty-eight bite-sized chapters, each of ten pages or so, and many of those chapters focus just on a single scheme or action that Mao, they claim, was able cannily to exploit to his own advantage. Thus we find Mao using the Nationalist Party leader Wang Jingwei to bolster his own role in the United Front; playing lackey to the Comintern; betraying his comrades' trust at Wuhan in 1927; tearing apart the guerrilla base in the Jinggang mountains; sabotaging the military achievements of his fellow revolutionaries Peng Dehuai and Zhu De; instituting a wave of torture and murder in the Jiangxi Soviet; using the Long March to destroy his main Party rival Zhang Guotao; reducing Zhou Enlai to 'slavish' dependence; conniving with Stalin to push the Japanese into a war in Shanghai while refusing to fight them near his own base region in the northwest; mentally tormenting and trying to poison Wang Ming, his main intellectual rival in the Party; setting up a police state in the same base region; betraying his communist colleagues in central China so they could be wiped out by Chiang Kai-shek; developing a monolithic cult of Mao in the base; insisting on a murderous military policy in civil-war Manchuria, so that the casualties in some cities there exceeded the entire total of those killed by the Japanese in the rape of Nanjing; betraying China by letting Stalin keep vast areas of formerly Chinese territory in the north and west; duplicitously forcing his senior colleagues to enter the Korean War even without Soviet air support; tricking the intellectuals of China with his fake 'Hundred Flowers' promises; needlessly raising grain requisitions from his people during the terrible famines that followed the Great Leap; destroying Chinese resources in order to pay for his mad global ambitions; deliberately destroying his own most talented colleagues in the Cultural Revolution purges, in some cases after treating them with great brutality, while also succeeding in 'wiping out culture from Chinese homes' as 'frightened citizens burned their own books'; and, near the end, ordering that Zhou Enlai be refused treatment for his bladder cancer, lest Zhou outlive him and try to reverse his policies.

All of the above episodes are elaborated versions of situations that did exist in some form or other, though not necessarily in a form at all like that presented by the authors. Take for example their eye-catching title to Chapter Nineteen: 'Red Mole

Triggers China-Japan War.' This chapter offers the argument that the Nationalist General Zhang Zhizhong, commander of the Shanghai-Nanjing region, was in fact a 'long-term Communist agent,' 'activated' by Stalin in August 1937 in order to broaden the war with Japan. The authors argue that General Zhang's success in forcing the Japanese into all-out war in the Shanghai theatre 'in effect, legitimised' the CCP as an ally of the Nationalists fighting the Japanese, and means not only that 'this was probably one of Stalin's greatest coups' but also that Zhang 'can arguably be considered the most important agent of all time'. These are huge claims, and are worth some reflection.

Certainly no historian working on twentieth-century China can deny that there were 'moles' at work in many sections of the Nationalist Chinese army and intelligence agencies, moles placed either by the Nationalist Party, the communists, or pro-Japanese sympathizers, and at times they influenced events in a decisive way. There were also double agents, on all three sides. All three sides had their own assassination squads.

This situation arose, in part, because the nature of the United Front was such that both communists and Nationalists attended the same military training academy at Whampoa near Canton in the early 1920s, where Comintern agents were intensely active. Chiang Kai-shek served as commandant of the Whampoa academy, and Zhou Enlai was political director. Chiang Kai-shek had visited the Soviet Union to study their military training methods, while Zhou Enlai was from an educated family and had lived for some time in France. Zhou and Chiang, like thousands of other ambitious young Chinese, had also studied in Japan. General Zhang Zhizhong did rise rapidly in the Nationalist army and was clearly a favourite of Chiang Kai-shek, as the authors write; he also much later, in 1949, did surrender to the communists rather than retreat to Taiwan with Chiang Kai-shek.

But there are many aspects of the authors' dramatic claims that still need much clarification: How, for example, did Stalin 'activate' General Zhang in order to broaden the war with Japan? Were there Shanghai-based Comintern agents still in touch with Moscow by secret radio channels and in a position to give instructions to General Zhang? And what exactly was General Zhang's job before he was 'activated'?

In his own memoir, published in Beijing in 1985, General Zhang writes that as early as February 1936 Chiang Kai-shek had authorized him to undertake confidential planning with senior officers in the National Military Academy (of which Zhang was dean) to defend the Suzhou-Shanghai region against the Japanese. This work continued into 1937, when Zhang went for medical treatment in the northern city of Qingdao. But on 9 July 1937, after hearing news of the Japanese assaults in north China, Zhang hurried back to Nanjing and Shanghai, to coordinate the defenses there.[3] This does not sound like a mole surreptitiously working away; in fact, as General Zhang also writes in his memoirs, he had been active in the fighting against the Japanese in Shanghai in early 1932, and Chiang had greeted him with an honor guard when he returned to Nanjing airport from the front. Chiang seems to have known Zhang's views, and to have consistently trusted him.

One other linked point merits attention. The authors say that because of his aggressive position against Japan, General Zhang was 'forced to resign, in September [1937], by an angry, frustrated and undoubtedly suspicious Chiang'. Zhang, however, states – and other sources confirm – that after the initial Japanese victory in the Shanghai region, he was transferred to be the governor of Hunan province. This does not seem to have been a disgrace, since Chiang Kai-shek's plan for a general retreat suggested that the inland province of Hunan, south of the Yangtze with major river links to the southwest, would be a key region in China's future. Zhang adds in his memoirs that it was in Hunan, in November 1937, he finally met up again – after a ten-year gap – with some of the communists (including Zhou Enlai) he had known from the old days in Whampoa. The authors cite General Zhang's memoirs as one of their sources, and there is of course no reason why they should agree with General Zhang on all these details. In this, as in many of the other bold scenarios in *Mao: The Unknown Story*, a tighter historical context would have been helpful to the reader.

3

Any historical approach naturally reflects the times and locations where it was constructed, and Edgar Snow's benign vision of Mao's revolutionary goals and methods was never uncontested. Criticism of his position mushroomed after Chiang Kai-shek's retreat to Taiwan in 1949; in the following year, the grim realities of the Korean War, and the mounting horror and the hellish evidence then emerging of Stalin's Soviet Union, sharpened the critical commentaries on Snow's version of Mao. The domestic American arguments concerning the 'loss of China' and the victimization of the Americans believed to be responsible for it were only part of the story. As Hong Kong under British rule became a haven for refugees fleeing from Mao's China, social scientists flocked to interview them, and to develop the analyses that would delineate the nature of 'brain-washing', and the institutional and emotional underpinnings of the Chinese state and society.

In Taiwan, as the Nationalists dug in and tried to maintain the belief that they would soon be returning to the Mainland, evidence of Communist excesses and atrocities was collected and codified, and made available to researchers. In the People's Republic, each purge or mass movement was accompanied by the compilation of dossiers on those who were charged or implicated, and this 'proof' of their crimes became part of a secret but permanent record. In Japan, though in-depth research into the nature of the Japanese occupation was hesitant, there was extensive collation and reprinting of the field studies undertaken by the Japanese researchers who had lived and worked in Manchuria and north China. The dawning of the Sino-Soviet rift after 1956 also led researchers to explore anew the differences between Soviet and Chinese revolutionary tactics and ideology.

As new materials have become available, the historiography has shifted and deepened. The largest new body of materials related to Mao – on which the authors of *Mao: The Unknown Story* draw liberally – are the floods of memoirs and reminiscences that have recently poured from Chinese presses: originally in Taiwan and Hong Kong, but now on an immense scale from publishers within China itself.

General Zhang's memoirs can be taken as an example of this trend, but the first of these really to catch major Western attention was the memoir by one of Mao's doctors, Li Zhisui, published in Taiwan in 1994 and in English translation by Random House the same year, under the title *The Private Life of Chairman Mao.*[4]

This book sharply highlighted the biggest difficulty of evaluating the memoir literature on Mao: Was it true or not? That it ought to be true was not the key factor – when the bits all seemed to fit in a certain way, could we be sure that some alternative pattern of events might not be equally valid? Li's memoir was coherent and forceful, and with time his depictions of Mao have come to be widely accepted. Dr Li presented a Mao who was totally self-absorbed: erratic and dictatorial, full of opinions and slogans, not especially talented intellectually, fleshly by inclination, innately luxury-loving. Mao's cruelties were shown to have sprung sometimes from random whims, at other times to have been the results of cold calculation. The comparatively measured tone of Li's book encouraged acceptance of its main claims.

I do not feel that the same is true of the unstintingly hostile accounts in *Mao: The Unknown Story*, even though many of its materials are also drawn from Chinese memoir literature, and from interviews with a wide and richly varied cast of characters – among them Mao's former girlfriends, his private secretaries, his bodyguards, his daughter, and the spouses of some senior colleagues who have miraculously survived. Particularly hard to evaluate are materials that appeared in China in conjunction with the purging and kangaroo trials of senior political figures such as the former president Liu Shaoqi and his wife, Wang Guangmei, or Lin Biao and his wife, Ye Qun, who allegedly tried to assassinate Mao in 1971 and died in a plane crash as they fled to the Soviet Union shortly after their coup failed.

During the period between 1973 and 1975 the entire country was mobilized by Mao to criticize the former army marshal Lin Biao and his family, and as had been true so often in the past with other fallen leaders, people hastened to create condemnatory documentation that would brand each new victim with his or her due level of infamy. Here, for instance, is part of an allegedly bugged telephone conversation between Lin Biao's wife, Ye Qun, and the army's chief of staff, Huang Yongsheng, a man Lin Biao himself appointed in 1968 when he and Mao were in close partnership. As the authors explain, Huang was 'a well-known womaniser' and 'soon became Mrs Lin's lover'. Mrs Lin herself was then a powerful figure who soon became a member of the Politburo. The authors write:

> Ye Qun was a woman of voracious sexual appetite, for which she had little outlet with the clearly impotent marshal, whom she described as 'a frozen corpse.' The relationship between her and her lover is revealed in a three-hour telephone conversation that was bugged.

> YE QUN [YQ]: I am so worried you might get into trouble for pursuing physical satisfaction. I can tell you, this life of mine is linked with you, political life and personal life. ... Don't you know what 101 [Lin Biao's code name] is like at home? I live with his abuse. ... I can sense you value feelings. ...

The country is big. Our children can each take up one key position! Am I not right?

HUANG: Yes, you are absolutely right.

YQ: ... Our children put together, there must be five of them. They will be like five generals and will get on. Each will take one key position, and they can all be your assistants.

HUANG: Oh? I am so grateful to you!

YQ: ... I took that measure [implying contraceptive]. Just in case I have it and have to get rid of it [implying baby], I hope you will come and visit me once. [Sound of sobbing]

HUANG: I will come! I will come! Don't be like this. This makes me very sad.

YQ: Another thing: you mustn't be restricted by me. You can fool around. ... I'm not narrow-minded. You can have other women, and be hot with them. Don't worry about me ...

This transcript is quoted by the authors from a Chinese volume published in 1993, the title of which the authors translate as *Super Trial (Chaoji Shenpan)*. But that volume, a slamming indictment of the Gang of Four led by Mao's wife Jiang Qing, and of all members of Lin Biao's family who conspired with them, gives no sources at all. The transcript is simply printed there with no attribution save for the vague remark that it was 'listened to clandestinely' by Lin Biao and Ye Qun's own son, so that he would have a hold over his mother.[5]

Since all three of these people were allegedly involved together in a plan to assassinate Mao in 1971, and were all killed in a getaway plane that crashed in Mongolia later that year, little verification is possible. Even if this passage is cited in *Super Trial* as a genuine transcript, it still seems to me much closer to the bawdy Chinese popular storytelling tradition than to an actual bugged conversation between two of China's top political figures: this, after all, was during the Cultural Revolution, in a society rife with spies and informers of every stripe, where discretion was essential to survival. Though we are comparatively used to sexual vagaries in our own society, the situation in China was surely incomparably different. We can imagine such an account being used, at some point, to discredit Ye Qun and her husband, but we should know more about its provenance before accepting it on its face.

Mao: The Unknown Story contains many other examples of 'secret' conversations between the top leaders of China which somehow have made their way into the memoir literature and thus become 'sources'. It is rare that the authors show the candor that they do on one occasion, where, citing some remarks about foreigners' sexual habits made by the wife of the guerrilla leader Zhu De, they comment that her 'information reflected the gossip of the day'.

Despite its length, *Mao: The Unknown Story* avoids seriously grappling with other factors that made the twentieth century such a terrible one for tens of millions of Chinese, irrespective of what Mao may have done: these would include the depth and savagery of the Japanese assault on China, the nature of the Chinese labour movement, the realities of peasant deprivation in republican China, the collapse of local order and the spread of banditry, the strength of organized criminal gangs, the significance of Chiang Kai-shek's lack of political and military skills, the social, regional, and class differences that separated the communists from one another, and the technical aid, including police training methods, spycraft, and military communications, furnished by the United States to the Nationalists.

By focusing so tightly on Mao's vileness – to the exclusion of other factors – the authors undermine much of the power their story might have had. By seeking to demonstrate that Mao started out as a vile person and stayed vile throughout his life, the authors deny any room for change, whether growth or degeneration, for subtlety or the possibilities of redemption. The countless Chinese who did struggle for change are denied any role in their own story, and become mere ciphers, their lives and deaths without purpose. With few exceptions, particularly General Peng Dehuai, who stood up to Mao on several key occasions and was eventually tortured and killed, Mao's senior colleagues and would-be comrades are presented here as pathetic figures, easily manipulated, unable, apparently, to fathom even Mao's grossest and most far-fetched power plays and deceptions. Locked into their misery by the force of one man's personality, the Chinese people as a whole are denied all agency. And Mao himself ceases to be absorbing. How far can Mao have to fall, when he is at the bottom already?

As I was reading this book, I kept asking myself why historians should feel that they ought to be fair even to pathological monsters, if that is truly what Mao was. The most salient answer is perhaps structural as much as conceptual. Without some attempt at fairness there is no nuance, no sense of light and dark. The monster, acute and deadly, just shambles on down some monstrous path of his own devising. If he has no conscience, no meaningful vision of a different world except one where he is supreme, while his enemies are constantly humiliated and his people starve, then there is nothing we can learn from such a man. And that is a conclusion that, across the ages, historians have always tried to resist.

Part II

Reviews in *The China Journal*

4 The portrayal of opportunism, betrayal and manipulation in Mao's rise to power

Gregor Benton and Steve Tsang

An expanded version of a review first published in *The China Journal*, January 2006.

To look at China's revolution through the prism of a man whom CCP politics long revolved around is not in itself a bad idea. Pro-Maoists have too often abbreviated the revolution to a hagiography of Mao, so a book that examines the complex interplay between a leader's life and the historical context would be welcome. Regrettably, Chang and Halliday merely invert the error of the Mao worshippers. Where the worshippers imply that Mao sprang from the womb a Marxist, Chang and Halliday argue that Mao sprang from the womb a monster. Armed with this opinion, they simplify complex causalities in favour of a myopic focus on the machinations of a single tyrant.

Such methods make for bad history and worse biography. History requires a catholic regard for facts, especially those that subvert one's prejudices. It calls for a judicious assessment of the evidence and the setting of events in context. Biography needs an all-sided grasp of its subject and an awareness of his or her coherence and integrity, as well as a sense of empathy to enable the biographer to understand why the subject does what he or she does. The authors depict Mao (before 1949) as a power-hungry sadist, a bandit, a coward, an idler, an egomaniac, a cunning fool, a hopeless orator, an utterly selfish 'leader' who was despised more than respected by his comrades and followers, and an incompetent and cruel military commander, as well as an opportunist who ended up by accident a revolutionary and leader of a movement that seized power in the world's most populous country. They ignore or misconstrue his ideas and fail to analyze the interplay between him and his political, social and intellectual environment. They attribute the CCP's success first and foremost to Mao's building of a reign of terror from the first moment he had access to power in it, as well as to massive assistance and long-standing guidance by Moscow and the Comintern's adroit planting of three moles in the Kuomintang.

Chang and Halliday make much of the decade they spent researching this book, which lists a formidable number of sources and informants. We therefore devote the bulk of our review to scrutinizing their research. We concentrate on issues we know from our own work and on extreme claims that are easily checked. We stick to the period up to 1949 (in which we are specialists). We find that the authors make numerous flawed assertions, both about Mao and the broader context. They misread sources, use them selectively, use them out of context, or otherwise trim or bend them to cast Mao in an unrelentingly bad light. They also make claims about other important events and personalities that distort rather than illuminate a crucial period in China's modern history.

Individualism and self-interest

Chang and Halliday maintain that Mao before 1927 was wholly indifferent to the sufferings of peasants, workers and women, although this opinion is belied by a mass of evidence in Mao's writings. Their thesis culminates in the claim that Mao equated morality with absolute selfishness and irresponsibility (pp. 13–14), an argument they base on a tendentious reading of his notes on Friedrich Paulsen. Like many Chinese in the 1910s, Mao believed in the redemptive power of individualism. Exalting individuality was essential not just to destroy Confucianism's rigid hierarchies but to create altruism and connect with the 'greater self'. Mutual aid represented 'fulfilment of the individual. … Self-interests are indeed primary for human beings, but it does not stop here. It is also our nature to extend this to helping others … so working for the interests of others is in my own self-interest'.[1] These ideas are wholly missing from Chang and Halliday's caricature.

A communist of the Soviet type?

> [Mao's] instincts were those of a Leninist. Some other Communists – especially the Party leader Professor Chen [Duxiu], who flew into a rage when he heard about mob atrocities and insisted that they had to be reined in – were ultimately not Communists of the Soviet type.
>
> (p. 43)

Chen did oppose 'excesses', but not for the reasons Chang and Halliday think. He was afraid that attacks on landlords would 'frighten society' and alienate Nationalist army officers. He took this stand under the influence of the Russian Borodin, who feared that excesses by 'local rascals' might bring down the united front that Moscow favoured.[2] Later, after falling out with the Russians, Chen regretted having accused the peasants of 'going too far' and called Moscow's China policy 'shameful'.[3] So Chen was the real 'Communist of the Soviet type' in 1927, while Mao's glorification of 'excesses' as a necessary part of revolution put him at odds with the Comintern.

Mao and Putonghua

> Mao was no good at languages and all his life spoke only his own local dialect and not even the Putonghua – 'common speech' – that his own regime made its official language.
>
> (p. 16)

Mao did speak Putonghua – though with a very strong accent. Had he spoken only his local dialect, no one outside Shaoshan would have understood him. Like others of his generation, he strongly supported the national language. In 1917, he proposed using it in workers' classes. Editing a magazine in 1919, he insisted articles were in the national language. He asked a former teacher to send him materials about the national language, and he promoted it in schools.[4] In this respect, he was a child of his age and not the parochial obscurantist Chang and Halliday portray him as.

The start of the Long March

No one wanted to be left behind in the Central Soviet in late 1934. ... Xiang [Ying] argued strongly against taking Mao along.

(pp. 127–9)

There is no reliable evidence that Mao was afraid to remain in Jiangxi because he wanted to stay near the party's centre of power. Otto Braun (Chang and Halliday's source for the claim) does not in fact say Xiang wanted to keep Mao in Jiangxi.[5] (Why would Xiang have wanted to share the rearguard with a man he loathed?) Some of those left behind in Jiangxi were Mao supporters, others were not. Later, people depicted the rearguard as a death legion, but at the time no one knew whether it was safer to go or stay.[6] There has been much gossip about the selection of the rearguard, most of it factional or self-interested. It can be used to support almost any theory.

Chiang 'let the Long Marchers go'

[General He Jian] manned the fourth fortification line, situated at an ideal place to wipe out the Reds, on the west bank of the Xiang. There were no bridges, and the Reds, who had no anti-aircraft guns, had to wade across the wide river, easy targets from land and air. But again they went completely unmolested. ... Chiang let the CCP leadership and the main force of the Red Army escape. ... He wanted to drive the Reds into [Guizhou and Sichuan], so that their warlords ... would allow [him] in to drive the Reds out. ... Letting the Reds go was also a goodwill gesture on Chiang's part towards Russia.

(pp. 136–40)

It is true that Chiang used the Long March to weaken the warlords and that many warlords did little to resist it. But did Chiang loyalists let the marchers escape across the Xiang River? The Taiwan historian Kuo Hua-lun (Warren Kuo) quotes Chen Jan (a Long Marcher and Kuo's main informant) and Liu Bocheng to show that the communists 'had to fight with resolve' to break through at the Xiang and lost 50,000 men.[7] Peng Dehuai, Chang and Halliday's 'most honest' communist, mentions hard fighting.[8] Braun, whom they also trust, reported huge losses and said Chiang wanted 'to destroy our main force while crossing the river'.[9] The book ignores this firsthand and seemingly reliable testimony.

Chiang chose the destination for the Long March

> Chiang did not want the Reds to cling on in the rich heartland of China. His aim was to drive them into a more barren and sparsely populated corner, where he could box them in ... [in] the northern part of Shaanxi province. ... The main person Chiang used to implement this scheme was none other than Shao Li-tze. ... Shao was appointed governor of Shaanxi in April 1933. ... At the exact moment the Long March began, in mid-October 1934, Chiang came to Shaanxi province for a visit.
>
> (p. 141)

This theory assumes that Chiang had decided, at least in general terms, as early as April 1933 to drive the communists from their southern bases to northern Shaanxi, a year and four months before he launched the campaign that finally overwhelmed the Jiangxi Soviet. In April 1933, Japan's Kwantung Army was on the move in north China and two of Chiang's divisions suffered a major reverse at the hands of the communists in Jiangxi. On 11 April, Chiang privately told senior officers that 'the key to China's survival was not the external threat but the internal one' – hardly an indication that he would tolerate the continued weakening of national unity by the communists while he worked out a long-term plan to resist Japan.[10] In this period, Chiang carried out a wholesale reorganization of his army to prepare to resist the Japanese.[11] Even if he had had the imagination, ability and time in 1933 to work out a strategy and find a suitable place to box in the communists, could he have spared the military resources necessary to drive the Long Marchers to Shaanxi, particularly after the Japanese stepped up their military pressure in 1935? According to his official diary in the Chiang Kai-shek Papers at the Academia Historica, which Chang and Halliday consulted, Chiang did not think the Long Marchers would go to Shaanxi. He expected them to try to join up with their Soviet patrons and head towards Outer Mongolia, by way either of Qinghai or of western or northern Sichuan and Ningxia.[12] As for his visit to Shaanxi in 1934, this was part of his effort to promote the New Life Movement, which took him to ten provinces in forty days.[13]

The Dadu River 'myth'

> There was no battle at the Dadu bridge. ... Chiang had left the passage open.
>
> (p. 159)

Chang and Halliday quote a 93-year-old local woman to prove Mao invented the Dadu fighting and claim that Nationalist communications made no mention of it. However, another surviving witness among the local residents, 85-year-old Li Guxiu, told an Australian journalist who wanted to check the Chang and Halliday account that she recalled fighting at the bridge.[14] Whatever the case, the personal recollections of civilian bystanders after such a long time are probably unreliable. Mao certainly exaggerated the battle, but there is plenty of evidence that one took place. Braun (a Mao-hater whom they quote frequently – but not here) reports fighting on 25 May (on the water – an event they barely mention), which he watched from an 'elevated place'; and on 29 May, at the bridge.[15] Braun's story is similar to Mao's. He says the Nationalists removed some foot-planks and tried to burn the rest. Chang and Halliday cite a vague statement by Peng Dehuai to prove there was no fighting, but ignore his firm recollection elsewhere that the marchers defeated Liu Wenhui, crossed the Dadu River, and captured the Luding Bridge.[16] *Zhanshi bao* (Soldier), a Red Army magazine, reported the river fighting on 26 May, the day after it happened. On 30 May, *Hongxing* (Red Star) described the bridge crossing and *Zhanshi bao* listed those who spearheaded it.[17] Chengdu's *Chuan bao* (Sichuan Daily, 17, 22 and 25 May) and *Xinxin xinwen* (New News, 15 and 18 May and 8 June) mention deployments to defend the river.[18] On 22 May, Chiang ordered the 90th Division to annihilate the remnants of the communists near the Dadu River.[19] Military dispatches say Chiang appointed Yang Sen as river commander.[20] In a telegram sent in May, Chiang ordered Liu Wenhui 'on pain of a court martial' to hold fast at the Dadu River in order to enable Xue Yue's 100,000-strong army to catch up with the Red Army and destroy it south of the river.[21] Yuan Guorui, one of Liu's brigadiers, ordered Li Quanshan to guard the bridge.[22] Zhang Boyan (Liu's chief of staff) and other former Nationalist officers describe the battle. On 28 May, Li positioned a battalion at the Luding Bridge. It arrived in the evening, and controlled both sides of the bridge. The soldiers started to remove planks. As it was raining and dark and the soldiers were tired and suffering from opium addiction, they stopped. Li and the rest of his regiment arrived the following morning, on 29 May. By then, the Red Army was at the other end of the bridge, so Li was unable to remove the rest of the planks. In fighting, Li's regiment lost fifty men. By the evening, the Red Army main force had arrived. Li telephoned Yuan for instructions, saying the bridge was difficult to hold. Yuan was himself engaged in fighting. When the telephone went dead, Li panicked and ordered a withdrawal. He left behind a squadron and ordered the burning of the bridge.[23] Chang and Halliday say Li Quanshan was not at the bridge, but early CCP sources describe his defence of it.[24] On 30 May, a Nationalist Division reported that the Reds 'besieged Luding and fought a fierce battle with Liu Wenhui'.[25]

Chang and Halliday's 'strongest evidence' that no fighting happened at the bridge is their claim that the 22-strong vanguard of bridge-crossers suffered 'no battle casualties'. If right, this would have been a good (though not necessarily conclusive) argument. Conversely, the fact of casualties would disprove their theory. So it is a shame that they apparently failed to consult the exhaustive four-volume history of the First Front Red Army, published in 2003, which says three members of the 22-strong vanguard 'died as martyrs'.[26] None of the sources cited in this paragraph figures in Chang and Halliday's book. Chiang did not leave the passage open.

The Xi'an Incident

> [Zhang Xueliang] plotted to supplant [Chiang]. ... He aspired to rule all of China [p. 182]. ... By the end of October 1936, the Reds were desperate. The Young Marshal saw an opportunity to rescue them, and gain favour with Moscow. His plan was simple, and extreme: to kidnap Chiang. ... And Mao very deliberately concealed the plan from Moscow, knowing that Stalin would be dead set against it. ... Mao gave the Young Marshal the impression that he, the Young Marshal, was their only possible partner, implying that Moscow would accept this.
>
> (p. 187)

That Mao double-crossed Stalin and Zhang would be a significant finding if true. However, Chang and Halliday's account of the Xi'an Incident lacks credibility, for in good Maoist style they airbrush out a key player. Nowhere do they mention General Yang Hucheng, Zhang's co-conspirator and a participant in some of Zhang's discussions with the communists, who was in charge of security in Xi'an at the time of Chiang's arrest.[27] Yang repeatedly prevented Zhang from releasing Chiang.[28] When Chiang was still his prisoner, Zhang admitted he had not made up his mind to detain him until 10 December 1936, less than two days before the kidnapping.[29] Chang and Halliday's only reference to Yang is in a footnote (p. 141) where they refer to him as a 'fellow traveller' who collaborated with the supposed communist mole Shao Lizi. Why do they erase him from the record? Perhaps because their theory of a Zhang-Mao conspiracy would otherwise collapse. As for Zhang, they inform readers that they interviewed him in 1993. However, we find nothing in the archives or in Zhang's other recollections after his release from house arrest half a century later to suggest that his motive in kidnapping Chiang was to supplant him, with Soviet backing. Zhang was the only leading warlord to swear allegiance to the central government on his own initiative after Chiang's forces took Beijing at the end of the Northern Expedition, unlike many who did so because of Chiang's military intimidation or the prospect of spoils. Zhang kidnapped Chiang not to supplant him but because he disagreed with his strategy of first pacifying China before resisting Japan.

The New Fourth Army (N4A) Incident, January 1941[30]

> [By January 1940] the N4A, operating under Liu [Shaoqi] near Shanghai and Nanjing, had tripled, to 30,000.
>
> (p. 225)

The Jiangnan troops (south of the Yangtze) were not under Liu. Most of the N4A was north of the Yangtze. It was twice as big as Chang and Halliday say.

> Mao set Xiang Ying's group up to be killed by the Nationalist army, in the hope that the massacre would persuade Stalin to let him off the leash against Chiang.
>
> (p. 236)

Chang and Halliday argue that Mao mounted his trap because Xiang had opposed him in the past, and because he wanted an excuse to turn on Chiang. Just before the incident that led to Xiang's destruction, in January 1941, Chiang told him to cross the Yangtze by a guaranteed direct route. Mao, however, ordered him to go north along a vetoed route that veered east, and kept the order secret. He also withheld a message by Xiang to Chiang about the route. Xiang marched unannounced into a Nationalist force, which thought it was under attack and hit out. Xiang asked Mao to get Chiang to stop the fighting, but Mao did nothing. Not until 12 January, the day before the ceasefire, did Mao tell Zhou Enlai (in Chongqing) to get the siege called off – by which time it was too late.

Chang and Halliday's claim that Mao set Xiang up to be killed is not supported by the evidence. Did Mao tell Xiang to go north along a route Chiang had vetoed, and keep the order secret? On 25 December 1940, Mao told Zhou to ask Chiang to let Xiang use two routes, including the easterly one. The next day, Mao told Xiang to work out for himself how to go north. On the 28th, the Jiangnan leaders told Mao they would go by an easterly route, copying an earlier instruction from Yan'an. On the 29th, Zhou told Mao the easterly route was safe. Mao passed on the message to Xiang. The next day, Liu and Chen Yi said they were urging Xiang to go by the easterly route, and asked Mao to do the same. On 31 December and 1 January, the Jiangnan leaders said they were preparing to march east. Did Mao withhold Xiang's message to Chiang? Even if he did, Ye Ting, the N4A Commander, told the Nationalists on 2 January that he was preparing to send a regiment east. On the 3rd, Ye asked Fang Riying, a Nationalist general on the easterly route, to free a passage for the marchers. Instead, Fang blocked the area. Ye and Xiang stayed incommunicado after 3 January, but Fang was obviously ready for them.

Did Xiang frantically ask Mao between 6 and 9 January to get Chiang to stop the firing? Chang and Halliday seem not to know that Xiang went AWOL on the 8th and hid in the mountains for three days, out of contact with Ye and his command. On the 10th, Ye asked Mao and Zhou to negotiate an end to the offensive. Ye and Xiang (by then reunited) told Mao they could hold out for a week and asked Yan'an to threaten Chiang with a split. On the 11th, Ye told Mao he planned to break out of the siege. On the 12th, Mao told Ye to hold talks, prepare to break out, and not to bank on negotiations in Chongqing. On the 13th, Ye's messages to Liu stopped. On the 14th, Mao said Chiang had ordered a ceasefire, but Ye was by then a prisoner. On the 11th, Ye had drafted a note requesting Chiang to lift the siege and asked Yan'an to decide whether to send it on. Mao decided not to. Perhaps he thought the message pointless, since Zhou was negotiating anyway.

Mao's view of Xiang's presence in Jiangnan changed repeatedly in 1940. When he feared that Chiang was thinking of surrendering to Japan, he urged Xiang to go north. When he thought Chiang would continue to resist, he told Xiang he could stay put for the time being. But Mao's reasoning was flawed, for Chiang's hostility to Japan did not erase his anticommunism.

Then there was Xiang's self-interest. Xiang was no cat's-paw and had his own reasons for wanting to stay south. The contradictions in Mao's directives were partly a result of deals he struck with Xiang, in what was a process of negotiation.

One can at best say that Mao was complicit in Xiang's procrastination – he was certainly not its cause. In the fog of war, mistakes happen. N4A sourcebooks are littered with discrepant messages between Mao, Zhou, Xiang and Liu from this period. Chang and Halliday think they have solved the mystery, but all they have really done is reduce a complex situation to a schema to support their prejudice.

The allegation that Mao engineered the N4A 'massacre' to persuade Stalin to unleash him against Chiang is doubly hard to credit. It is true that Mao decided to launch a political and military counteroffensive in the heat of the moment, on hearing that Ye faced destruction, but he swiftly dropped the idea on the advice of Zhou, Liu and the Comintern. He knew that Stalin's foremost interest in Asia at the time was to ensure Chiang would continue to resist the Japanese and thus reduce the danger of Japan attacking the Soviet Union. Indeed, in the immediate aftermath of the Incident, Stalin offered Chiang aircraft that he had refused to supply a few months earlier.[31]

> Communist propaganda claimed that up to 10,000 [N4A] were massacred. In fact, the total casualty figure was around 2,000. Three thousand had managed to escape back to their own side by turning round and taking the North Route across the Yangtze, the one designated by Chiang. They were unmolested. ... [Chiang found it hard to condemn the N4A incident, for] he had not protested publicly about the many earlier and much larger clashes in which his troops had been the victims.
>
> (p. 241)

Actually, no one knows how many casualties there were. Mao mentioned 7,000. A CCP official said 6,000. For the Nationalists, Chen Cheng talked of 10,000 and Leng Xin of 3,000 to 4,000. Chiang's official diary listed 4,400 communists captured, including 900 officers.[32] Chang and Halliday claim the northern route Chiang had set for the marchers was safe, but in fact the Nationalists had stationed strong forces along it and planned to destroy the N4A on the Yangtze. The Japanese were informed of the route. Far from being 'unmolested', the marchers who about-turned along this route suffered fierce attacks. Chiang had in principle authorized Gu Zhutong to deal with the N4A in early November 1940, though only if Gu was fully prepared and confident of success so the communists would be unable to exploit the incident to their own ends.[33] Chiang made this decision after his army had suffered heavy losses in a N4A attack a month earlier, in which the 33rd Division was partly destroyed and its commander and a brigadier were captured.[34] It is untrue that Chiang had not publicized earlier N4A attacks on his troops.

Three communist moles

Planting moles was one of the most priceless gifts that Moscow bequeathed to the CCP. Mostly these moles joined the Nationalists in the first half of the

1920s. ... Infiltration worked on several levels. As well as overt Communists working inside the Nationalist movement, as Mao did, there were also secret Communists. ... For the next twenty years and more, they [the latter] ... played a gigantic role in helping deliver China to Mao.

(pp. 138–9)

It is well known that the Kuomintang failed to prevent communist infiltration, so the authors' account of the planting of three super agents is not in itself implausible. The three alleged moles were Shao Lizi, Zhang Zhizhong and Hu Zongnan. In Chang and Halliday's account, Shao saved the CCP from destruction by taking Chiang's son Ching-kuo to Russia in November 1925 on Moscow's instructions, as Stalin's hostage (p. 139). As a result, Chiang accepted the 'survival of the CCP [in exchange] for Ching-kuo' during the Long March (p. 140). As for Zhang, he is said to have started a full-scale war with Japan and thus greatly weakened Chiang's regime and given the CCP the chance to rebuild and expand. He is supposed to have done so because Stalin was concerned that 'Japan's swift occupation of northern China in July [1937] posed very direct danger' to the Soviet Union (p. 208). As for Hu, he is said to have allowed the communists to destroy large parts of his 500,000-strong army after seizing Yan'an on Chiang's order in 1947. He sealed the Nationalists' fate in the Yan'an war theatre and helped turn the Civil War against Chiang. But in all three cases the authors' evidence is mainly circumstantial and their arguments lack analytical coherence.

Shao Lizi

The authors make much of Chiang's supposed deal with Stalin to trade Ching-kuo for the survival of the CCP, but they produce no evidence even of a 'gentlemen's agreement'. They premise their case on Chiang's obsession with preserving his biological heir. But while Ching-kuo was indeed Chiang's only biological son and Chiang cared deeply for his sons, neither the Chiang Papers nor the writings of Ching-kuo and Wei-kuo, Chiang's younger and non-biological son, suggest Chiang treasured Ching-kuo more than Wei-kuo. In fact, they suggest he doted more on Wei-kuo. In November 1943, when Wei-kuo was with the Chinese Army in India, Chiang three times pressed him to return to China, but to no avail. On his way home to Chongqing from Cairo, where he agreed that the Chinese Army in India would attack Burma in coordination with the British, Chiang arranged to stop over in Ramgarh, where he picked up Wei-kuo.[35] In contrast, he did not hesitate to send Ching-kuo on highly dangerous missions, such as going to Kunming on 22 September 1949, to make sure General Lu Han, thought to be about to defect to the communists, would not kidnap Chiang, who was scheduled to arrive a few hours later.[36] If, as the authors claim, Chiang was so angry with Shao that he took revenge by having Shao's son killed in 1931 – 'a son for a son' (p. 140), another Chang-Halliday assertion unsupported by hard evidence – why did Chiang continue to work closely with Shao after Ching-kuo returned to China in 1937? Chiang's diary records that Chiang received Ching-kuo back with no great show of emotion.[37] Is that likely if the price he paid for his son was the CCP's survival? Chiang was old-fashioned, but he had no dynastic ambition. Ching-kuo only became his heir after Chen Cheng died in 1965. Chiang came to rely on Ching-kuo heavily only after he proved his worth as a 'revolutionary comrade' in the crises of 1949. In the 1920s, Chiang was merely Commandant of the Whampoa Academy and only became Commander of one of the six Corps of the new National Revolutionary Army in August 1925, when Ching-kuo had already decided to go to the Soviet Union. Why was Chiang's son picked to be a Soviet hostage while other more senior leaders were spared?

Zhang Zhizhong

The authors assert that Zhang was a sleeper activated by Stalin after the Marco Polo Bridge Incident of 7 July 1937. However, they give no evidence to show how this was done. They claim that as garrison commander in Shanghai Zhang triggered a full-scale war by staging an incident at Hongqiao Airport on 9 August to provoke the Japanese and that he disobeyed Chiang's orders on 14 and 16 August by attacking Japanese forces in Shanghai (pp. 208–9). But the Japanese had already seized Beijing and Tianjin and were reinforcing their army in north China when the Hongqiao incident occurred. While some Japanese diplomats might have wanted to avoid an escalation in the fighting, the authors' assertion that the 'Japanese gave every sign of wishing to defuse the incident' (p. 209) is false.

Eleven days before the incident, on 29 July, the Japanese High Command issued a directive to crush the Chinese army in the Beijing-Tianjin area and to prepare to use force in Qingdao and Shanghai.[38] On the day of the incident, the Japanese requested marine reinforcements within five hours of the shooting, and deployed them in Shanghai less than forty hours later.[39] On the day after the incident, the Japanese Cabinet ordered an additional three army divisions to Shanghai.[40] On the Chinese side, as far back as 11 July, Chiang had put his forces on a war footing, designated 100 divisions for frontline duties with 80 more as reserve, and ordered six months' ammunition and supplies to be distributed along the Yangtze.[41] On 13 July, Chiang ordered Zhang to prepare Shanghai for a Japanese attack. In early August, Chiang made sure the Air Force was deployed in airfields that could defend Shanghai despite north China's desperate need for air support.[42] On 7 August, two days before the incident, Chiang and top regional military leaders had decided to resist Japan, although they also agreed that diplomacy would continue while China mobilized.[43]

On 12 August, the day after the first Japanese Marine reinforcements landed in Shanghai, Nanjing put its High Command on a war footing and Chiang deployed two crack divisions in Shanghai in contravention of the agreement that ended the 1932 Shanghai Incident (under which no regular Chinese forces were allowed in the city). On 13 August, with a land force of 12,000 (compared to 3,000 Marines before the incident) and more naval firepower and air cover than was available to the entire Chinese Navy, the Japanese started hostilities, though 'it was the Chinese who took swift, decisive and well-coordinated action once hostilities started'.[44]

When Zhang allegedly attacked the Japanese against Chiang's instructions on 14 and 16 August (p. 209), the Shanghai campaign had already started and both sides were rushing reinforcements to the front. The rapid escalation in Shanghai does not support Chang and Halliday's assertion that 'war became unstoppable as large Japanese reinforcements began to arrive on 22 August' (p. 209).

Chang and Halliday forget that Chiang had decided in 1935 that when war came, Chinese forces would maintain an in-depth defence in the north while using mobile forces to defend the Yangtze basin.[45] A stand in Shanghai was critical, for Chiang wanted to expose Western interests to Japanese aggression to win Western support. In constructing their Stalin-Zhang spy plot, the authors disregard Japan's overwhelming military superiority in 1937. Few if any military observers believed Chiang's forces could hold out for long. Why should Stalin think that spreading the war from north China to Shanghai would make the Soviet Union safer? Would the Japanese not be freer to threaten the Soviet Union after subjugating China, which would be made more likely by opening a new front in the south? Did Zhang really stage the Hongqiao incident? Chang and Halliday cite Zhang Zhizhong's memoirs as a source, but the page cited and Zhang's account of the Shanghai campaign provide no basis for such an assertion.[46] Did Zhang disobey the two orders? Zhang's memoirs merely record his disagreement and unhappiness with some of Chiang's directives.[47]

Hu Zongnan

Chang and Halliday's case against Hu is even flimsier. To say Hu was a spy because Mao learned that Chiang had ordered Hu to attack Yan'an on the day the order was issued (p. 313) ignores more likely explanations. The information could have come from real communist moles whose identity we (as well as Chang and Halliday) know, such as Liu Fei and Guo Rugui, who occupied offices that could have allowed them to tip Mao off. More likely, the communist party's own explanation is correct: the source was Xiong Xianghui, a communist agent in Hu's office.[48]

Why do the authors ignore Xiong's account of his role, although they list his autobiography in their bibliography?[49] Given that they provide no evidence to show that Hu contacted Mao, why do they think their own explanation more plausible? As for Hu directing his army to be destroyed piecemeal by Mao after capturing Yan'an, why did Hu, by then in command of the largest field army under Chiang, not simply declare his real allegiance and turn against Chiang? Why did Hu continue to fight for Chiang all the way from Shaanxi to Sichuan until he was airlifted out of Xichang in March 1950? And why did he not arrest Chiang when Chiang was under his protection in December 1949?[50]

Chang and Halliday believe that the common strands that linked the three 'moles' were their sympathy for the communist cause during the United Front of the 1920s and their actions in holding the Kuomintang back from destroying the CCP, directing Chiang's attention elsewhere, or allowing their own forces to be destroyed by the communists. Following this line of reasoning and using the same standard of proof, Chang and Halliday should have gone on to unmask the fourth and biggest mole – Chiang Kai-shek. As the leading 'Red General' in Guangzhou up to 1926 and the man who can be said to have actually delivered all that Shao, Zhang and Hu allegedly delivered, he was without doubt the biggest gift 'Moscow bequeathed to the CCP'.

Conclusion

After checking Chang and Halliday's sources against our own research, we conclude that their book fails to provide a judicious reconstruction or a fair evaluation of Mao. Nor does it tell us much of value about Mao or the history of China that we did not already know. It reduces to Mao's personal wickedness and his terrorizing of his comrades and the Chinese people the complexity and real forces that shaped the CCP and enabled it to seize power. We do not disagree that Mao authored atrocities and suffering and that he bullied and murdered party members and others to advance his own or the party's cause. But the CCP's rise to power, Mao's success in establishing and retaining leadership over the other party leaders, and his skilful turning of Soviet aid to his own ends cannot be explained by the authors' one-dimensional formulation. Their view of Mao is not much less prejudiced and distorted than Beijing's official line, though it lies at the other end of the spectrum.

Some of the authors' most important claims for the period up to 1949 are controverted by the evidence. Others, such as the large-scale aid the CCP received from the Soviet Union or the cultivation of opium in the Yan'an years, have already been noted by other scholars. The book's biggest problem is its one-sidedness and improper use of sources. As a result, we feel it does not represent a reliable contribution to our understanding of Mao or of twentieth-century China.

5 The new number one counter-revolutionary inside the party

Academic biography as mass criticism

Timothy Cheek

First published in *The China Journal*, January 2006.

Michael Oakeshott famously described education as a conversation. That insight speaks to the heart of the matter in Chang and Halliday's biography of Mao, and particularly the part under review in this section (chs 20–32), which covers the period 1937–49. These are the years of the Japanese invasion, the years of the second United Front between the CCP and the KMT, the years of Yan'an and rectification and the rise of Mao to supreme, indeed deified, leadership, the years of massive expansion of the CCP in land, labour and military might, and the years of the final Civil War with the Kuomintang that ended in victory for the CCP and the establishment of the People's Republic of China under the leadership of the party and Mao. There have been many stories about this portion of Mao's life and of the life of the CCP and of the history of China from war and revolution to national reintegration.[1] None of those stories, however, appears in this book. Instead, we get a single line, the one met in the first nineteen chapters: Mao the monster making history by nefarious deeds, along with Stalin and a handful of moles, traitors and American fools.

Despite its impressive reference apparatus, Chang and Halliday's book is not a history in the accepted sense of a reasoned historical analysis. It is, ironically, a Maoist denunciation of Mao himself, done in the florid style of the Cultural Revolution denunciations of Liu Shaoqi, Deng Xiaoping, Peng Zhen and so many others of Mao's discarded colleagues in the mid-to-late-1960s. The deceptive show of primary research belies a distorted and unprofessional refusal to take account of contrary information in the primary and secondary sources cited, or to give established scholarship the due of an explicit engagement and rebuttal. There is no Oakeshott-style conversation, and the result is a great waste of effort. For Jung Chang and Jon Halliday have been industrious: they select their details from a daunting array of sources, and yet their story actually tells us very little that is new and that historians can, upon inspection, believe. There really is an 'unknown story' related to this book: it is the story that remains unknown to the non-specialist reader, the story of the world in which Mao lived, a sense of the agency of other actors in Chinese history, an appreciation of the difference among particular historical moments, a recognition of change over time. We are given no convincing account of why Marxism-Leninism became so powerful an organizing force on a nationwide level in the 1940s nor of Mao's role in the development of so disconcerting an ideology, initially so alien to Chinese tradition, yet fatefully so effective when combined with it. We don't learn much about China at all, not to mention how the party Mao came to lead operated (beyond the uniform claims that it ruled by terror alone and always). While Mao is consistently demonized in this text, we really get nothing of the tragedy of the dark side of Chinese communism, because we have no contrast, no reasonable assessment of its achievements by which to judge the costs.

Given that this biography of Mao reads like an entertaining Chinese version of a TV soap opera – *Dallas* (Mao as 'J.R.') for the older generation or *The O.C.* for younger readers – and in light of the considerable publicity effort by both the publisher and the authors (Chang, herself, remains widely admired by the general reading public for her immensely popular biographical book *Wild Swans*), this book will have an impact on popular images of China and most probably on the students in the classrooms of teaching China scholars. As such, I recommend teaching this as a flawed work in conjunction with other, more scholarly, accounts.

The 'Evil Man' school of history

Chang and Halliday portray Mao as an evil, power- and sex-hungry sadist who works for his personal advantage in the most despicable ways, relying on trickery, manipulation and terror. In the middle of Part Three of the book, 'Building His Power Base', we are introduced to a Mao bankrolled by the Soviet Union to fight Chiang Kai-shek and not the Japanese (ch. 20) and ultimately to carve up China with Stalin (ch. 21). Mao dispatches his bothersome lieutenants in the New Fourth Army Incident (ch. 22), builds his power within the CCP by raw terror in the rectification campaign and spy purges in Yan'an (ch. 23), and poisons one of his main rivals for leadership, Wang Ming (ch. 24). Next we see Mao enjoying this 'realm of persecution' as supreme leader, toying with his toadies (Kang Sheng and Liu Shaoqi) and playing with his women while building up his personality cult (ch. 25). In Part IV, 'To Conquer China', we see Mao run a rapacious regime of excessive grain tax and opium production (ch. 26) and observe Stalin once again keeping the evil affair going from a distance (ch. 27). When that doesn't work out, foolish Americans are duped into providing life-saving support to the communists (ch. 28). Meanwhile, a newly uncovered 'red mole', Kuomintang general Hu Zongnan, joins the KMT's Manchurian supreme commander, Wei Li-huang (also, it is suggested, a communist agent), in bringing down the resistance of the Nationalist forces (ch. 29). Mao takes Manchuria by dint of his 'most formidable weapon', his pitilessness (ch. 30). The story, for this section, winds up with Mao's establishment of the totalitarian state through the 'campaign to suppress counter-revolutionaries' while personally enjoying an extravagant lifestyle (ch. 31). Chapter 32 begins Part V, 'Chasing a Superpower Dream', with a battle of wits between Mao and Stalin, the duelling dictators.

This quick summary indicates what the reader can expect from the 140 pages devoted to these years. The most obvious problems with the story have been met in the first two hundred pages: an unrelenting *People*-magazine storyline in which all action derives from Mao or Stalin or moles or traitors, all of whom are completely and consistently bad, bad, bad. This is an astonishing revival of Great Man historiography as 'Evil Man' history. It is also monolithic history, or in the Chinese parlance, *yiyuanhua*. These Evil Men, both the Greatly Bad (Mao and Stalin) and a cast of lesser Badlings (traitorous generals and credulous Americans), have simple, bad motivations: they are either evil or monumentally stupid. No other factors are particularly relevant to this story of China's revolutionary history. Unexplained is how this strange group of professors and radical students became a potent political force, how the party they founded came to lead forces in rural China, how it developed an ideology that in the 1940s and 1950s was persuasive to millions and brought national reunification and economic development, or how it self-destructed in the late 1950s only to recover and dive again in the mid-1960s, only to recover and build an astonishingly fast-growing economy in a stable country that is wracked by the contradictions and inequalities of capitalism under an authoritarian state. Describing what a truly, deeply, completely nasty person Mao was doesn't explain this complex history.

Mass criticism history: the historiography of denunciation

The other great weakness of these chapters is a deceptive impression that the given story is built upon massive and impeccable documentation. The impression, fully accepted by non-specialist journalists writing book reviews over the past six months in major newspapers such as the *New York Times* and *Globe and Mail* (Toronto), is that whether or not you agree with Chang and Halliday's point of view you have to admire the 'definitive' detail they have brought to their case. There is, after all, an impressive-looking scholarly apparatus of some 150 pages of detailed notes, lists of interviews and a massive bibliography (in tiny print). However, this is not sound history and the notes too often do not support the major points. In the end (as argued by Benton and Tsang earlier in this volume) the critical reader cannot trust the documentation.

For example, Chang and Halliday have interviewed hundreds of people (listed on pp. 661–74), including major Western scholars. The impression, naturally, is that they have benefited not only from the data but from the perspectives of senior scholars. However, Frederick C. Teiwes' reflections give the reader real cause to doubt how Chang and Halliday have used the many interviews they ask us to trust:

> During the early stage of their research, I met with the authors to exchange views. It quickly became clear that the party line was fixed, and would not change. The authors (to be precise, Jung Chang) had no interest in alternative views, not simply in an overview sense, but on specific events where inconvenient evidence existed. It was apparent to me even then that any attempt at balance was simply not in the game plan.[2]

Indeed, the historical method used in this book is astonishingly similar to that used in Maoist denunciations from the Yan'an period to at least the 1980s – the orchestrated denunciations of Wang Shiwei in 1942, the campaigns of the 1950s, the Cultural Revolution denunciations, and even those against intellectuals such as Fang Lizhi in the mid-1980s. Each of these denunciations was associated with a rectification campaign that entailed mass criticism. The archetype was the June 1942 anti-Wang Shiwei 'Diary of Struggle' in Yan'an's *Jiefang ribao* (Liberation daily), described by previous scholars as Mao's 'logic of criticism' or 'textual analyses'.[3]

These Maoist denunciations employ three rhetorical devices to blacken their targets and convince their audience. First, they establish a black-and-white dichotomy. Without firm documentation, they start by asserting that the subject is bad, has always been bad, and has never done a good thing. Second, this prima facie assertion is 'documented' by plausible but erroneous lines of argument, usually based on selective use of sources and quotation out of context. Third, such denunciations indulge in cheap shots, slurs, sexual innuendo and sometimes crude puns and animal characterizations.[4] What is amazing about this form of denunciation is that it has always included substantial reprinting of the writings of the person being denounced. Indeed, under the information blockade of the 1960s, Merle Goldman was able to obtain information for criticizing the CCP's attacks on Wang Shiwei from materials published by the CCP. However, the gap (at least in independent scholarly eyes) between the complicated documents reprinted and the simplistic denunciations never seems to have bothered CCP authorities. Clearly, the power of party officials to enforce their interpretation on Chinese citizens through the mechanisms of thought reform was very real. Since this form of denunciation was almost always accompanied by mass criticism – indeed, the texts were produced as study materials for such mass meetings – I call this 'mass criticism history'.

Chang and Halliday's misuse of sources includes the use of tainted sources (KMT propaganda from the 1950s and Soviet propaganda in the anti-Mao years), cherry-picking from sound sources to fit their story-line while ignoring inconvenient contrary evidence, resting key assertions on interview data that cannot be checked, and flatly failing to give references for some major claims. None of this is immediately obvious when one flips back to p. 677 and sees that for every page of the book there are three to ten citations with specific page numbers. It seems a mind-boggling exercise in documentation. Yet it adds almost no new reliable information to our understanding of Mao.

How does this work in detail? Chapter 20, for example, depicts Mao's well-known rivalry with Zhang Guotao[5] and the convening of the very important Sixth Plenum of the Sixth CCP Central Committee in September 1938. However, Chang and Halliday's story focuses on personalities and does not even mention the name of the plenum, its role in CCP development (military strategy in the anti-Japanese War and solidification of CCP organizational structure), or its major policies. What we get is a battle of personalities, divorced from these broader historical issues, and a central narrative assertion: that the key agency for CCP survival and Mao's rise to full power was Russian support. Page 218 begins with this search for Russian arms supplies via Outer Mongolia. Zhang Guotao's army is called the 'Western Contingent' and sent on a hopeless mission that gets most of them killed. Indeed, the few who made it back to Yan'an were brutally murdered. This atrocity is documented by the direct quote of an observer:

> When they were chased into our [area], we first of all gave them a welcome party and took over their arms. Then we said to them: 'Comrades, you have been through a lot. You are transferred to the rear to have a good rest'. We took them in batches into the valleys, and buried all these grandsons of turtles [i.e., bastards] alive. It was such fun burying them. At first, we said to them with smiles, 'Comrades, dig the pits well, we want to bury Nationalist troops alive'. They really worked hard. ... After they finished, we shoved and kicked them all in.
>
> (p. 219)

This is rough stuff, but it is not documented by reliable sources. In fact, this quote comes from a 1952 anti-communist propaganda text by Sima Lu published in Hong Kong.[6] Chang and Halliday have a penchant for using unreliable but lurid reminiscences and pseudo-histories, especially the popular 'wild histories' (*yeshi*) purporting to expose the escapades of the rich and famous that have long appeared in the Hong Kong press and have been published in the PRC since the early 1990s.

The use of Sima Lu's dramatic story is a case in point: uncritical use of clearly biased and otherwise uncorroborated Chinese texts. This is matched by a similarly uncritical use of reminiscence sources and Soviet sources from the Brezhnev period – a time of well-known mutual denigration between the USSR and PRC. Thus, for the key assertion that Mao was relying on Moscow's money Chang and Halliday use Yang Kuisong's *Xi'an shibian xintan* (New study of the Xi'an Incident) published in Taipei in 1995 and A. Totov's three-volume *Materials Toward a Political Biography of Mao Zedong* (in Russian), published in Moscow in the early 1970s. No attempt is made to evaluate the accuracy of these sources. We do not know the origin of Yang Kuisong's claims. Does it rely mostly on reminiscences or on documents? What sort of documents? In short, Chang and Halliday undertake none of these key tasks of source criticism required of the professional historian, for this chapter or any chapter. The neophyte reader is left to assume that if the text is in Chinese, it must be true and if it is Russian it must be a newly discovered secret. Once again, Chang and Halliday avoid the relevant context. The Russians did provide the CCP with financial support, and this is not news. But they also funded the KMT, and the Soviet support for Chiang Kai-shek is only a secret to Chang and Halliday. Lyman Van Slyke reports in the 1986 volume of *The Cambridge History of China*: 'Paradoxically, it was Soviet Russia that became the Nationalists' first and remarkably generous friend. ... During 1937–9, the USSR supplied a total of about 1,000 planes, 2,000 "volunteer" pilots, 500 military advisers, and substantial stores of artillery, munitions and petrol ... totalling US$250 million.'[7] Does this make Chiang Kai-shek Stalin's pawn?

Joshua Fogel warned colleagues over a decade ago of the dangers and limitations of PRC reminiscence literature (*huiyilu*). These reminiscences are not archives of raw data; rather they are wonderfully detailed accounts produced for a reason. They do not give all the news fit to print, but rather just the news that fits their story. Historians can still make use of them, as these PRC publications are most likely not outright fabrications. But they require source criticism – checking assertions with other known information, checking for internal inconsistencies, and comparing stories with other available stories. 'There are still villains and unwritten agendas at work', writes Fogel, 'and we must not allow them to influence our research overly much'.[8] These problems of source criticism apply just as much to the spate of unofficial (and usually undocumented) histories published in the PRC's increasingly commercialized press since the early 1990s.[9]

In addition to taking dubious sources at face value, Chang and Halliday build their narrative by assertion and innuendo. For example, Chang and Halliday blithely tag Wang Jiaxiang as 'The Red Professor' for no documented reason. They further claim that the entire Sixth Plenum was a battle of wits between Mao and Wang Ming over control of the party and the relationship with Moscow. Thus, they write, 'As his strategy [concerning the United Front] directly contravened Stalin's instructions, Mao was afraid that the news might be leaked to Wang Ming, and through him to Moscow. So he ordered his speeches to be kept absolutely secret ...' (p. 224). This is distorted reasoning. CCP meetings and inner party documents had always been confidential, because the CCP was a revolutionary organization that was being hunted by the KMT state. However, within the CCP, the documents of the Sixth Plenum were by no means secret. Indeed, this 'secret' plenum reaffirmed the military strategy of two of Mao's most famous essays, 'On Protracted War' and 'Problems of Strategy in Guerrilla War'. That Mao and the CCP relied so heavily on material support from Russia – and would otherwise not have survived – is thus mere assertion.

A fundamental disappointment of Chang and Halliday's text is that it ignores the content of Mao's policies and ideology. That the CCP transformed experiences in guerrilla warfare into policy is widely regarded as an important factor in CCP survival and ultimate success.[10] Since Chang and Halliday think this established view is wrong, they need to engage the current scholarship by Frederick C. Teiwes and Warren Sun, Tony Saich and David Apter, David G. S. Goodman, Joseph Esherick and several others, in addition to well-documented and clearly reasoned research from the 1970s and 1980s by Mark Selden, Raymond Wylie, David Holm, and Teiwes' monumental *Politics and Purges* (first published in 1979). But Chang and Halliday address neither Mao's policies nor the earlier writings on them.[11]

Equally absent is discussion of the development and impact of Mao's 'Thought'. Stuart Schram is just now finishing the series of complete translations of Mao's pre-1949 writings.[12] Of Mao's many writings, the Yan'an corpus is notable not only for his articulation of military policy (noted above) but for his articulation of Chinese Marxist dialectics and his writings on party reform: 'Reform Our Study', 'Oppose Party Eight-Legged Essays' and 'Talks at the Yan'an Forum on Art and Literature'. These are critically important documents that set the tone for CCP administration not only in the 1940s but well into the PRC years. Additionally, it is clear that Mao's writings on party history were central to his rise to power, to the identity of leading colleagues and to the rank and file in Yan'an – as shown by Saich and Apter.[13] None of these texts, or Mao's ideas in them, gets serious attention from Chang and Halliday.

Chang and Halliday lead the reader to believe that mainstream scholars are uncritical of Mao. Anyone familiar with the work of Frederick Teiwes and Warren Sun or Tony Saich will know that this is hardly the case. For example, the outrages of the Wang Shiwei case and the anti-spy terror of 1942–43 in Yan'an appear clearly in their works; this is not an unknown story in 2005.[14] It has also been available to English readers since 1994, in a vivid account, with accompanying documents, compiled by Dai Qing and Song Jinshou.[15] With these tools general readers can do what specialists do – compare the astonishing idealism and energy of Mao's rectification writings with the sordid tale of Wang Shiwei's destruction under mass criticism and the horrors of the 'rescue campaign' (now blamed on Kang Sheng, the security chief but, as Teiwes and Sun in particular document, clearly Mao's fault).

Another of Chang and Halliday's major claims is that the CCP armies didn't really fight the Japanese. No systematic data is presented to substantiate this claim. Chang and Halliday ignore the brutal CCP–Japanese fighting all across North China in the Jinchaji, Taihang and other base areas over some seven years. They claim that 'Chiang's armies, on the other hand, had fought large-scale battles with the Japanese in Burma, they had put more Japanese out of action in one campaign than the entire Communist army had in eight years in the whole of China'. This is a startling assertion and potentially an important 'unknown story': but Chang and Halliday offer no documentation. The endnote for this page (which appears on p. 710) offers only documentation for six unrelated points. Instead of careful documentation of this key assertion, Chang and Halliday simply stick to the rhetoric of repetition: 'By studiously avoiding combat with the Japanese, Mao had ended up with an army that could not fight a modern war' (p. 298).

Chang and Halliday do bring together a stunning list of sources, even if they fail to assess them and insist on using them in dubious ways. To ignore this book would be foolish and the working scholar – able to read Chinese – should pore through the sources to see what may be new. I certainly found several relevant texts. For example, as one of many who have done primary research on Yan'an and particularly the Wang Shiwei case, I was keen to see in Chang and Halliday's bibliography the collection by Wen Jize and colleagues on the Wang Shiwei case published in 1993. But, in truth, with one exception I did not see any major source on the history of Mao in their bibliography that has not been exploited by major Western scholars in the past ten to fifteen years, including in careful treatments of the problematic memoir and unofficial history genres.[16] The one exception is the new Russian material. The assessment of the new sources from the Russian archives and the post-USSR reminiscences will need the help of comparative scholars able to read Russian. It would be a great boon to the field if Halliday would make his archival and interview material open to other scholars for independent assessment.

Conclusion

Given the problems with Chang and Halliday's biography and the widespread publicity for it, what is a scholar to do? First, teach it; second, write something better for the same audience.

Mao: The Unknown Story is a page-turner, at least at first. Students will probably enjoy reading a couple of chapters, even fifty or a hundred pages. The plot structure is very similar to popular TV dramas. For teachers of modern Chinese history, Chinese politics or world history, this book can offer a useful lesson in what does and does not constitute good history-writing. While I suspect the distortions in Chang and Halliday's book will become evident quickly, I don't imagine that the alternatives will come off without criticism, either. Too much of academic history-writing is deadly dull and even the most cautious and documented historical monograph is subject to unexamined assumptions.

While their methods are suspect, Chang and Halliday sound a clarion call to bring Mao to account for his crimes. This book forces us to clarify how we come to terms with the inspirational quality of some of Mao's revolutionary writings in light of the terrible suffering caused by the CCP under his leadership. This is a classic and painful opportunity to confront ourselves and our students with the moral as well as professional and scholarly questions involved in historical judgement. How do we balance Mao's ability to inspire a generation to build a new China, the military victories of the People's Liberation Army, and the good things that have happened under CCP rule (from land to the tiller, to improved women's rights, to impressive economic growth) with the terrors of Maoist campaigns, the Great Leap Forward famines, and the fratricide of the Cultural Revolution? Chang and Halliday may have answered badly, but they have set the question well, and in a fashion that I hope we will not ignore.

The central irony of *Mao: The Unknown Story* is that it has been told before, except that it was told by Mao, about others. Chang and Halliday's book conforms disappointingly to the norms of Maoist mass criticism historiography from the worst of his thought-reform campaigns. Since Jung Chang was a Red Guard in the Cultural Revolution, we can conclude that she is familiar with this form in a visceral way. But why Halliday has chosen to pick up a neo-Stalinist denunciatory narrative to write for an English-reading audience is beyond my ken. Chang and Halliday's Maoist denunciation of Mao at least has the poetic justice of giving the Chairman a taste of his own medicine. But it is not history; it is propaganda.

It is disturbing to me, then, that major Western commercial media can conclude that this book is not only history, but terrific history. That Random House in Britain and Australia and Knopf in North America publish such a flawed book as history is a sorry reminder that we cannot trust the commercial press to distinguish reliable scholarship from pseudo-scholarship. As always, they will publish what sells. That Philip Short has already written a very readable and more judicious biography of Mao matters little to them.[17] The need for the strict peer review of university presses is nowhere more clear than in this case.

For that reason I strongly endorse Joseph Esherick's call to assign fifty or a hundred pages of this book to our students, with time to look at the notes, read the other stories that this book ignores, and consider what makes reliable history. After that, the task falls to us – professional historians and scholars of modern China – to write books aimed at the same audience. The failure of the 'actually existing academic freedom' in Western universities and grant agencies to support or reward intelligent popular writing is the deeper problem revealed by the case of Chang and Halliday's bizarre story. That challenge, our lack of contribution to popular knowledge, will still confront us long after *The Unknown Story* is eclipsed by the next commercial revelation.

6   Pitfalls of charisma*

Lowell Dittmer

First published in *The China Journal*, January 2006.

I think the reason that this book has engendered so much critical attention, along with such heroic efforts by PRC authorities to preclude its penetration of the mainland (by banning even reviews), stems from its sharp focus on Chinese political corruption. Corruption is more commonly associated with the marketization and privatization of the post-Mao era, in contrast with the sweeping drive for moral purity inaugurated by Liberation in 1949. But Chang and Halliday make the case that the Maoist era was afflicted by corruption of a quite different sort, concentrated right at the charismatic core of the leadership, where Mao emerges as a living embodiment of Lord Acton's epigram that power corrupts and absolute power tends to corrupt absolutely.

As such, the book is an odd hybrid. On the one hand, it represents the culmination of well over ten years of impressively extensive research, shown in 139 pages of references, 363 interviews with people who at some point impinged on Mao's long career, however tangentially (ranging from actor Michael Caine as a soldier in the Korean War, to two former American presidents, to Mao's former maids or girlfriends), along with an extensive bibliography of the Chinese archival collections and 23 pages of sources, many of them new, in at least six languages. On the other hand, this is not a work of objective scholarship but a passionate polemic, consisting of the vacuum-cleaner assemblage of every bit of information conceivably damaging to Mao's revolutionary reputation.

The result is a picture that will certainly be shattering to its intended Chinese audience, where Mao's portrait still graces Tiananmen. As Geremie Barmé notes in this volume, the current leadership is quite filial towards Mao. To some degree it is also revealing to Western China-watchers, although we have already been exposed to some of the more unsavoury aspects of Mao's private life in, for example, the memoirs of his former personal physician.[1] In a way it is the biography the Chairman deserves, having in his career as leader presided over the systematic character

---

* For their helpful comments on an earlier draft of this review, I wish to thank Richard Baum, Jing Huang and Brantly Womack.

assassination of so many of his political opponents (often with injurious physical repercussions as well, to which Mao's crystal sarcophagus remains proof). Though a high-risk research strategy, Chang and Halliday's approach may have in some cases facilitated their investigation, reassuring prospective interviewees with something explosive to disclose by making the authors' non-acceptance of CCP conventional political wisdom quite clear. Having critically identified the Procrustean polemical framework as a major liability for this ambitious work, I propose to say no more about it, as it has already been amply documented by my colleagues in this volume as well as by other distinguished reviewers.[2] To contemporary China scholars, by now accustomed to such one-sided presentations, the challenge will be to sort out the nuggets of genuinely new material and plausible, if not always verifiable, hypotheses while provisionally suspending judgement on the encompassing interpretive superstructure, the overall theme of which is of course that Mao was a power-hungry megalomaniac who cared for nothing but his own glory.

The pre-Cultural Revolution period to be reviewed here, corresponding to Part V of the authors' book, is disproportionately focused on Chinese foreign policy, presumably reflecting their (not unreasonable) judgement that this was the policy arena of chief concern to Mao at this time. Domestic political developments are covered as well, but in chapters that alternate with those on foreign policy, giving the narrative a somewhat disjointed, episodic quality. We shall consider the foreign policy chapters as a whole before turning to the chapters on domestic politics, briefly summarizing those points where the authors reinforce existing interpretations while focusing on their original contributions. Finally, in conclusion, we relax our suspended judgement and return to the elusive but inescapably central issue of Mao's character and cumulative historical impact.

Mao, the Soviet Union and the bomb

Within the foreign policy arena, the Sino-Soviet relationship takes pride of place, relying heavily on Jon Halliday's Russian-language skills for interviews and on documentary research taking advantage of the post-1992 opening of Russian archives. The overall picture that emerges departs from the authors' pre-1945 emphasis on a close Stalin-Mao connection to depict an intensely suspicious Stalin warily admitting this eager but unpredictable supplicant to his presence, having been burned by the recent secession of Tito from the bloc. Having shown China's mettle in the Korean War (whose initiation he strongly encouraged, sacrificing his drive for Taiwan), Mao then moves from an initially cordial relationship with the younger Khrushchev to a far more fractious one, each convinced that he alone should lead the international communist movement. The authors thus concur with recent Western scholarship in dismissing the 'lost chance' for early Sino-American friendship as a tactical feint to minimize American aid for the Nationalists and to impress the Kremlin (initially, Stalin was inclined to retain the Sino-Soviet treaty he had negotiated with Chiang Kai-shek in 1945, agreeing to see Mao only reluctantly after protracted delays).[3] New here is the emphasis the authors place on the primacy of the strategic component of the relationship: the alliance was, from

Mao's perspective, oriented less towards economic development than towards strategic objectives, chief of which was his 'secret superpower programme', which he seems to have launched as soon as it became clear that in the Korean War an opponent had been encountered which the USSR was afraid to confront directly and which China could not defeat. Although it has long been clear that China embraced the 'Soviet model' of catch-up development, consisting of a centrally planned economy with a focus on heavy industry, according to Chang and Halliday the emphasis was not just on heavy but almost exclusively on military industry. They claim that arms-related industry amounted to no less than 61 per cent of the budget during the first Five-Year Plan, surprising even Stalin.

And in contrast to Mao's well-known public dismissal of nuclear weapons as a 'paper tiger', he also seems to have been almost obsessed with their acquisition right from the outset. Indeed, Mao's determination to acquire this technology, and various Soviet delays in responding to Chinese demands, are for Chang and Halliday the glue of vexation that held the relationship together. Thus they explain three otherwise puzzling Chinese *démarches*. First is the Chinese role in the Korean War. Responding far more readily to Kim Il-sung's request to launch the invasion than had the cautious Stalin, Mao's massive intervention (despite the reservations of a majority of the CCP Politburo) was based not on socialist solidarity, or even the wish to demonstrate Chinese reliability after Tito's betrayal, but on Mao's calculus that, if China were to become involved in a war involving the United States, then the Soviet Union would give the PRC the weapons it needed to fight the premier capitalist military power in the world, rather than involve itself or see China collapse. And, indeed, this logic seemed to pay off, as the Russians, initially willing to sell weapons but not the ability to manufacture them, finally agreed to transfer the technology to produce seven types of small arms. And as soon as Eisenhower threatened use of nuclear weapons against China in his inaugural address (Chang and Halliday claim preposterously that this threat was 'music to Mao's ears'), Mao demanded the bomb as well. Rather than accede, Stalin decided just before his death to end the war (though Mao then allegedly prolonged it two more months, until Moscow threatened otherwise to expose Chinese 'germ warfare' accusations as fraudulent).

The second puzzle is Mao's initiation of an artillery duel with Taiwan over the offshore island of Jinmen (Quemoy) in 1954, and again in 1958. Otherwise puzzling in light of subsequent research indicating he had no plan or capacity to invade Taiwan at the time, this attack seems to have been based on the same logic: by provoking a confrontation with the US in which the latter threatens a nuclear attack on the mainland, China could demand nuclear aid from Moscow as a more palatable alternative to the nuclear umbrella contracted in their mutual defence alliance. The initiation of artillery bombardments in 1954 did provoke a US nuclear threat in March 1955, and in the same year Moscow agreed to build China a cyclotron and a nuclear reactor. But Soviet reluctance to follow through may be inferred from Beijing's recurrent use of such blackmail: in 1957, Khrushchev needed Chinese support in the wake of a challenge from the Stalinist right, and Beijing agreed, in exchange for a prior written agreement to hand over 'the materials and the models for the production of a nuclear weapon'. Yet again in August 1958, Mao launched an artillery bombardment of Jinmen, once more provoking nuclear threats from Washington (casually dismissed by Mao with the boast that both the USSR and the US might be annihilated in a nuclear exchange and communism would still triumph, thanks to Chinese demographics). The bombardment was suspended only after eliciting from Moscow a pledge to supply nuclear submarines and submarine-launched ballistic missiles. Khrushchev reneged on this commitment the following year, and in 1960 withdrew all Soviet advisors from China. Yet Mao, whose public criticisms of Soviet leadership had instigated the break, maintained debt repayments and some semblance of diplomatic amity for two more years (along with continuing ideological polemics), because he found that he now needed Soviet missile technology to deliver the bomb. Only after Moscow joined the Nuclear Test Ban Treaty in July 1963, thereby promising to forswear all nuclear proliferation, did Mao give the order to denounce Khrushchev publicly as a 'revisionist'.

Third is the massive Third Front relocation of China's heavy industrial base to central and western China. This relocation absorbed two-thirds of the country's total investment capital and a decade of hard work on a project that made no economic sense, and has been understood in Western scholarship to have been motivated by security as well as developmental considerations.[4] Chang and Halliday attribute it more specifically to Mao's fear of a pre-emptive attack associated with China's acquisition of nuclear weaponry (the Third Front was launched in June 1964, the first nuclear test detonated on 16 October). Mao rationalised Chinese assistance to Vietnam, too, in terms of providing 'hostages' against the possibility of a US nuclear attack. Thus it appears that China's acquisition of nuclear weaponry was greeted with at least as much consternation by the powers of the day as is the case regarding contemporary Pyongyang or Teheran – the option of a pre-emptive strike was seriously considered at various times in both Washington and Moscow. True, the empirical evidence linking this series of confrontations to Mao's consuming desire for nuclear weaponry is only fragmentary and involves the imputation of motives, but it does provide a plausible framework to interpret three otherwise puzzling high-risk foreign policy ventures.

Other Chinese foreign policy concerns of the day are also reviewed here – the Sino-Indian territorial dispute, China's efforts to inspire a revolutionary constituency in the Third World, the split with Cuba – albeit without offering much new. The Sino-Indian border war of 1962 was allegedly timed to take advantage of the Soviet-American confrontation over nuclear missiles in Cuba, with Mao declaring a unilateral ceasefire upon the lifting of the American naval blockade (then abrogating the informal deal he had with Moscow by publicly lampooning Khrushchev for cowardice in withdrawing the missiles). Mao allegedly also hoped to use the 1965 Indo-Pakistan war as an opportunity to resume the fight, but the early ceasefire precluded this.[5] The origins of the dispute are examined only from the Chinese perspective, with Nehru uncritically depicted as innocent.

Chang and Halliday are most impressed (even appalled) by Beijing's eleemosynary contributions to the world revolutionary struggle (6.92 per cent of GNP in 1973, by far the highest percentage of foreign aid per capita the world has seen), particularly during the great famine of the 'three bad years' (1959–61), and blame Mao for squandering precious domestic assets for foreign adventurism. Yet it is conceivable that Mao was not fully aware of the plight of the peasant masses when the PRC was making such magnanimous loans and grants. With the possible exception of Peng Dehuai, the Zhongnanhai elite had grown increasingly isolated from the populace; as late as 1961, even Liu Shaoqi was shocked when he returned to his home province for a visit (as the authors illustrate in two graphic photos). Clearly Mao's reformist successors have learned from this revolutionary profligacy, as China was not to return to the ranks of the world's donor nations until the 2005 Asian tsunami relief effort.

Domestic politics and the Great Leap Forward

With the exception of the Great Leap and the ensuing famine, Chang and Halliday allocate little space to the content of the policies of 'socialist reconstruction'. They sweepingly dismiss the 'socialist primitive accumulation' strategy and socialization of the means of production (around which there was probably elite consensus) for the somewhat contradictory reasons that on the one hand it robbed the peasants of their agricultural surplus for the sake of investment in heavy (mostly military) industry and foreign aid, and on the other it failed to increase productivity sufficiently to generate such a surplus. Chang and Halliday's main focus is on the elite struggles and purges Mao's policies occasionally precipitated, about which they do make some original contributions.

The Gao Gang-Rao Shushi struggle has been interpreted to date primarily in terms of a split between Red-area forces (those who spent the war years in the revolutionary base areas) and White-area or enemy-occupied-area forces (those who spent the war years behind Japanese lines or in Chongqing), or as a premature succession struggle resulting in the break-up of the Yan'an round table.[6] Chang and Halliday, relying on Soviet sources, view the fight chiefly in terms of the Soviet connection.[7] Gao Gang, as party boss of Manchuria, had a lot to do with the Russians, with whom he allegedly discussed inner-party machinations a bit too freely. The factional explanation, in which Mao initially encourages Gao to challenge Liu Shaoqi and Zhou Enlai but then, when Zhou's supporters counter-mobilize, rescinds his support, is in my judgement still the most persuasive. It is, however, striking that Mao does not move against Gao until the death of Stalin.

The 1956–57 intellectual enlightenment campaign around the slogan 'let a hundred flowers bloom, let a hundred schools of thought contend', is presented here as an exercise in sheer political cynicism: namely, a mousetrap, in which intellectuals are encouraged to speak out freely not in order to deal seriously with their complaints but only to incriminate those gullible enough to take the exercise seriously. Evidence supporting such an interpretation has long been available, based, however, exclusively on statements after the event, permitting the possible interpretation that Mao had reconstrued his motives. After all, there were people, like Zhou Enlai, who were genuinely interested in encouraging greater intellectual contributions to socialist reconstruction. After the crackdown the rules of democratic centralism would have required Mao to recant any 'liberal' sympathies and reaffirm the leadership consensus. To my knowledge this is the first time Mao has been cited clearly explicating his 'lure the snakes out of their holes' strategy before the 'blooming', in early April conversations with Ke Qingshi and others. Although it is still conceivable that Mao was tailoring his message to persuade a suspicious elite audience to open up, the cynical interpretation is in my view more convincing. This allows us to interpret Mao's famous February 1957 text 'On the Correct Handling of Contradictions Among the People' somewhat differently, and to add this variant of 'luring the enemy in deep' to his arsenal of intramural political tactics.

In recounting Mao's confrontation with Peng Dehuai, the authors rely strongly on Li Rui's revealing memoir of the 1959 Lushan plenum.[8] The two men had long had a complex relationship, Mao reportedly holding the general responsible for the death of his son in Korea. (Delia Davin argues persuasively, contra Chang and Halliday, that it seems inaccurate as well as unfair to assume Mao's complete indifference to the loss of his son.)[9] Whereas the authors' sympathies clearly lie with Peng, it was through no fault of his own that his attack on the Leap fell short of true factional conspiracy. Within the party, Peng's case ironically elicited far more sympathy after his purge than before, precipitating a move in the early 1960s to rehabilitate him, which Mao vetoed.

In any case, in 1959 the full magnitude of the Leap disaster was perhaps not yet sufficiently clear to anyone save Peng and a few scattered supporters (Zhou Enlai, Liu Shaoqi and Deng Xiaoping all joined in the criticism of Peng at the time). But by 1962 it had become inescapable, inspiring a surprisingly bold challenge to Maoist developmental priorities by the CCP vice-chairman and then chief of state (and personally designated successor) Liu Shaoqi. The full dimensions of this challenge are for the first time limned in this book, based primarily on interviews with Liu's widow Wang Guangmei. Deeply shaken by a return visit to his hometown in Hunan in April–May 1961, Liu was moved to apologise to the local peasantry for CCP misrule, and he apparently resolved to do something about it. At the January 1962 Conference of Seven Thousand, Mao had prepared and circulated a draft keynote speech to the delegates upholding and continuing existing policies, anticipating only minor editorial revisions before it was delivered by Liu Shaoqi. But on 27 January, with Mao sitting directly behind him in the chair, Liu with breathtaking audacity substituted his own draft for the circulated text he was expected to deliver. This was presumably not visible to earlier analysts of CCP power politics because only the final drafts were published, about which Mao of course voiced no dissent.[10] In this new draft, which was reportedly met by 'torrential' applause from the 7,000 delegates, Liu criticized the Leap far more vigorously than in Mao's original draft (including in particular a focus on nameless deviations from 'democratic centralism') and, instead of endorsing a continuation of Mao's confiscatory food procurements and adjuring future Leaps, introduced the first corrective policies.

This may be a somewhat melodramatic (in any case very elliptic) account of what took place. To have accorded with party rules, Liu's draft must also have been circulated to the rest of the central leadership to solicit their views, which (assuming they concurred) would have thereby in effect constituted a policy coup by the 'first front'. Although Mao, in Chang and Halliday's words, immediately 'plunged into damage control', blaming all sorts of factors beside himself and bringing Lin Biao in with an unqualified endorsement of his infallible leadership, he felt constrained to provide an almost unique 'self-criticism' at this conference. This self-criticism, mentioned here only in passing, elicited a stalwart defence from Lin Biao (who said the leadership had failed only by not following his directives correctly) and more qualified endorsements from Zhou Enlai (who assumed responsibility on behalf of the State Council), Deng Xiaoping (the whole central government was responsible) and even Liu Shaoqi.[11]

If this account of the Conference of Seven Thousand withstands further critical scrutiny, it throws the next five-year period leading to the Cultural Revolution into new relief. The relationship between Mao and Liu had been irreparably breached by Liu's 'ambush', even if others did not necessarily realize what had occurred. Yet Liu was too powerful for Mao simply to eliminate, which was not in any case his style. Mao sought legitimacy as well as power. Thus he began to circle and stalk his prey. Anticipating Mao's assault, Liu began building an independent base of support, rehabilitating many of Peng Dehuai's supporters and even some of those condemned in the 1957–58 anti-Rightist movement, for the first time authorizing the cultivation of his own 'personality cult' with the issuance of a new edition of his *How to Be a Good Communist*, publishing side-by-side photos of 'two chairmen', even taking public swims. With the support of Deng Xiaoping, Peng Zhen, Chen Yun and other members of the 'first front', he also proceeded to implement an alternative 'revisionist' policy platform setting the country back on the road to economic recovery.

Mao of course could not but interpret these moves as a direct threat to his own leadership position, all the more infuriating for using some of his own tactics. He encouraged Lin Biao, his recently promoted minister of defence, to insert his radicalized PLA into increasingly prominent political positions, pushed his own cult to unprecedented heights, encouraged Jiang Qing's 'revolutionization' of culture and the arts, and continued the public polemic against 'revisionism' and 'taking the capitalist road' in the Soviet Union despite the fall of Khrushchev. Thus, ironically, Chang and Halliday revive the old 'two-line struggle' model all but repudiated by the reformers at the Sixth Plenum of the 11th Central Committee in June 1981. And although this takes us beyond our brief, the Cultural Revolution itself becomes open to reinterpretation as well, making its construal as the culmination of an elite factional conspiracy that emerges in the third volume of MacFarquhar's trilogy more plausible.[12] Of course, Mao continued to insist to his dying day that launching a cultural revolution had always been his great dream, but Mao's vision may have been inextricably linked in his own mind to the public humiliation and destruction of his opponents. Even so construed, Mao's motives were not, however, exclusively power-political, but culturally iconoclastic as well.

Concluding remarks

In sum, what are we to make of Mao's 'unknown story'? Surely the depiction is overdrawn. It is easy to pick it apart by citing the incessant imputation of evil motives leading to implausibly complex interpretations of what may often more parsimoniously be construed as simple blunders, and to point out the small-minded refusal to recognize Mao's equally impressive gifts (he was a great poet and one of modern China's most powerful and influential prose stylists, whatever one thinks of the substance) or his country's undeniable achievements during his tenure (relatively impressive economic growth, life expectancy doubled, poverty, corruption and illiteracy greatly reduced). The interpretation of Mao's personality is moralistic and simple-minded. It fails to take into account his glaring contradictions: though absolutely determined to have his own way and crush all opposition, he was sneeringly contemptuous of those (like Zhou Enlai) who fawned on and flattered him; though a well-read intellectual, he called intellectuals pedantic ignoramuses and tried to consign them all to lifetimes of manual labour, and so forth. Chang and Halliday also tend to over-personalize a situational context or institutional culture: thus, intraparty struggle was a fierce, zero-sum game, but the rules were known and shared by both sides (for example, just as Mao withheld information of Zhou's terminal bladder cancer, Zhou knew and withheld the diagnosis that Mao was stricken with Lou Gehrig's disease and had but two years to live). The consuming Chinese interest in modern weaponry antedates Mao all the way back to China's nineteenth-century self-strengtheners ('rich country strong army') and survives him through to Jiang Zemin and Hu Jintao, now courtesy of Russian arms merchants.

Still, the cumulative picture is convincing and in my view quite devastating – it could conceivably alter forever our historical picture of the revolutionary origins of the PRC. What emerges is a story of absolute power leading to political corruption, assuming two distinct forms, one conventionally personal, consisting of the indulgence of omnivorous sexual appetites, untrammelled paranoia resulting in an army of tasters, guards and handlers, private trains, planes and helicopters and the sybaritic construction of over fifty hidden palaces, all in concrete-bunker style with hidden exits. The more costly, however, was policy corruption, consisting of the power to realize fantastic charismatic visions and ignore negative feedback, with often tragically unanticipated consequences, the Great Leap famine and the Cultural Revolution turmoil being only the most obvious examples.

Yet the real challenge is how to reconcile the political monster that emerges from the text with my sense that, in the minds of his countrymen, Mao's image may yet survive this latest assault intact as well. This charismatic resilience relates to three of Mao's unusually strong qualities. First, though not an impressive public speaker, Mao displayed a skill in public relations that has seldom been equalled. Not only did he put together one of the world's great personality cults (all the more effective for belying his own seemingly self-effacing charm), but he trained the world's largest populace to parrot his world-view in unison, underwriting an often indelible branding of national villains and model heroes as well. Relying on endless repetition and the 'big lie', he linked his message with simple but highly effective symbolism and neo-traditional rituals. This public-relations genius made Mao the PRC's first millionaire, living high on the royalties of his *Selected Works* (obligatory in every Chinese household) while menacingly enumerating in meetings how many catties of meat his Politburo colleagues ate per week.[13]

Second, whatever his win-loss record on the field of battle, he was a highly resourceful and innovative lifelong political-military thinker and writer in the 'realist' school of Sun Zi or Cao Cao, whose impact on Chinese strategic culture will outlast the shelf-life of 'people's war'.[14] Among the inventors of modern guerrilla warfare, he was also an innovative contributor to modern terrorism, using violence not in *Nacht und Nebel* fashion but in public humiliations, public interrogation under duress, public executions. Little wonder this military amateur could remain so confident of the political loyalties of the PLA – whatever the odds, he was ever ready to lead them into battle. A lover of paradox, he was able to string together such unlikely hybrids as violence plus negotiation, violence plus work, violence plus education. In the end, continuous violence may have proved too much for the irenic Chinese masses and, like Hitler, near the end of his life Mao self-pityingly reflected that his people had ultimately failed him.

Third, Mao did have a simple, unoriginal but compelling revolutionary vision of equality and selfless commitment to the greater good, which he was able to realize in terms of some of the world's most impressive Gini coefficients (along with an antlike cultural uniformity). This vision is badly slighted here, based on the implicit argument that ideals were not a motivating factor but a mere rhetorical cover story for ruthless ego-tripping. I think this was a mistake. The failure to live up to the ideals one espouses for others is not after all an unusual shortcoming, and the validity or political efficacy of an idea is logically distinct from the motives of its promulgator. For those to whom Mao remains relevant, his noble, impractical vision, undimmed by time, redeems all his other transgressions and follies. Some of the problems currently perplexing China's far more economically successful reform and opening movement – notably the waxing corruption and inequality – seem to have given that vision new purchase on the imaginations of his compatriots.

7 'I'm So Ronree'

Geremie R. Barmé

A revised version of an article first published in *The China Journal*, January 2006.

He's back

With the accession of Hu Jintao to the dual roles of State President and General Secretary of the Chinese Communist Party's Politburo in 2002, many presumed that the relatively lax ideological rule of the Jiang Zemin years would continue. Ever-optimistic observers even thought that here, finally, China had a Soviet-style reformist of its own (recall putative Sino-Gorbachevs past, Qiao Shi, for example).

It was probably the 2003 commemoration of the 110th anniversary of Mao Zedong's birth, and the speech that Hu Jintao made at the Great Hall of the People in December that year, that put paid to such a notion. Ten years earlier, in 1993, the party had also commemorated Mao, using the centenary to extol the virtues of Deng Xiaoping theory and the direction the country had taken since the Cultural Revolution. In part, the authorities were also attempting to redirect the popular Mao cult that flourished from the late 1980s, especially after 1989 (a cult evident in nascent form in the 1989 mass protests), an unruly outcrop of mass sentiment chronicled in my study of the 'posthumous career' of the Great Leader, *Shades of Mao* (M. E. Sharpe, 1996).[1]

In a speech delivered on the occasion of the centenary celebrations of Mao's birth in December 1993, Jiang Zemin had at least made mention of Mao's errors.[2] For Hu Jintao, on the other hand, the banner of Mao Thought had 'always to be held high, at all times and in all circumstances',[3] and he had nothing but praise for the man who, with his death in September 1976, had bequeathed his country a legacy of arrant politics, economic ruination and profound social anomie.

Hu Jintao has pursued a politics that was evident in his pro-Mao speech of 2003, ushering in a period of increased ideological policing. It is therefore perhaps a good time for there to be renewed work and thought devoted to Mao Zedong and his abiding – I would argue inescapable – patrimony, whether it be in Chinese or some other international language. Chang Jung and Jon Halliday's *Mao: The Unknown Story* (or *The Untold Story*, in the North American edition) promises, among other things, startling revelations about one man's monomania, diabolical ego and tireless cruelty. It is a work that provides the reader with a Mao in verso, a dark negative of the CCP's account. The hyper-marketing strategy of its publishers has allowed the book to enjoy a near dream run in the mass media of the Anglophone world. But is *The Unknown Story* a serious contribution to our knowledge and understanding of a crucially important figure of the twentieth century and the history of a country with which his personal story is so profoundly commingled?

Bandit Mao

It was, I recall, in 1980 that I first heard one of my mainland friends use the expression 'Bandit Mao', or Mao *zei*, to describe the dead chairman. The friend was a veteran writer who had suffered terrible persecution from 1957, and whose wife had been brutally beaten and disabled during the opening months of the Cultural Revolution. We had met shortly after the arrest of the 'Gang of Four' at a gathering of literary *bon-vivants* who had been kept apart by two decades of political persecution. From then on, this particular friend – a man now lauded in the Chinese media as a great talent abused during the years of 'leftist' supremacy and one that, despite his constant criticism of the party authorities, was courted by Jiang Zemin in his later years – would often refer to Mao as Mao *zei*, even, according to both him and other friends, at meetings where pro-Maoist party elders were present. He was also an early and strident proponent in favour of removing Mao's corpse from his mausoleum, and taking down the portrait that to this day looms over Tiananmen Square.

He was only one of many men and women of conscience, people who had endured the brutalities of the Mao years, who would speak out in various forms against the Chairman and his baneful legacy. There was Wang Keping of the Stars avant-garde art collective, who produced the memorable sculpture of Mao as Buddha in 1978; Bai Hua who published the scenario 'Unrequited Love' (*Ku lian*) in 1979; and then, in January 1980, the Sichuan writer Sun Jingxuan, who wrote a powerful poem on the lingering leader. In it he ominously warned his readers that 'A loathsome spectre/ Prowls the desolation of your land ...'.

Despite Deng Xiaoping's canny move to put Mao in his place and party Central's decision on post-1949 history that provided a final official ruling on the leader's historical role (and mistakes) – a ruling that Hu Jintao used to his own ends in his 2003 commemorative hagiography, throughout the 1980s Chinese writers and thinkers continued, as best they could, to excoriate and interrogate the burden of Mao. Among my favourites is Li Jie, who used his particular adaptation of psychoanalytic theory and cultural studies to pierce the 'fog that Mao shrouded himself in, both intentionally and unintentionally'.[4] This Shanghai author's analysis of Mao paralleled the Russian philosopher Alexander Zinoviev's cogitations on Stalin and Stalinism, in which he considers the powerful and complex psycho-political intermeshing of the Russians with their Soviet ruler. As Li says of China's own leader, 'Mao utilised the weakness of the Chinese to further his own Mao-style revolution'.[5]

I mention here in summary some early attempts by mainland Chinese cultural figures to deal with Mao, despite the pressures of intermittent and egregious official censorship, because if there is one overarching flaw in the Chang-Halliday tome, it is that the authors give scarcely a hint of the complex binding relationship between Mao, his colleagues and those who participated in, created, benefited and suffered from the Chinese Revolution, especially following the founding of the People's Republic of China.[6]

Another reason that 1980s and 1990s Chinese-language works on Mao, many of them colourful and fanciful, seem relevant to a review of this book is that in many ways *Mao: The Unknown Story*, with its histrionic tone and its unwavering certainty, is reminiscent not of, say, the more balanced prose of other recent popular dictator biographies like Ian Kershaw's work on Hitler, but rather of the bitter glee of so much post-Cultural Revolution mainland Chinese historiography and pop sensationalism. While anyone familiar with the lived realities of the Mao years can sympathize with the authors' outrage over the atrocities of the time, one must ask whether a vengeful spirit serves either author or reader well, in the creation of a mass market work that would claim authority and dominance in the study of Mao Zedong and his history.

Troubles with the telling

Having spent some long years working with colleagues in Boston to make a film, and create a website, related to the history of the Cultural Revolution era,[7] and having encountered many knotty issues in the process, I began reading with some anticipation the relevant sections of Chang-Halliday's Mao, entitled 'Unsweet Revenge' (pp. 523–654), which the editors of *The China Journal* have asked me to concentrate on here. Given the authors' avowed in-depth research into the machinations of the party elite, and Mao in particular, I was looking forward to at least some new information or consideration of the questions related to the origins and unfolding of the Cultural Revolution, Mao's motivations, and the history of that period.

My problems and doubts began on the first page of 'Unsweet Revenge', and they just kept increasing:

Jiang Qing is immediately dubbed 'police chief for stamping out culture nationwide' (p. 523). Further on the authors tell us that: 'In the annihilation of culture, Mme Mao played a key role as her husband's police chief in this area. And she made sure that there was no resurrection of culture the rest of Mao's life …' (p. 542). This reduces to a parody the long-term and important debates about reform versus revolution, and mass as opposed to bourgeois values, in the Chinese arts that can be traced back to the May Fourth era (1917–27) and which found a clear, if shrill, re-articulation in Jiang Qing's speech at the PLA arts forum of 1966 (which Chang-Halliday call a 'kill culture manifesto'). But then, some sixty pages later, the authors contradict themselves and speak of the partial revival of culture years before Mao's death (p. 586). One would have thought that given the energy devoted to trouncing Jiang Qing in this book (indeed, a whole chapter is devoted to her role in the Cultural Revolution, see pp. 622–33), it is curious that the authors overlook her role in the denunciation of the film *A Life of Wu Xun*', a key moment in the cultural ructions of the early 1950s. More generally, their lambasting of cultural debates (no matter how convoluted or driven by power they were) make it hard, no, well-nigh impossible, for the interested reader to discern any sense or logic to the Cultural Revolution, or its origins outside of Mao's supposedly twisted pathology, and Jiang Qing's mania.

The reader is presented with a confusing rehearsal of the history of the Hai Rui incident and the involvement of the Ming historian and deputy mayor of Beijing, Wu Han, in the complex prelude to the Cultural Revolution proper (see pp. 525–26).

The account of how high-school students became involved in the early phase of the Cultural Revolution, and how the crucially important Red Guards came into being, is perfunctory (p. 532).

The authors claim that teachers and administrators 'were selected as the first victims [of the Red Guards] because they were the people instilling culture' (p. 534). This overlooks the fact that the first victims of the young rebels included some of the rabid Maoist pedagogues who instilled violent and radical ideas in the minds of the young people in the first place. Chang-Halliday remark that 'the seeds of hate that Mao had sown were ready for the reaping' (p. 535), failing to acknowledge the existence of a collective enterprise devoted to social engineering, or to appreciate that Mao was hardly the only gardener who tilled the rich field of mass discontent and rebellion.

The way the writers deal with the fascinating and complex case of Song Binbin, the young woman who famously pinned a Red Guard armband on Mao at the 18 August 1966 mass rally at Tiananmen, is glib (p. 537). Commonplace sources are relied upon and there is no consideration of Song's view (one that she put on the record for the first time in the film *Morning Sun*, a full two years before the publication of this book).

Here and elsewhere in the text the authors indulge in unprovable or factually incorrect generalizations such as 'there was not one school in the whole of China where atrocities did not occur' (p. 538); or, again, 'virtually no new dwellings had been built for ordinary urban residents under the Communists' (p. 541).

The complex, and fascinating, relationship between Mao and Confucian thought (and indeed the century-long tussle involving Confucius and the Chinese intelligentsia) is summarized in what can only be described as burlesque: 'Mao did, indeed, hate Confucius, because Confucianism enjoined that a ruler must care for his subjects' (p. 542).

Etcetera, etcetera, etcetera …

The text of the book is supported by a panoply of devices, presumably employed to assure the reader of its academic authenticity, even though the authors aver that they are writing a popular biography, not a scholastic work. There are sixty-seven pages of footnotes and a large bibliography of monographs and articles cited in various languages, and of archives used. The particular sources for 'Unsweet Revenge' cover a wide range: standard works by scholars in the field, the occasional unpublished paper, numerous books and articles produced on the mainland, some by more sober writers, and many issued by what is little more than the gutter press. Added to these are the numerous 'insider' interviews which were conducted in many places over many years, and through which the authors have gathered a veritable cornucopia of detail.

A sample of interview citations alone will give the reader some indication of the difficulty that any historian faces when dealing with sources for what is often quite sensational new information. Take the notes on pages 731–33, for instance. Here we have, among others, an 'interview with Mao's personal staff, 19 Apr. 1999'; 'with a local official, 13 Apr. 1996'; 'interviews with locals'; 'interview with the girlfriend of Mao, 2 Nov. 1995'; and, 'interviews with many high officials' children'. Often the source is simply given as an 'interview with an insider' followed by a date; or an 'interview with a member of Mao's personal staff', followed by a date; 'interview with an economic manager', followed by a date. Or, in regard to Li Na, Mao and Jiang Qing's daughter, and the crucial details of her Cultural Revolution career, information is based on, among other things, 'a conversation with Li Na', an interview 'with a colleague', 'interview with a friend of hers who visited her', 'interviews with a friend and former servant', 'interviews with members of Mao's personal staff', and 'interviews with people close to Mao's family' (p. 742), with various dates supplied.

All this is fascinating stuff, to be sure, and much may well be credible. However, without providing readers and specialists with more detail, or the wherewithal to verify, cross-check and interrogate the credentials of these materials, I would suggest that Chang-Halliday seem to be wending their way through a territory profitably traversed by the noted American political biographer Kitty Kelly. Perhaps when the Chang-Halliday archive of interviews (detailing the time and place of interviews, the interviewees' names and relevance to the subject matter under discussion, with full, not selected, recordings, and transcripts, etc.) is opened to public scrutiny, these churlish quibbles will be swept aside.

When considering the authors' eclectic, and sometimes idiosyncratic, use of sources, in particular Chinese language materials, I believe that we should be mindful of a grand, if not always palatable, tradition of Chinese historical writings, that of *waishi*, or 'informal histories'. These are exogenous, non-official, or salacious accounts of the workings and machinations of court politics, or heterodox versions of historical incidents. Such works are also known as *yeshi*, or 'stories from the wild', that is, unofficial histories, or *baiguan yeshi*, which are opposed to or can be contrasted with officially condoned and scripted narratives. More often than not such accounts appear after the fall of powerful ruler, or even following the decline of a dynasty or regime dominated by such a ruler. The *yeshi* or *baishi* have, from their origins, been linked to novelization or semi-fictional accounts. Nonetheless, *yeshi* have sometimes been used to provide alternative material on events, people and historical moments. Some have even treated them with a measure of credence more usually accorded archival sources. *Yeshi* accounts of events, while not necessarily of value in the writing of reliable historical narratives, have upon occasion acquired a certain cachet. It is in light of this tradition of Chinese historical writing that, perhaps, *Mao: The Untold Story* will gain currency in Chinese, allowing it to enjoy a greater longevity in that language than in English.[8]

As I write this, I unavoidably think of another famous account of Chinese court politics, one that also caused an international sensation when it appeared nearly a century ago. This is *The Diary of His Excellency Ching-shan*, supposedly an insider's record of events surrounding the Boxer Rebellion of 1900. This work had an inordinate impact on international views of late-imperial China and in particular the life, attitudes and activities of the Empress Dowager, Cixi. However, the *Jingshan Diary* was a confabulation, a mystification, the product of the fecund imagination of Edmund Backhouse. It is contained in its entirety in the book Backhouse co-authored with J. O. P. Bland (who edited Backhouse's 'translation' of the diary), *China Under the Empress Dowager* (Heinemann, 1910). The forgery was only uncovered in 1936 (a final, fatal blow, being struck in 1940), after having enjoyed exultant praise in the Western press and long years of influence.[9] The excited international media response to the *Jingshan Diary*, what my late colleague Lo Hui-min called 'the tidal wave of eulogies', is worth recalling here:

> The popular press led the way in ensuring the book's success: newspapers and journals in which China had hitherto found no place now rushed into print to hail its appearance. Critics everywhere, not to be outshone by their peers, showered it with extravagant expressions of appreciation, as if no praise were high enough. In a seemingly unending crescendo, readers from Glasgow to Dunedin, from Toronto to Johannesburg, were told that this was 'an indispensable guide through the bewildering maze of Chinese politics'; that it was 'the most informing book on Chinese affairs that has appeared within a decade'; that it 'throws more light on the internal history of Peking than all the books written about China during the last quarter of a century'; that it was 'without question one of the most important contributions to contemporary historical literature which has been made in our time'.[10]

The latest twist in the *Jingshan Diary* fraud is that you can now buy a classical Chinese translation of the text (one based presumably on the 'original' that was deposited in the British Museum) touted by its publisher as being an important *yeshi* that contains information about the inner history of the late-Qing court.[11]

But as I read Chang-Halliday's *Mao*, I was also reminded of another rollicking romp through the workings of a post-imperial totalitarian inner court; an account that describes in great detail the cupidity, cowardliness and bullying of Josef Stalin. Simon Sebag Montefiore's 2003 biography of the Soviet leader, *Stalin: The Court of the Red Tsar* (Weidenfeld and Nicolson), is based on official and personal accounts, and although it dwells on the horrors of a tyrannical regime and indulges in the kind of flip hyperbole familiar to us from the Chang-Halliday screed, the author does at least show what layered depth is possible when archives are trawled in tandem with a careful reading of the correspondence and diaries of key historical figures. With the addition of interviews with family members and a careful attention to the politics of the era he is describing, Montefiore's Stalin is no less a monster, but his pathology is made clearer to the reader, not obfuscated as is the case with the present text.

Back in China, I would recommend rather the work of a true insider: the treat-and-tell account produced a decade ago by Mao Zedong's physician, Dr Li Zhisui. Although that text was generated for international consumption, with a gimlet authorial eye trained on the Roderick MacFarquhar rendition of the Maoist era, Li Zhisui and Anne Thurston's *The Private Life of Chairman Mao* (Random House, 1994) can be usefully re-read as a corrective to the book under discussion. The Li-Thurston narrative enjoyed the attention of a number of reviewers, including myself, in *The China Journal* in January 1996. For all its faults, and possible lapses of veracity, the Li-Thurston book is an atmospheric account that provides some hint as to the awe Mao inspired, as well as affording some insights into the world he and his fellows created in the sequestered environment of Zhongnan Hai, or the Lake Palaces in central Beijing, during his years at the helm.

As for the abiding valency of Mao in the popular realm of China, and the need for writers of serious intent to return to him, both in historical detail and through cultural analysis, I still believe that 'Li Zhisui's book will not alter the fact that Mao is, to many people, EveryMao: he is the peasant lad made good; warrior-literatus as well as philosopher-king'.[12] Moreover, I would question the contention voiced by a number of prominent reviewers of *The Unknown Story*, regardless of whether they found worth in the historicity of this account or not, that this book will make any significant contribution to some future, second wave, of Chinese de-Maoification.

The Monkey King

Reading Chang-Halliday's *Mao*, one is hard pressed to find any cogent account of Mao Zedong's own motivations during the first three decades of the People's Republic (except that he was a megalomaniac bent on world domination), or why he gained such support then, or continues to enjoy any popular influence today. While Jung Chang has offered a gruesome précis of her findings in media interviews and believes she has gained insights into the workings of Mao's mind, the reader is faced with little more that a depiction of a pathological 'evil genius', a monumental ego with an unbridled lust for power. That is not to say, however, that the authors do not essay some explanation of Mao's character.

In 'Unsweet Revenge' one can glean a hint about Mao's contradictory political and personal impulses. On p. 565, for example, the writers describe a famous encounter between Mao and Kuai Dafu, the Red Guard leader of the Jinggang Shan Regiment at Tsinghua University ('Mao's point man' at the institution, p. 549) that took place as Mao Thought Worker's Propaganda Teams moved on the campus. The leader and the Red Guard firebrand met in the Chairman's suite in the Great Hall of the People. After introducing Kuai, who was in a highly wrought-up and tearful state, the authors offer the following: 'Mao, too, apparently cried, quite possibly out of frustration at his own inability to reconcile his impulses with practical needs'. They then proceed in what for the reader has by now become their trademark clumsy prose to aver that: 'The impulse side of Mao wanted the many "Conservatives" he knew were out there to be beaten to a pulp. But the practical side recognised that in his own interest he had to restore order'.

Sadly, even this hard-won observation on the leader's ambivalent motives is little more than a refraction of Mao's own famous evaluation of himself. In a letter to Jiang Qing supposedly written on the eve of the Cultural Revolution (but not released for internal party consumption until after the fall of the chairman's hand-picked successor Lin Biao), Mao remarked that his personality combined a 'kingly air' (*wangqi*), one that demanded to dominate and suborn, with a 'monkey spirit' (*houqi*) that urged him to run riot and throw all into disorder.

As for any of the ideas that motivated the Cultural Revolution, excited so many well-educated young people and inspired the rather particular culture of the era (and yes, whether you like it or not, it did spawn a culture whose roots far pre-date Jiang Qing's speech at the February 1966 PLA Forum on the Arts), they are all dismissed out of hand. The Nine Critiques of the early 1960s that articulated the Chinese Communist Party's in-principle divergence from the Soviet Union, the long (and admittedly tedious) theoretical essays on culture, the discussions and warnings about the fatal mismatch between the country's economic base and its superstructure (the legal and educational systems, the arts and the media) that appeared in the press as the expression 'cultural revolution' (inspired as it was by political theorists in the Soviet Union of the 1920s) gained currency, and the writings of party theoreticians (virtually none of which are even named), or, for that matter, the activities of Mao's secretaries (Hu Qiaomu, Tian Jiaying, et al.), rate no mention at all.

Chen Boda, a cunning theoretician who wrote many of the key articles in the lead up to the Cultural Revolution, only appears in a cameo role as a co-conspirator, while Zhang Chunqiao, who would come to prominence as a theoretical writer in the 1970s, having promoted the 'Commune of China' at a key moment in the early history of the Cultural Revolution, is blithely dismissed. Someone merely possessed of an 'ability to churn out articles that dressed up Mao's self-serving deeds in Marxist garb ... Zhang was the person largely responsible for the texts that caused many people in China and abroad to entertain illusions about the true nature of the Cultural Revolution' (p. 575). Thus, in their haste to evacuate entirely ideas, ideology and non-personal motives from modern Chinese history, the authors effectively cut that country off from the twentieth century, except when its leader is dabbling in international power politics, or besting his foreign rivals in infamy by slaughtering his own people.

And what about the 'banner-bearer of the Cultural Revolution', Jiang Qing? What of her notorious involvement, first in culture and then in politics during those long years, or that of Lin Biao's wife, Ye Qun? Why, of course, they both got embroiled in venomous power play because they were not getting enough sex! They took a shine to pitiless revolutionary violence because their concupiscent comrades-in-arms were holding out on them. As the authors opine: 'Like Mme Mao, who was also hysterical from frustration, Mrs Lin [*sic*] now sought compensation and fulfilment in political scheming and persecution, although she was less awful than Mme Mao' (p. 533).

It is hard to know how to proceed at this point. Should I applaud the occasional authorial *aperçu*, ponder further the validity and weigh up the relative worth of the writers' archive-based investigations and personal interview 'revelations'? Should I marvel anew at the ghastly toll of Mao's personal and ideological rule? Or should I expend myself interrogating every exaggeration, chide each simplification or point out every factual error? Should I just deride the breezy tone of an obnoxious work whose authors glide cockily between knowing self-righteousness and glib journalese? Or, should I instead do my bit as an historian and talk magisterially about the general problems of writing this kind of despot-centred history, one that elides the agency of all others, treats the reader to a snuff-fest of outrages, and yet leaves us none the wiser as to what the hell it was all about?

No one left to dance with

Mao danced on. One by one, as the days went by, his colleagues disappeared from the dance floor, either purged or simply having lost any appetite for fun. Eventually, Mao alone of the leaders still trod the floor (p. 546).[13]

The part of the book I like the most (although it sports a particularly ungainly title: 'Nixon: the Red-baiter Baited', pp. 601–13), and one that sits most comfortably with the authors' ohmygod! style of prose, is that related to the clandestine Sino-American rapprochement. Here we have two autocrats – one effective, Mao Zedong, and the other, Richard Milhouse Nixon, a mere wannabe, along with their cunning enablers, Zhou Enlai and Henry Kissinger – negotiating one of the most dramatic shifts in geopolitical relations. This is readable *Realpolitik*, comic and grim in turn. The exchanges – all readily available in other sources – are delicious, and the devil dance between the North American superpower and the People's Republic provide the observer with dialectical delight. It is also the part of the narrative on which I am least qualified to offer an informed opinion.

But when leaders meet sparks may fly. And in Chang-Halliday's Mao we are presented with the Oriental Despot *redux*.[14] Page after page Mao careens through plots, counter-plots, ploys, machinations and manipulations, whipping up in his wake his very own *Sturm und Drang*. The book details a cavalcade of horrors and lies, and the 'take-home message' of the volume is clarion clear both on the first page of the narration, and in the numerous media interviews Chang Jung has given in relation to the book: 'Mao Tse-tung, who for decades held absolute power over the lives of one-quarter of the world's population, was responsible for well over 70 million deaths in peacetime, more than any other twentieth-century leader' (p. 3).

China becomes thereby something of a world leader in despotic atrocities. But I fear I detect in the sensationalist prose of this book the unmistakable stench of 'competitive body counting'. There seems to be a certain *Schadenfreude* at work here, a sense reinforced by such utterly distasteful sentences as: 'It was, it seems, a good day if the boss waived a few million deaths' (p. 504). The horror, suffering and deaths of countless numbers of innocent (as well as not so innocent) people can literally shock the mind into numb incomprehension. Even in my personal experience, I well recall the mounting panic, frantic depression and emotional suffocation that I experienced upon encountering dozens of returnees from camps, cadre schools and jails during the late 1970s and early 1980s, and hearing them recount their tales of suffering, loss and death. The high dudgeon of the authors of *Mao: The Unknown Story* seems to me, however, to serve ill the memory of the victims of this wretched history, encouraging in the reader an unsettling and breezy lassitude in regard to the origins, scale and meaning of the repeated terrors and their impact on real people, families and communities, a history that still reverberates through the lives of Chinese people today.

Not only do Chang-Halliday bruise the protocols of serious history writing and reinforce, albeit unintentionally, a callousness in regard to the nature and ongoing problems of China's situation, but they also employ a language that all too readily evokes the image of oriental obliquity. Mao's colleagues are spoken of as a court, the Chinese people are his subjects (p. 337, 500); the mayor of Shanghai, Ke Qingshi, is 'a favourite retainer' (p. 515); PLA Unit 8341 charged with the security of Zhongnan Hai is dubbed 'the Praetorian Guard' (p. 274 ff.). Wang Dongxing is the leader's 'trusted chamberlain' (p. 532), and Zhou Enlai his 'slave' (pp. 271–2). Even when Mao employs the pronoun of faux party collectivity, the authors claim that, as usual, he is using the 'royal we' (p. 589). To emphasize Mao's rank inhumanity, however, the writers also observe that his 'girlfriends were not treated like royal mistresses and showered with gifts and favours. Mao used them, as he did his wife. They provided him with sex, and served him as maids and nurses' (p. 628). Nonetheless, the admix of courtly Victoriana, Claudio-Julian terminology, along with the echoes of China's own parlance of palace intrigue, leave us with a metaphorical schema that places Mao firmly at some quaint, incomprehensible oriental remove, reducing a complex history to one of personal fiat and imperial hauteur. Although, I should note that there are moments when the terminology of court politics gives way to that of the bestiary: Zhang Chunqiao is 'the Cobra' (p. 575) and the 'Gang of Four' are collectively described as 'Cultural Revolution Rottweilers' (p. 637).

One must wonder whether readers have been presented a Mao tailor-made for the Age of Terror; though on second thought, Mao's impugned obsession with world domination (*vide* the long descriptions of this in the section entitled 'Launching the Secret Superpower Programme', pages 396 ff: 'Mao's determination to preside over a military superpower in his own lifetime was the single most important factor affecting the fate of the Chinese population' [p. 397]) brings to mind a lesser oriental despot, one who is dealt with far more adroitly in another pop culture product.

The creators of the TV animation *South Park*, well known for their debunking satires and knowing parodies, gave birth to their own 'mini-Mao' in what J. Hoberman writing for *Village Voice* called a marionette-driven 'equal opportunity offender', *Team America: World Police* (Paramount, 2004). The dominant personality in this film is not the group of terror-quelling, butt-kicking hi-tech patriots-on-a-string, 'Team America' (fuck, yeah! – as their theme song bellows), nor is it one of the bleeding-heart Hollywood A-B list celebs who are mocked and murdered. Rather, it is the North Korean anti-hero, Kim Jong-Il. In one short song sequence in this feature-length spoof, Trey Parker, Matt Stone and Elle Russ manage to create a compelling portrait of a self-pitying and psychologically twisted potentate.

Having dispatched Hans Blix, the UN weapons inspector, in his wide-screen size shark tank, the diminutive dictator wanders through the corridors of his socialist kitsch palace. Moving past frescos of banner-bearing workers rushing towards a communist future, and then by a display case of action figures, Kim is shown lying mournfully on a capacious bed. Finally, he appears at the end of a corridor dominated by a portrait of his father, Kim Il-sung, framed by a moon gate. All the while Kim the Younger sings his own version of 'I'm So Lonely'.

> I'm so ronree, so ronree
> so ronree and sadree arone.
> I have no one, just me onrey
> sitting on my rittle throne.
> I work very hard, and make a great friend
> But no body ristens, no one understands.
> Seems rike no one takes me seriousree
> And, so, I'm ronree
> A bitter ronree, horrid old me.[15]

Part III

Reviews in other specialist academic journals

8 Mao and *The Da Vinci Code*

Conspiracy, narrative and history

David S. G. Goodman

An edited version of an essay first published in *Pacific Review*, vol. 19, no. 3 (September 2006), pp. 359–84.

There would seem to be little point in taking Dan Brown to task for his lack of historical accuracy. *The Da Vinci Code* on most levels is avowedly a work of fiction – an adventure story that delivers a heavy dose of escapism. Its primary concern is conspiracy, which almost necessarily permits conjecture as evidence, a relationship that history usually handles more cautiously. Two conspiracies are at the heart of *The Da Vinci Code*. One is the conspiracy of The Priory, said to be a secret society protecting reason and the 'sacred feminine' of the early Christian Church. The other is the conspiracy of the mainstream Roman Catholic Church to maintain its dogma and organization, particularly through the more recent manifestation of Opus Dei, described by Brown in this book as a 'deeply devout Catholic sect' but more usually referred to within the Church as a prelature – an organization independent of location that includes both ordained priests and lay members.[1]

There can be little doubt that part of the popularity of *The Da Vinci Code* is indeed its concern with conspiracy. Conspiracy, like celebrity, has become a social obsession. The past few decades have seen the growth of conspiracy theories, or parapolitics, about a vast range of social, cultural and political activities. These include suspicions about the roles of governments, government agencies, multinational corporations, scientists and 'those in the know' in attempting to mislead across issues such as fluoridization, artificial sweeteners and access to this planet by extraterrestrial beings (Levy 2005; Vankin and Whalen 2004). Indeed, so great is the desire to find conspiracy that the strongest evidence for the existence of a conspiracy often becomes the total absence of evidence (Wright 1998). Explanations of this phenomenon are often linked to the impact of industrialization on communities, the waning of the importance of organized religions and the loss of faith, as well as a growing distrust of politicians (*Sydney Morning Herald*, 8 October 2005).

These tendencies have also been well observed in and with respect to the People's Republic of China (PRC) since 1978 and possibly for many of the same reasons. Towards the end of that year a series of high-level meetings in the party-state introduced the retreat from both Mao-dominated politics and the previous introversion of the Chinese state. The introduction of a reform agenda and an opening to the rest of the world started a process that led domestically to rapid industrialization, urbanization and economic growth; severely challenged belief in the political system; and made people more sceptical, both within the PRC and among external analysts, not least because the Chinese Communist Party (CCP) deliberately and purposively revised its own history. From the early 1980s onwards, academic, political and editorial commentators in the PRC have often talked about the resultant crisis of faith and confidence in the political system, not least because they have been concerned to reinforce regime legitimacy (Goodman 1985).

Certainly, too, the secretive nature of CCP politics has made it a field ripe for conspiracy theorists in the period of greater openness (particularly in publishing within the PRC) of the last twenty-five years. Alongside some similar concerns to those to be found in the rest of the world (especially those related to spies, multinational corporations and extraterrestrials) there has been a whole range of PRC-published books exposing the inside story of CCP politics and the lives of individual celebrities.[2]

Outside the PRC, too, the earlier certainties of dealing with China, the PRC and the CCP have been challenged in a variety of ways. In particular, in the last decade or so, the search for revisionist history and conspiracy has delivered a number of books in China Studies that identify the conspiracy of the political system at the heart of their subject of study, as well as (to some extent even more importantly by implication) the conspiracy of academics and scholars who have chosen not to reveal the truth as now revised by each of these authors. The most recent is Jung Chang and Jon Halliday's *Mao: The Unknown Story*, which portrays Mao as a self-obsessed dictator whose behaviour was in every respect even more extreme and excessive than either Stalin or Hitler.

Chang and Halliday's *Mao* has become controversial for a variety of reasons. It is to a remarkable extent sensationalist in the claims it makes and in the ways it makes them, and its marketing has reflected this. In particular, it has been presented as completely revising knowledge and understanding, not just of the phenomenon directly at the heart of investigation but also of China as a whole. Its revisionism has been presented as coming from outside the mainstream, particularly of academic scholarship, thereby reinforcing the apparent anti-establishment thrust of the analysis. Possibly in part as a response, it has been attacked by academics for its poor scholarship, which almost necessarily it would seem has added not only to the authors' self-belief but also to the confidence of their (usually non-academic) supporters in the case being argued and their sense of moral superiority. This academic criticism has of course not stopped *Mao* becoming a mainstream literary best-seller around the world.

Apart from its obsession with revising history and its sensationalism, it shares a number of additional common characteristics with other such books. It *has* clear academic pretensions, though it is clear from the very start that its authors are not prepared to obey normal academic rules of engagement. Quite apart from other functional aspects of academic writing, the more formal and basic architecture is absent. It has no introduction, no conclusion. Again like other such books, it has a view of history as the past waiting to be discovered, which of course facilitates the imagination of conspiracy, since the emphasis focuses on 'truth' rather than a process of more open discussion and interpretation with less certainty.

The style of writing could in no sense be said to be dispassionate, and is extremely polemic. Moreover, the principal author is involved personally in the story, as victim. A consideration of the book, and of its claim to revisionist history, provides more than simply the opportunity to detail and demonstrate poor scholarship, satisfying though that may be under the circumstances. More interestingly, it stimulates consideration of the characteristics of academic scholarship, particularly of history, and its differences from other kinds of writing more generally. It raises questions about the nature of evidence and argument that are fundamental to academic endeavour. These questions also touch on issues about the use of narrative and the nature of conspiracy, as well as raising questions about the relationship between history as past events and history as interpretation of the past.

It is far from easy to find a term that appropriately describes the kind of writing represented in this book. A charitable starting point would seem to be its identification as 'popular scholarship'. There is a clear distinction to be made between fiction, even where that fiction uses historical events and characters (such as *The Da Vinci Code*) or is based on historical scholarship, and scholarship, including popular scholarship. The dimensions of scholarship necessarily vary from field to field and discipline to discipline. Nonetheless, it would be difficult to think of scholarly writing without three functional characteristics: verifiable evidence; contextualization in a corpus of knowledge; and a theory (at least implicit) of knowledge, including an understanding of how law-like generalizations (often aka proof) are established. In history and social science, which might at best always be regarded as less precise areas of knowledge, proof is an argument not simply that a particular case can be demonstrated but also that its counter-arguments would appear to be less likely.

It is possible that the term 'popular scholarship' is meant to imply an approach to knowledge that does not respect these basic characteristics of scholarship. More usually it suggests a more immediate and reader-friendly way of delivering the message of scholarship that avoids some of the more idiosyncratic aspects of academic writing. Certainly, the book under consideration does not qualify under the more usual description of popular scholarship. It seems to accept that 'the truth is out there somewhere', lacks any apparent theory of knowledge, and does not engage with logical as opposed to metaphysical proof. Like Lewis Carroll's Bellman it relies on repeated statement rather than argument – 'What I tell you three times is true' (Carroll 1876). Whatever its other defects, it is characterized by constant overstatement. Conjecture frequently replaces evidence and evidence is too often not verifiable. Moreover, the writings of others are in large measure ignored, even when they (remarkably) would appear to support the case being made.

Like other such books, *Mao* is strong on narrative. Indeed, it could be argued that a strong narrative is its substitute for evidence and argument. It is also highly polemical. If something had been the case, then these are the consequences that might have followed: except that doubt has been totally exiled. All the same, as readers start to consider their response to this book, they are also likely to reflect on the essentially contested nature of evidence and knowledge. How we know what we know depends not only on records but also on interpretation of those records, and that is often more dependent on the spirit of the times than even those who accept the necessary influence of contemporary factors may sometimes admit. Though many historians are undoubtedly positivist, history more reliably remains a continuing discussion about the interpretation of the past, including engagement with earlier scholarship. Writing of all kinds – fiction as well as academic writing – contributes to the creation of an intellectual environment. In that context *The Da Vinci Code* and other assorted conspiracies take on a new importance. As it becomes far from straightforward to maintain a distinction between fiction and scholarship then it would seem safer to argue that not only scholarship but even historical fiction should not deliberately mislead and that in so far as either fiction or popular scholarship lay any claim to historical legitimacy they too should evince both integrity and a grounding in the contemporary state of historical knowledge.

The Mao Conspiracy

Take a charismatic and best-selling author who is Chinese but who now lives in England and writes in English; add a husband who has knowledge of the Russian language and a research record; and have them write a biography of one of the major figures of the twentieth century. It is an undoubted formula for literary success, and so it has proved. Jung Chang and Jon Halliday's biography of Mao Zedong was one of the literary sensations of 2005 throughout the English-speaking world. Jung Chang is the author of *Wild Swans*, a family history of China in the twentieth century that is justifiably credited with introducing many people to that country.

The publication of *Mao: The Unknown Story* was greeted by a series of extremely favourable reviews which made comments along the lines of (in the title words of one) 'This book will shake the world' (Allardice 2005). All have confirmed its importance in reassessing Mao's place in China's history, even when noting that the book is more than a little polemical (Chellany 2005; French 2005; Kristof 2005; Link 2005; Monk 2005; Spence 2005; Waldron, in this volume; Windschuttle 2005). Even the authors of the later, more considered reviews have for the most part hesitated to be too openly critical (Davin, in this volume; Nathan, in this volume; Wasserstrom 2005).

Certainly it would seem that a high standard of scholarship has been set for the book. According to the publishers, *Mao: The Unknown Story* is a groundbreaking biography ... the most authoritative life of Mao ever written ... full of startling revelations ... exploding the myth of the Long March, and showing a completely unknown Mao. ... This is an entirely fresh look at Mao in both content and approach. It will astonish historians and the general reader alike.[3]

Jung Chang herself (in publicity interviews, though not in the book) goes even further in her claims to have revised history, citing the failure of others to see the truth. Here is another author claiming privileged access and the ability to reveal knowledge of which others are not only ignorant but have also been complicit in ensuring that it remains unrevealed:

> 'All the historical events like the Long March, the war with Japan, how Mao came to power, the Great Leap, the Cultural Revolution – our story is completely different. Nobody has explained Mao like us. … Bits of the information were around but they were like pieces of a jigsaw that didn't make any sense. Nobody has put them together into this coherent picture of Mao. People looked but they didn't see.'

Much is made of their access to sources, in China as well as elsewhere.

> The Chinese government warned surviving members of Mao's inner circle to watch what they said to Chang and Halliday, but the threats backfired. 'People were dying to say things. They realised that if the government was that bothered, their story was going to be heard. I always gave them a copy of *Wild Swans* so they knew this was the kind of person I am, the kind of book I would write. They knew it wouldn't be the party line'.
>
> (Allardice 2005, p. 11)

Jung Chang read the Chinese sources, Jon Halliday the material in Russian archives. And why could these two authors succeed where others feared to tread? The answer is a high level of personal involvement and motivation that led to the need to inquire how the Mao-conspiracy had come about. As Jung Chang revealed in an interview in Hong Kong:

> Mao dominated my earlier life. I saw him bringing disaster to my family. Both my mother … my father and my grandmother died in the Cultural Revolution, and I saw him turning the lives of a quarter of the world's population upside down. And yet I felt the world knew astonishingly little about him, and I certainly didn't know much. I didn't know what drove him, what went on in his head, how did he become the supreme leader of the Communist Party and then China, and what was he up to after he took power. I wanted to find out a bit more.
>
> (Hahn 2005)

The flavour of the Mao portrayal is rapidly established by the authors. The book starts:

> Mao Tse-tung, who for decades held absolute power over the lives of one-quarter of the world's population, was responsible for well over 70 million deaths in peacetime, more than any other twentieth-century leader.
>
> (p. 3)

The reader is left in no doubt that this will be no hagiography. This impression is reinforced in short order by details of Mao's notes in the winter of 1917–18 taken from his reading of Paulsen's analysis of ethics, and the authors' comments:

> In these notes, Mao expressed the central elements in his own character, which stayed consistent for the remaining six decades of his life and defined his rule. Mao's attitude to morality consisted of one core, the self, 'I', above everything else: 'I do not agree with the view that to be moral, the motive of one's actions has to be benefiting others. Morality does not have to be defined in relation to others. ... People like me want to ... satisfy our hearts to the full, and in doing so we automatically have the most valuable moral codes. Of course there are people and objects in the world, but they are all there only for me.' ... 'Some say one has a responsibility for history. I don't believe it. I am only concerned about developing myself. ... I have my desire and act on it. I am responsible to no one.' Mao did not believe in anything unless he could benefit from it personally.
>
> (p. 13)

> Absolute selfishness and irresponsibility lay at the heart of Mao's outlook. These attributes he held to be reserved for 'Great Heroes' – a group to which he appointed himself. ... The other central element in his character which Mao spelt out now was the joy he took in upheaval and destruction.
>
> (p. 14)

In short, this is to be a demonography – there is to be not an ounce of good behaviour, not a scintilla of high purpose, to be found in Mao. Chang and Halliday's *Mao* has a sense of manifest destiny, a great capacity for destructiveness alongside personal as well as political nastiness, and is both opportunistic and excessively selfish. These themes are then played out throughout the book, organized by episodes of evil rather than strictly through a more conventional chronological biography. In each of the six broad periods assigned to Mao's life there are separate chapters dealing with specific events that overlap in time. For example, the period from 1937 to 1945 (the era of the War of Resistance to Japan) is dealt with by nine chapters across two major sections of the book. The structure and flavour of this exercise is readily demonstrated through chapter titles and descriptions:

... PART THREE – *Building His Power Base*
18 New Image, New Life and New Wife (1937–38; age 43–4)
19 Red Mole Triggers China – Japan War (1937–38; age 43–4)
20 Fight Rivals and Chiang – Not Japan (1937–40; age 43–6)
21 Most Desired Scenario: Stalin Carves up China with Japan (1939–40; age 45–6)
22 Death Trap for His Own Men (1940–41; age 46–7)
23 Building a Power Base through Terror (1941–45; age 47–51)
24 Uncowed Opponent Poisoned (1941–45; age 47–51)
25 Supreme Party Leader at Last (1942–45; age 48–51)

PART FOUR – *To Conquer China*
26 'Revolutionary Opium War' (1937–45; age 43–51)

It is an unusual method of narration, and from the perspective of highlighting instances of Mao's apparent perfidy and moral turpitude works well. In the process it is possible to read apparently new stories and interpretations in almost every chapter, some of which are quite sensational. To take just three of the most surprising (from a series of) examples: Mao apparently amassed a considerable personal fortune during the Jiangxi Soviet of the early 1930s, a period somewhat better known previously for the establishment of the first (extremely localized) CCP state (p. 117). The famous battle to cross the Dadu River (in southwestern China) during the Long March (in 1935) previously credited with enabling the revolution to continue because it ensured the CCP escaped from its Nationalist Party pursuers, is here said to have been 'a complete invention' (p. 159). During the Cultural Revolution (1966–69) Mao clashed with Liu Shaoqi, a CCP leader and president of the PRC before his fall from grace. A report to the CCP Central Committee recommended the death sentence for Liu, who had been imprisoned, starved and humiliated in a variety of ways, to the extent that his health had deteriorated substantially. According to Chang and Halliday this was rejected by Mao on the grounds that he preferred a 'slow, lingering death' for Liu (p. 556).

On the other hand, the book's claims to scholarship and integrity are at the very least questionable. There are essentially three kinds of problem: the novelty of its approach to the subject is overstated; there are problems with its use of evidence; and it has, at best, a very confused theory of knowledge. The claim that this is in some sense Mao's 'unknown story' is certainly debatable. There is certainly much new detail revealed in the text, and, as already noted, many new stories and interpretations of specific events. The publication of information, particularly personal memoirs, in the PRC during the last twenty years as the CCP has rediscovered its own history has ensured that, compared to the era of Jung Chang's adult life in China, considerably more is now known about internal CCP politics generally, as well as about Mao himself. At the same time, the idea of a destructive, self-centred, nasty Mao is not at all new. Both Mao's doctor (Li Zhisui 1994) and Philip Short (2003) have produced portraits of Mao as monster in the last decade. Perhaps more remarkably, Lucian Pye produced a very early revisionist biography of Mao along these lines in 1976, highlighting Mao's psychological profile as a first-born son who later felt rejected by his parents, especially his mother, once other children were born, and who reacted adversely to relationships of all kinds in consequence. In this context, Pye's study is remarkable because despite their extensive research Chang and Halliday appear not to have read it, or at least *Mao Tse-tung: The Man in the Leader* is not listed in the forty-four pages of bibliography (pp. 745–89). Nor for that matter are recent biographies by Delia Davin (1997) and Shaun Breslin (1998), as well as that by Short (2003), and there are some similarly remarkable omissions of literature written in the PRC (Jing Fuzi 1990; Shan Shaojie 2000).

It is easy to claim to be both novel and authoritative if other books and writings are discounted. Scholarship more usually proceeds by engaging with other accounts, often quite explicitly. *Mao: The Unknown Story* does not, even where other biographies and accounts of Mao's life and work are listed in the bibliography. At the same time, if the demonizing of Mao presented here is justified then it may be possible to argue that the intensity of his nastiness was not properly understood before this book. The proof of that equation, though, depends on the validity of the evidence, and quite clearly much of that is extremely problematic.

The more controversial any topic the more the evidence will be expected to be both verifiable and reliable. In *Mao: The Unknown Story* the evidence is too often neither. Andrew Nathan, who has written about internal CCP politics during the 1980s and 1990s, comments: '... many of their discoveries come from sources that cannot be checked, others are openly speculative or are based on circumstantial evidence, and some are untrue' (Nathan, in this volume).

The problem of verifiability and reliability is well demonstrated by reference to the three examples already cited of the book's more sensational findings. As already noted, it is claimed that Mao amassed a personal fortune during the Jiangxi Soviet. Nathan's concern on this point is worth quoting in full:

> Chang and Halliday cite four sources to support their statement that Mao amassed 'a private fortune' during the Jiangxi Soviet period of the early 1930s. One is an anonymous interview which cannot be checked. The second source is a book in Chinese by a writer called Shu Long, which says that Mao ordered his brother, Zemin, who was president of the communists' state bank, to disperse money from a 'secret treasury' to the various communist military units when a gathering enemy offensive threatened the money's security. The third is *The Long March* by Harrison Salisbury (1985), which says similarly that Zemin took part in hiding the Red Army's money and treasure in a mountain cave for two years until it was removed shortly before the Long March and divided among the communist armies that were about to set off on the March. The fourth source is a file in the Harrison Salisbury papers at Columbia University. However, the citation is garbled, so the file Chang and Halliday used cannot be located in Columbia's Rare Book and Manuscript Library (nor can the correct citation be reconstructed from the information given).

The Chang and Halliday claimed fiction of a battle at the crossing of the Dadu River is even more straightforwardly contested. In the book, Chang and Halliday cite an interview with an unknown 'sprightly 93-year-old when we met her in 1997' standing at the spot who is reported as denying that there was any battle (p. 159). More recent visitors to the location report not simply that they could not find the unknown source but also that no one there was able to assist in identifying who she might have been. Moreover, they did manage to find Li Guixiu, an eyewitness and survivor of the incident (who was fifteen years old at the time):

> The KMT warned us that the Reds would eat the young people and bury the old. ... Many fled up the mountainside. But when we saw them, they told us not to be afraid, they only opposed bad people. I remember they were wearing

straw shoes, with cloth wound around their shins. The fighting started in the evening. There were many killed on the Red Army side. The KMT set fire to the bridge-house on the other side, to try to melt the chains, and one of the chains was cut. After it was taken, the Red Army took seven days and seven nights to cross. Later, I was told that someone we had seen was Mao Zedong.

(McDonald 2005: 7)

Mao's apparent decision to let Liu Shaoqi die a lingering death is also tendentious. The sources are apparently an interview with Liu Shaoqi's wife in November 1995, and an apparent interview with an (unnamed) member of Lin Biao's family in October 1995. Delia Davin, one of Chang and Halliday's discounted alternative authors on the life of Mao, accurately highlights the problems involved in using much of this kind of evidence. She notes that Chang and Halliday

ignore substantial contrary evidence. ... Their bibliography is impressive – but what is lacking is any attempt to evaluate sources and their relative reliability. We are not made aware that different witnesses and participants have their own axes to grind and are rarely reminded that much of the history of the CCP is contested.

(Davin, in this volume)

Especially when dealing with the necessarily hidden politics of the CCP, where rumour and innuendo abound, sources have to be evaluated and comments put in context. It would be foolhardy in the extreme to always assume that single items of apparent evidence could be taken at face value. Yet that is largely the *modus operandi* of Chang and Halliday. These problems in the use of evidence are related to the book's weak understanding of scholarship and its confusing theory of knowledge. There is no introduction; no discussion of biography or history, or the processes of social and political change and the role of the individual in those processes. Scholarship is not mechanistic, and methodology need not be explicit (particularly if a book is being written to be popular). Nonetheless, in a controversial book of this kind one could reasonably expect an appendix on methodology and the evaluation of sources. In particular, it is crucial to understand how the authors are so certain they have avoided the ecological fallacy on so many occasions. Fred Teiwes is probably universally regarded as the most accomplished historian of the CCP outside the PRC. In his various writings on the inner workings of the CCP, much of which has been centrally concerned with Mao, he has gone to considerable pains to explain the complex processes that attend the evaluation of dubious or potentially unreliable sources. Asking what else is known that may confirm, deny or confront any available information or source is central to scholarship.

The theory of knowledge that seems embedded in *Mao: The Unknown Story* is less than convincing. In the first place, from interviews associated with publicity for the book, it is clear that Chang and Halliday believe that it is possible to gather all the facts about Mao dispassionately and that this constitutes scholarship and the writing of history. Or at least they explicitly argue that this is what they have done (Allardice 2005; Hahn 2005; *The Brian Lehrer Show* 2005). The construction of history is usually regarded as a more controlled process, necessarily involving selection and judgement. In contrast, *Mao: The Unknown Story* is then presented more as an exercise in data-mining. It is as if the reader has been given an assurance that nothing has been left out. Fatally, though, explanation (as opposed to description) is absent. There is a major paradox at the heart of this book. Mao was power crazed, venal, incompetent, disastrous for China and the CCP, and instilled so much fear and hatred in those he came into contact with throughout his life. Yet nonetheless he was able to exercise absolute power and authority. At the very least there needs to be some explanation of the political behaviour of those in the leadership around Mao that takes account of their autonomy as human beings.

In the second place, *Mao: The Unknown Story* is not consistent in its identification of Mao the subject of the biography. Sometimes Mao and his actions are differentiated from those of the CCP, and sometimes they are equated. Thus, when Mao was on the outer fringe of CCP politics during the early 1930s (p. 115) or apparently opposed by Liu Shaoqi in 1962 (p. 509) or Deng Xiaoping in and after 1974 (p. 634) (even more unlikely given Deng's close relationship to Mao from 1933 that ensured that any later reinterpretation of Mao's role in China's history would be severely limited after his death), Mao is identified as an independent actor. On the other hand, when the CCP is engaged in nefarious activities, most notoriously the production and sale of opium in Yan'an, the communist capital during the War of Resistance to Japan (p. 283), there is no daylight to be seen between Mao's actions and those of the CCP. Mao may have been responsible for the policy on opium production and trade but at the very least in a detailed (and authoritative) biography one might expect analysis of whether this was by commission or omission. It might even add to an understanding of his exercise of leadership.

Mao: The Unknown Story is a vast compendium of information about its subject. Its authors have made much in interviews and publicity material associated with the book about the quantity as well as the quality of their sources. In addition to secondary sources there are documents, archive material, published memoirs and several hundred interviews with people, often well known in other contexts, who had met Mao. The book is full of detail, interpretation and conjecture. Some of it is almost certainly accurate, some of dubious authenticity, and some just plain false. (For example: the CCP was not founded in 1920, and Nelson Rockefeller was not Nixon's Vice President in 1972, however many times Chang and Halliday may choose to say otherwise.)[4] Ultimately, though, the book is a self-defeating exercise. The authors, again in interviews, have said that they set out to write an accessible account (explicitly like *Wild Swans*) of Mao (Allardice 2005). This volume is so focused on Mao as monster that it is not readily understandable other than by those with expert knowledge of the histories involved. For those without, it requires reading alongside a history of the CCP or of China in the twentieth century.

Martyrs to daytime TV chat shows

Strip away the pretension, the pomposity and the poor scholarship and it is clear that the authors of *Mao* have sacrificed intellectual reputation on the altar of instant celebrity. They emphasize the time and effort they have expended in research and production. In interviews, Chang mentions often that she had the idea for a biography while completing *Wild Swans* sometime in the early 1990s.

Nonetheless, it is clear that publication was too rushed. Leave aside the infelicities that might have been avoided by more careful reading by publishing houses, authors' friends or colleagues. Chang and Halliday could have produced a view of Mao based on their extensive interviews of the famous and the powerful, but a possibly good book waiting to be written was rushed into print and the opportunity was lost. The book was produced with inadequate consideration, so that it cannot continue to be taken as seriously as its subject matter demands. This is doubly unfortunate since in dealing with China there is clearly a quite explicit control of history being exercised by the CCP, with which historians need to engage if they are to understand the dynamics of China's social, cultural and political development. The search for the apparently more immediate and sensational conspiracies, while entertaining, runs the risk of obscuring that understanding.

If publishers can call this scholarship, as they do, then academics can request that similar rules apply to historical fiction, or at least request that fiction be published in a historically responsible manner. To return to *The Da Vinci Code*, its presentation is more than a little ambiguous as to where it stands in the relationship between fact and fiction. There is a note at the front of book in which the author states: 'In this work of fiction, the characters, places and events are either the product of the author's imagination or they are used entirely fictitiously'. At the same time, the paperback edition appears with reprints of reviews claiming (for example) that it transmits 'several doctorates' worth of fascinating history and learned speculation' (*Chicago Tribune*) and incorporates 'massive amounts of historical and academic information' (*The Mystery Reader*). The text of the story also starts with the existence of its two main conspiracies presented as 'Fact'. It is small comfort that the 'facts' in *The Da Vinci Code* are about as reliable as those to be found in *Mao: The Unknown Story*.

References

Allardice, Lisa (2005) 'This book will shake the world', *The Guardian*, 26 May, p. 11.
Breslin, Shaun (1998) *Mao*, Harlow: Longman.
Brown, Dan (2003) *The Da Vinci Code*, Sydney: Corgi.
Carroll, Lewis (1876) *The Hunting of the Snark*, Fit One – The Landing, stanza 2.
Chang, Jung and Halliday, Jon (2005) *Mao: The Unknown Story*, London: Jonathan Cape.
Chellany, Brahma (2005) 'Neo-Emperor of Evil Genius', *Japan Times*, 4 September, p. 23.
Davin, Delia (1997) *Mao*, Yeovil: Sutton Publishing.
Feng Chongyi and Hans Hendrischke, eds (1999) *The Political Economy of China's Provinces: Competitive and Comparative Advantage*, London: Routledge.

French, Howard W. (2005) 'Putting a Knife into the Heart of the Chairman's Legend', *San Francisco Chronicle*, 23 October, p. 17.

Goodman, David S. G. (1985) 'The Chinese Political Order after Mao: "Socialist Democracy" and the Exercise of State Power', *Political Studies*, vol. 33, no. 2, pp. 218–35.

Hahn, Lorraine (2005) Interview with Jung Chang, *TalkAsia*, 23 July.

Jing Fuzi (Gu Hua) (1990) *Mao Zedong he tade nürenmen* (Mao Zedong and his women), Taipei: Lianjing chuban shiye gongsi.

Kristof, Nicholas (2005) 'The Real Mao', *New York Times Book Review*, 23 October, p. 82.

Levy, Joel (2005) *Conspiracies: Fifty Reasons to Watch Your Back*, Sydney: Allen and Unwin.

Link, Perry (2005) 'Mad, Bad Mao', *Times Literary Supplement*, 20 July.

Li Zhisui (1994) *The Private Life of Chairman Mao*, New York: Random House.

McDonald, Hamish (2005) 'A Swan's Little Book of Ire', *Sydney Morning Herald*, 8 October, p. 7.

Monk, Paul (2005) 'So Vile a Thing as Mao', *Australian Financial Review*, 26 August, p. 11.

Pye, Lucian W. (1976) *Mao Tse-tung: The Man in the Leader*, New York: Basic Books.

Shan Shaojie (2000) *Mao Zedong zhizheng chunqiu (1949–1976)* (Mao in power [1949–1976]), Hong Kong: Mingjing chuban she.

Short, Philip (2003) *Mao: A Life*, London: John Murray.

Spence, Jonathan D. (2005) 'Portrait of a Monster', in this volume.

Sydney Morning Herald (2005) 'Conspiracy Theorem', 8 October, p. 40.

Teiwes, Frederick C. (1990) *Politics at Mao's Court*, Armonk, NY: M. E. Sharpe.

The Brian Lehrer Show (2005) WNYC, 19 October.

Vankin, Jonathan and Whalen, John (2004) *The 80 Greatest Conspiracies of All Time*, Lincoln, NE: Citadel Press.

Wasserstrom, Jeffrey N. (2005) 'Mao as Monster', *Chicago Tribune*, 6 November, p. 43.

Windschuttle, Keith (2005) 'Mao and the Maoists', *New Criterion* (October), p. 21.

Wright, Charles (1998) 'Web of Deceit', *Australian Financial Review*, 21 March, p. 8.

Yao Ming-le (1983) *The Conspiracy and Murder of Mao's Heir*, London: Collins.

9   Mao

A super monster?

Alfred Chan

A revised and expanded version of a review originally published in *Pacific Affairs*,
vol. 79, no. 2 (2006), pp. 97–103.

Any fresh consideration of the life and times of Mao Zedong – the revolutionary,
strategist, visionary, dictator, modernizer, intellectual and poet – should be
welcome, considering the national myth surrounding Mao that is still propagated
both officially and unofficially in China. At present, there is a mountain of Chinese
language material on the topic, including biographies, memoirs, histories, official
and unofficial documents and chronologies. Yet few Chinese scholars or writers,
with the exception of those who publish in Hong Kong and Taiwan, dare to cross
the party line. A large body of English academic materials also exist, including a
number of perceptive biographies published recently.[1]

Mao: The Unknown Story (hereafter *Mao*) claims to be the 'most authoritative
life of Mao ever written', intended to 'astonish historians and the general reader
alike'. This effort, by husband-and-wife team Jung Chang and Jon Halliday – she of
Wild Swans fame, he an academic writer on the Korean War and Japanese imperialism – represents a formidable research enterprise, and took a decade to complete.
The authors conducted extensive interviews in 35 countries with those who knew
or were connected to Mao, and their archival research took them to ten countries,
including Russia. The 58-chapter book includes 46 pages of bibliography and
86 pages of notes.

The book portrays Mao as a relentless schemer who exploited every situation
and opportunity to satisfy his ego and greed for power, and as a homicidal and
genocidal tyrant who would sacrifice anyone and anything. Manipulative and bent
on revenge, he is shown to be a sadist who enjoyed thuggery, torture and slow
deaths. As if this were not enough, he is depicted as lazy, bumbling and 'addicted
to comfort'. Furthermore, the authors claim that he was indifferent to ideology,
and unpatriotic.

Among the 'startling revelations' of a 'completely unknown Mao' offered up
are the following: Mao despised the peasants and workers; he needlessly sacrificed
his soldiers, even a brother, in order to gain power; and he poisoned rivals, terrorized followers and lieutenants, and amassed a huge personal fortune. The authors
also assert that Chiang Kai-shek let the Reds go because Stalin was holding his

son hostage; that the heroic exploits of the Long March were a hoax; and that Mao's incompetence resulted in many lost battles, including the claim that his siege of Changchun took more lives than the 1937 Nanjing Massacre carried out by the Japanese. When Mao was in power, the authors allege that he deliberately starved the peasants and told them to eat leaves, sold grain during famine to acquire arms, and set a trap to ensnare the intellectuals during the Hundred Flowers episode.

This litany of Mao's evildoing establishes the underlying theme of his relentless quest for power and world domination. Writing as if they have access to his inner consciousness, the authors go so far as to share with the reader Mao's last thoughts: 'in [his mind] stirred just one thought: himself and his power' (p. 630).

One would expect careful and responsible analysis of source material in such an iconoclastic work, but Chang and Halliday have taken great liberties in this regard, distorting, stretching and quoting their sources out of context. Despite its academic trappings, this work ignores much existing scholarship in English and Chinese. Many of the so-called 'startling revelations' are well known, and new information is manufactured by manipulating facts to absurd heights. The outcome is that the authors have reduced a complex, contradictory and multi-faceted subject to a one-dimensional caricature of unremitting evil.

Manipulation of sources

Consider Chang and Halliday's major thesis: that Mao was obsessed with promoting the 'secret Superpower Programme' (SPP) so that China could dominate the world. This plan, however, exists only in Chang's and Halliday's imaginations; it conflates disparate events from different historical episodes that were neither secret nor linked to superpower aspirations. At first, this programme is identified as the General Line, launched with much publicity in 1953, with the intention of promoting industrialization and the development of agriculture and commerce (p. 380). Later, the authors identify the SSP with the First Five-Year Plan (FFYP, 1953–57) and insist on its unquestionable 'military nature' (p. 426), because military and arms-related industries for this Plan, they say, made up of 61 per cent of the budget. To come up with this percentage, the authors simply added up the budgetary allocations for national defence (23.4 per cent) and capital construction (37.6 per cent); the result is a gross distortion, because the latter included investments in many spheres of industry, agriculture, education and health. Granted, defence allocations were high and perhaps under-reported, and some industrialization could have military applications, but the authors lack grounds to claim that all investments were military. On page 426, they further confuse Mao's call to accelerate fulfilment of the National Programme for Agricultural Development (NPAD, 1956–67), a comprehensive rural development project, with the acceleration of industrialization and an imaginary SPP.

Mao was ambitious and at times delusional, but no evidence exists to suggest that he considered China to be capable of projecting power worldwide in his lifetime. Even with the completion of the General Line, the FFYP and the NPAD, China would still, according to Mao, remain 'poor and blank'. The convoluted assertions of Chang and Halliday prove nothing.

The authors' argument that Mao intended to dominate the world (p. 426 ff.) by controlling the Pacific Ocean is similarly contrived. They cite as proof a line in Mao's June 1959 speech: 'Currently the Pacific Ocean is not peaceful. It can only be peaceful when we take control over it in the future', and Lin Biao's interjection: 'We must build big ships, and be prepared to land (sc. military) in Japan, the Philippines, and San Francisco'. But in this speech Mao was only talking about what China would have to do if attacked, if Beijing and Shanghai were hit with nuclear bombs. China would have to retaliate, he said, and that would require a navy. He then wondered aloud as to how much effort and time it would take to build such a navy.[2]

Chang and Halliday's citation of Mao's line, 'In future we will set up the Earth Control Committee, and make a uniform plan for the Earth' (p. 426), as proof of his superpower pretensions is equally absurd. Here, Mao was talking about solidarity with Vietnam, and urging those who went there to care for everything, because affairs in Vietnam belonged not just to Ho Chi Minh but to all labouring people and the Earth. It was as an advocate of central planning that he said that the Chinese, if necessary, would make uniform plans to deliver grain to any place globally with a grain shortage by setting up an Earth Control Committee.[3]

Mao's most formidable weapon, Chang and Halliday assert, was his lack of pity, and they cite the starvation tactics used in the city of Changchun during the siege of 1948, when its population shrank from 500,000 to 170,000 (pp. 312–14). The authors' version, however, is indicative of how they cherry-pick evidence to make one-sided claims. This assertion contradicts their own source, which paints a complicated and balanced picture of the five-month siege, with both sides contributing to the tragedy.[4] This source argues that the communists planned to use the siege to break the KMT forces, but it was Chiang Kai-shek who forbade the exodus of the population; who ordered the holding of the city to wait for rescue which never came; who failed to supply the city with air lifts; and who ordered the forced requisition of all civilian grain to feed the starving soldiers.

Anything goes seems to be Chang and Halliday's attitude when it comes to sources. They frequently rely on works of historical fiction that are dramatized with reconstructed dialogue, and that prioritize entertainment, sensationalism and titillation over historical accuracy. In such accounts, factual gaps and uncertainties that baffle historians are filled in with the authors' imagination to complete the narrative. One example is Ming Xiao and Chi Nan's *Mousha Mao Zedong de heise taizi* (The black prince who tried to assassinate Mao Zedong),[5] which the authors use, among other things, to support assertions that Lin Biao and his wife knew and acquiesced in Lin Liguo's alleged plan to assassinate Mao (pp. 557–8, 728–9).

Most of what *Mao* 'exposes' does not represent discoveries unearthed from the archives. For instance, discussion of the alleged terrorist methods used in Jiangxi is in Gong Chu's memoirs[6] and Mao's alleged perfidies can be found in Zhang Guotao's memoirs.[7] Many other revelations are also well known to academics – for instance, the importance of opium revenue to support economic development in

Yan'an (p. 276 ff.) has been studied by Chen Yung-fa,[8] and its brutal rectification campaign is chronicled by Gao Hua[9] and others.[10]

Chang and Halliday assert that Mme Sun Yat-sen was beyond doubt a Soviet agent, but their lone piece of evidence proves nothing (p. 134). It is well known that Mme Sun clung to her husband's 'unite with the Soviet Union and accommodate the communists' policy and that she was a staunch supporter of the Guomindang left who later threw in her lot with the communists, but the authors' grotesque assertion even contradicts their own hagiography of Mme Sun, published in English and then translated into Chinese.[11]

On the Tucheng battle (pp. 143–4, 674), the biggest communist defeat of the Long March, Chang and Halliday claimed that Mao ordered and insisted on the ambush, but one major source cited says that the decision was arrived at collectively by Mao, Zhou Enlai and Liu Bocheng. To demonstrate Mao's deceit, the authors charge that he watched the decimation of his troops and consented to withdraw only after a full day. This is inconsistent with the accounts offered in the sources they used. For instance, Guo Chen relates that it took the Reds three hours, starting at 3 pm, to successfully occupy Tucheng. Intelligence received at 6 pm showed that enemy reinforcements nearby numbered eight divisions, and not the four originally estimated. This information prompted the retreat and the subsequent defeat by pursuing Guomindang forces.[12] Chang and Halliday do not cite interviews as a source for their claim that Mao blatantly sacrificed his troops. Their assertion that the defeat was 'completely suppressed in public' and remembered only in 'private' because Mao was responsible is also inaccurate. Mao openly admitted to and took responsibility for the mistakes he made in his command of the four battles at Gaoxingwei, Nanxiong, Tucheng and Maotai.[13] While cover-ups and euphemisms are often used to describe these mistakes, they are certainly not unknown, as all have been discussed in detail in the works of Hu Zhefeng.[14]

The Mao portrayed by Chang and Halliday was indifferent to death. They cite his May 1958 speech, when he allegedly told his audience to welcome deaths that resulted from their party's policy (p. 439). Again, this quote is taken out of context to prove Mao's 'ghoulish philosophy'. In this speech, Mao was employing some humour as he contemplated the philosophy of dialectics and the unity of opposites in relation to issues of war and splits in the party. According to him, the Chinese are rather dialectical in their thinking: when people die, they mourn, but they also regard this as a cause for celebration. Mao stated with dry humour that 'if Confucius were alive today and wanted to be part of the meeting, it wouldn't be too wonderful, because he would be 2,000 years old'. He thus urged his audience not to think in absolute terms, because disunity, imbalance, death, destruction and calamity could also offer their opposites, leading to unity, balance, life and development.[15] Mao gave this speech during the optimistic heyday of the Great Leap Forward, when widespread starvation was as yet unknown. Chang and Halliday's juxtaposition of this quote with descriptions of famine conditions in 1960 and 1961 in Fengyang County is an unjustifiably crude way to make their point. Distortions like this abound in the book.

According to *Mao*, the 24-year-old Mao's extensive commentaries scribbled on the book, *A System of Ethics*, by German philosopher Friedrich Paulsen, demonstrate that Mao had revealed 'the central elements in his own character, which stayed consistent for the remaining six decades of his life and defined his rule'. Mao's philosophical musing on ethics and morality, Chang and Halliday say, reveals that Mao was an absolutely selfish and irresponsible egotist whose only concern was his personal benefit, who shunned all responsibility and duty, and who took pleasure in upheaval and destruction and was indifferent towards death (pp. 13–15). These assertions of an emerging monster set the tone for the book, but they do not stand up to scrutiny.

Mao's pre-Marxist-Leninist thinking was complex and evolving. According to Stuart Schram, the young Mao was wrestling with the dialectical relations between Western and Chinese ideas and the ways to integrate them into a synthesis. Schram divides Mao's thinking from 1912 to 1920 into three stages: '(1) supporting good rulers of a traditional type; (2) rebellion against this tradition, manifested in extreme individualism and the exaltation of the hero; and (3) the search for a new, revolutionary political power'. During the winter of 1917–18 when Mao was reading Paulsen he was shifting his emphasis from stage 1 to stage 2: from his ideas of the need for great statesmen to lead and change China to 'liberal' notions of the primacy of the self and the individual over the group, and the importance of freedom of the will. After stage 2 Mao's ideas continued to evolve to incorporate the populism and iconoclasm of the May Fourth Movement and eventually Marxist-Leninism.[16]

Mao's writings can be subjected to different interpretations, but, essentially, what the authors do is to mix and match a number of sentences from different paragraphs and then yank them out of context to make their assertions. Schram's translations of Mao's Paulsen commentaries are included in the bibliography of *Mao*, but the authors offer their own translations to better serve their purpose, often showing the opposite of what was intended. In the following, I match the truncated quotations and snap conclusions in *Mao* against its own source as translated by Schram in full. Readers can judge for themselves on the quality of the interpretations. I put in italics the Chang and Halliday quotations and their equivalents in the Schram translation so that readers can easily identify them.

On Mao's alleged egotism and 'absolute' selfishness, Chang and Halliday write

Mao's attitude to morality consisted of one core, the self, '*I*,' above everything else: '*I do not agree with the view that to be moral, the motive of one's action has to be benefiting others. Morality does not have to be defined in relation to others. ... People like me want to ... satisfy our hearts to the full, and in doing so we automatically have the most valuable moral codes. Of course there are people and objects in the world, but they are all there only for me.*'

Compare this with the full source as translated in Schram's anthology:

I too disagree with Schopenhauer. There are two points here. The first point is that natural man is only egoistic, and that since the existence of the individual is incompatible with the universe, he must preserve himself. I say this is not true. Self-interests are indeed primary for human beings, but it does not stop here. It is also of our nature to extend this to helping others. This is one and the same human nature, so working for the interests of others is in my own self-interest. Self-interest is primarily benefiting one's own spirit, and the flesh is of no value in benefiting the spirit. Benefiting the spirit means benefiting the feelings and will. For example, since I cannot forget the feeling I have toward the one I love, my will desires to save her and I will do everything possible to save her, to the point that if the situation is desperate I would rather die myself than let her die. Only thus can my feelings be satisfied, and my will be fulfilled. In all times, there are filial sons, faithful widows, loyal ministers, and devoted friends, those who die for love, for their country, for the world, for their ideals – all to benefit their own spirits. *I do not agree with the first point, that moral values apply only to those acts that are motivated by altruism. Morality does not necessarily depend on others.* What depends on others is objective moral law; what is independent of others is subjective moral law. *My desire to fulfil my nature and perfect my mind is the most precious of the moral laws. There are assuredly human beings and objects in the world, but they all exist because of the self,* and the image I have of them disappears when I close my eyes; thus the objective moral law is also the subjective moral law. If I were the only person in the world, I could not fail to fulfil my nature and complete my mind, simply because it would be no loss to others. I would still have to fulfil and complete them. Such things are not done for others, but for ourselves.[17]

On Mao as a totally irresponsible person, Chang and Halliday write:

Mao shunned all constraints of responsibility and duty. *'People like me only have a duty to ourselves; we have no duty to other people.'*

Compare this with the full source:

I, however, think that we have a duty to ourselves, and have no duty toward others. We have the duty to do whatever we have thought about, that is, we have the duty to do whatever we know. This duty arises naturally within my spirit, such as repaying debts, keeping promises, not stealing, not being false, and although they are things that involve other people, it is my wish that they be done. The meaning of duty to oneself means no more than just developing fully one's own physical and spiritual powers. Helping those in need, perfecting those things that are humanly beautiful, treading fearlessly in the face of danger and sacrificing oneself to save others, are no more than duty, since I desire to do them, and only then will my mind be at rest. If I see someone in danger and do not try to rescue him, even if not doing so would not be considered wrong, will I really think in my own mind that not helping him is right? The fact that I think it is not right is what makes it my duty to rescue him. We rescue those who are in danger to set our minds at rest, and to develop fully the capacities of our spirits.[18]

The transformation and destruction of the old order in favour of a new one is indeed a consistent theme in Mao's revolutionary thought. But in Chang and Halliday's out-of-context narrative, this merely reflects Mao's delight in upheaval, chaos and destruction for their own sake, his 'cavalier attitude toward death', and his lack of conscience.

Simplistic reasoning, faulty logic

Chang and Halliday's moralistic fervour blinds them to the necessities that drive the actions of politicians such as Mao, the need to use strategy, including tricks, manipulation and even treachery, as a normal means of leadership, especially in dealings with foreign powers. They are likewise oblivious to any possibility of multiple interpretations for their evidence. The authors deem Mao's reluctance to confront the Japanese directly to be cowardly and hypocritical. They fault him for 'preserving his forces' and waiting for Stalin to do the job for him (p. 204). They describe Mao as privately furious with Lin Biao's battle at Pingxingguan and Peng Dehuai's Hundred Regiment Offensive (with 9,000 casualties), both fought without his authorization, while publicly lauding the battles as indicators of the communists' determination to fight (p. 221). Chang and Halliday do not appreciate that Mao's tactic of conserving strength in the face of overwhelmingly superior Japanese forces and avoidance of set pieces was what made him a great tactician and earned him the respect of his followers. Indeed, if Mao had fought the Japanese, at a huge cost of lives, the authors, using their inherent bad faith model, would likely blame him for recklessness.

Similarly, manipulation and deception are said to be behind Mao's invitations to Nixon and Kissinger. In a chapter entitled 'Nixon: The Red-Baiter Baited', Chang and Halliday describe how Mao had Nixon 'thinking that he was the keener of the two' for the visit; Nixon bore 'many and weighty gifts, and asked for nothing in return'. These weighty gifts included promises of diplomatic recognition, abandonment of Taiwan and a guarantee of Chinese sovereignty, as well as Kissinger's offer to withdraw troops from Vietnam and Korea and to share intelligence on the Soviet Union. Kissinger's presence in Beijing also helped China regain its seat in the UN's Security Council, and Nixon helped reverse the demonization of Mao, turning him into an international figure of 'incomparable allure'. Leaving aside whether this is an adequate analysis, and whether the Nixon/Kissinger team was that gullible, the authors' evidence can be interpreted as showing a supreme mastery of diplomacy by the Mao/Zhou team, which is inconsistent with their view of Mao as either a dissembler or a bumbling fool.

Chang and Halliday's approach of focusing in on Mao and his alleged perfidies misses the cultural, historical and socio-economic contexts that conditioned Mao's behaviour and his era. For instance, the authors argue that Mao repeatedly terrorized his troops and supporters, only to rehabilitate them when he needed them (p. 247), but the reasons why and under what conditions Mao resorted to such measures are not adequately explained. China descended into chaos and disintegration during the first part of the twentieth century when life was nasty, brutal and short. Mao was undoubtedly a hardened revolutionary but his adversaries were as ruthless as the chairman himself. Yet, in *Mao*, Mao's counterparts – foreign leaders, adversaries, colleagues, peasants, etc. – appear merely as passive and docile pawns in Mao's machinations and his quest for supreme power.

One of the most sensational assertions that captured reviewers' attention in *Mao* is that Mao and some leaders were so privileged that they were carried on litters for much of the Long March, revelling at the experience but at the expense of the suffering carriers. Chang and Halliday write:

> Bamboo litters were authorised for a few leaders, each of whom was also entitled to a horse and porters to carry their belongings. For much of the Long March, including the most gruelling part of the trek, most of them were carried. Mao had even designed his own transportation. Mrs Lo Fu recalled him making preparations with the Red Prof, showing off his ingenuity. 'He said: 'Look, we have designed our own litters … we will be carried.' He and Jia-xiang looked rather pleased with themselves showing me their 'works of art'.
>
> (p. 139)

It is worth considering the authors' claims against available sources to give context and perspective to the 'litter' issue. That leaders and followers were carried in litters during the Long March is no secret and has been officially and extensively documented. But Chang and Halliday neglect to inform the readers that those being carried were usually so sick, injured or pregnant that they could not ride a horse or donkey. For instance, according to Harrison Salisbury, Mao, weakened by a long bout of malaria, travelled 'from time to time' in a litter. A 'Who's Who' of high communist leaders, such as Hu Yaobang, who also suffered from malaria, were carried in litters. Deng Yingchao (wife of Zhou Enlai), stricken with tuberculosis and splitting blood, was in a litter for most of the Long March. Mao, Luo Fu and Wang Jiaxiang carried out political discussion in the litters. The wounded Wang was carried during the entire Long March.[19]

Salisbury's account is consistent with the descriptions in many Chinese sources. According to another source, Wang Jiaxiang was severely injured during an air attack in 1934, and even after an eight-hour operation without anaesthetics, the shrapnel could not be removed. Wang was carried during the Long March with an open wound, infected intestines, and tube(s) coming out of his abdomen. Mao almost died from malaria, and was so weakened that he could not walk. Both were in litters.[20]

Leaders were also carried in litters so that they could rest during the day. Mao, Zhou Enlai and Zhu De used to work at night as briefings about the March and enemy logistics were not available until late and movement plans for the next day had to be coordinated at night.[21] In a country with a huge population, human power (including 'coolie' labour) has always been a common means of trans-porting goods and humans. Sedan chairs (including primitive ones consisting of two poles attached to a chair to be carried by two persons) and rickshaws were a common sight in China. Communist stretcher units were organized to carry the injured. According to Guo Chen's book on the 'litter company' cited by Chang and Halliday, at the beginning of the Long March the No. 2 Transportation Company was converted into the Litter Company, which was later merged with the Cadre Convalescence Company. Lower down were Litter Platoons, which were led by a leader as well as a Commissar in charge of recruitment and political work. The litter carriers were civilians recruited and let go on the way but some were recruited into the Red Army.[22]

Chang and Halliday's assertion that Mao was carried 'for much of the Long March, including the most gruelling part of the trek', cannot be supported by the sources they cited (p. 674) and can only be regarded as one of their embellish-ments. They write that '[w]hen climbing mountains the litter-bearers sometimes could move forward only on their knees, and the skin and flesh on the knees were rubbed raw before they got to the top. Each mountain climbed left a trail of their sweat and blood'. This is accurate, but it portrays a general state of affairs and was not specific to Mao. Guo Chen describes how Zhong Chibing was carried in a litter because he had only one leg. When difficult terrain made litters impossible, the leaders had to march along on foot. It's difficult to imagine healthy leaders insist-ing on being carried under such harsh conditions. Deng Liujin (nicknamed Red Mama and mother to Zeng Qinghong), one of the thirty women who took part in the Long March, notes that she and other women took over as carriers of the litters when the civilians were scared away by the bombardment and that the injured and the amputees had to be carried while the slightly injured had to walk with canes. Mao's wife He Zizhen, who was pregnant at the beginning of the March and was severely wounded by shrapnel, had to be carried.[23]

The litters, essentially modified stretchers, were hardly a luxury. According to Salisbury, a litter 'consisted of two long hollow bamboo poles … and a cross-part made of woven fibre. It was light and buoyant, swaying from side to side and down like a sailor's hammock'. That leaders and marchers were carried on the March demonstrated simultaneously desperation and determination. Although the Long March has been immortalized as an epic of military history – the 6,000 miles covered on foot is more than twice the width of the United States – it was also essentially a year-long retreat during which dissension, recrimination and deser-tions were rife. The communists were attacked by Guomindang bombardment and ambushes and of the 80,000-odd who began the march only about 8,000 reached the finally destination. Children, including two of Mao's, had to be left behind, never to be found again.

The 'litter' issue is just one of the numerous examples of the persistent efforts by Chang and Halliday to manipulate the sources to make their sensational assertions. This is ironic because the authors place themselves on high moral ground, passing judgement on Mao's deceptions. It is true that in interpreting Chinese sources, one often has to extrapolate and read between the lines, but the authors' treatment of their sources can only be said to be sloppy, wilful and irresponsible.

Mao is not the breakthrough it is made out to be. Its nuggets of information require sophisticated and responsible analysis. A subject as complex as Mao's life and times cannot be treated in stark black and white terms. Mao's charismatic ability to move millions was not simply based on terror, cruelty and oppression. No sensible person would want to act as an apologist for Mao and his autocratic and paranoid ways, especially when official censorship, relentless propaganda and cover-ups have prevented many Chinese from telling their stories. Nevertheless, those interested in the life and times of Mao can turn confidentially to a large body of ongoing Western scholarship that has accumulated over several generations. As for Chang and Halliday, they have created more myths than they debunked.

Part IV
Chinese reviews

10 Jung Chang and Jon Halliday, *Mao: The Unknown Story*

A review

Chen Yung-fa

Translated by Wenjuan Bi with Christopher A. Reed

This review first appeared in Chinese in the *Bulletin of the Institute of Modern History* no. 2 (2006), pp. 211–19. The English translation first appeared in *Twentieth Century China*, vol. 33, no. 1, pp. 104–13.

No matter how people judge him, no one can deny the importance of Mao Zedong in twentieth-century Chinese history; indeed, he also holds a significant position in twentieth-century world history. Mao studied the Soviet Union, led the Chinese communist revolution, overthrew the regime of the Nationalist Party (Guomindang), and constructed an unparalleled centralized party-state system. He made great efforts to create a country distinguished from capitalist countries and tried thoroughly to eliminate the competitive market economy based on private property. All of these practices influenced China's destiny. Even though the Mainland of China today is an inseparable part of the world economic system, we can still see there the continuation of the political system of Mao's era. Mao's thought was reinterpreted by Deng Xiaoping, yet it remains the source of legitimacy for the Chinese Communist Party (CCP). Hu Jintao's first step after he was appointed General Secretary of the CCP was to visit Xibaipo, the site of some of Mao's toughest experiences before Mao entered Beijing. In China, many people who have not benefited from the policy of Reform and Opening still yearn for the social status and welfare system of Mao's era. Some intellectuals also long for the equality of Mao's era and criticize today's wide gap between rich and poor. Of course, some intellectuals also fear the return of political struggle and thought control.

Regarding such an important historical figure, one cannot help but be a little curious. In the era of Taiwan's anti-communist and anti-Soviet policies, approximately 1949 to 1964, because of political propaganda we did not have a concrete understanding of Mao. Some people regarded Mao as a dictatorial emperor. Others condemned him as a contemporary Qinshi Huangdi (c. 259–10 BC), while some denigrated him as a Chinese Stalin or Hitler.

Even in Mao's era, however, Hitler was regarded on the Mainland as a vicious criminal. Qinshi Huangdi and Stalin, conversely, reaped eulogies. The former established the basis of China's territory and political system and the latter not only brought about thorough change in an undeveloped Russia but also offered a paradigm for socialist construction. When Chinese experts on CCP history narrate the life of Mao, they always emphasize his role as 'the teacher and the emperor'. They point out that Mao was the pioneer who discovered the truth of Marxism-Leninism. He not only Sinicized Marxism-Leninism and transformed it into a scientific tool that was more suitable for the practice of revolution; based on it, he analyzed Chinese society and framed a strategy for revolution. In different stages, Mao led the Chinese people to defeat Japanese aggression, overthrow the rule of the Guomindang, and construct a new socialist China.

The broad narrative developed by experts on CCP history emphasizes the universalism of Marxism-Leninism. It was Mao who inherited the legitimacy of Marx, Engels, Lenin and Stalin. In a country in which capitalism was little developed, Mao organized, led, mobilized and liberated peasants. Then, in the process of converting China into a progressive socialist country, in this view, he transformed them into a stable foundation. This macro-narrative emphasizes Mao's creative reinterpretation of Marxism-Leninism. Although it does not stress Mao's belief in nationalism, it crowns Mao by crediting him with the creation of Chinese nationalism.

Conversely, some China experts overseas have underscored Mao's persistent nationalism to refute the views that Mao was a puppet following Stalin and that the Chinese communist revolution represented a continuation of the Russian revolution. They not only give prominence to Mao's Sinicization of Marxism-Leninism – they depict Mao's promotion of nationalism. They consider this tendency to be the most important reason for the bifurcation and later irreconcilability of China and the Soviet Union.

Author and researcher Dr Jung Chang's parents were loyal communists. Her father was in Yan'an and served as vice-director of Sichuan province's propaganda department during the Maoist era. In the 1960s, during the Cultural Revolution, when Chang was still in middle school, her parents were attacked by both the Red Guards and the Rebel Faction. After Mao ordered urban youths to be 'sent down' to rural and mountainous areas, Chang herself went to a barren area inhabited by Chinese and Tibetans in south-western Sichuan. Once Deng Xiaoping implemented the Reform and Opening policy, Chang left China for England and studied history. She published a best-selling English-language book, *Wild Swans: Three Daughters of China*, which bore her Chinese name Hong. This book described the psychological experiences of three generations, including her grandmother, her mother and herself. Her husband Jon Halliday specializes in the history of the Soviet and East European communist parties. Chang and Halliday cooperated closely in writing this biography of Mao. In the last dozen years, they have visited not only every place Mao went but also many archives in Russia and Eastern Europe. They interviewed many elderly CCP members with some connection to Mao and visited many political leaders of that period. They interviewed many influential political leaders as well as some minor persons who served Mao in his daily life. In her former residence at Bancang, near Changsha, they even found letters and a memoir left by Mao's wife Yang Kaihui.

From these abundant materials, they claim to have discovered an unknown Mao whom they consider to have been 'an unprecedented madman'. In their view, he was concerned only with himself, with power, and with conquest. He was unfilial to his parents, unmerciful to his brothers, disloyal to his wife, perfidious to his friends, faithless to his comrades, unpatriotic to his country, unsympathetic to the workers and peasants, suspicious of Marxism-Leninism, and even unconcerned with whether he would leave a good or notorious name after his death. They find that he provided little leadership, little in the way of a political ideal, little communist morality, and little strategy. His seizure of the Chinese Mainland was based only on violent terror, fraudulent cabals, and secret police tactics. To defeat his opponents, he used all kinds of means, fair or foul. He was insidious and selfish. Chang and Halliday charge Mao with having been greedy and brutal, and argue that he enjoyed privilege, feared death, was a born lecher and was never sincere. From the image of Mao that Chang and Halliday summon up, we cannot see the influence of Marxism-Leninism on him nor can we find any trace of twentieth-century Chinese nationalism. He turns out to have been simply an individual who gained the favour of the gods.

The image of Mao portrayed by Chang and Halliday shatters the myths prevalent on the Mainland as well as overseas. They demonstrate that Mao pursued other women while still in love with wife Yang Kaihui. Soon after he arrived in the Jinggang Mountains, he fell in love with another woman and ignored his wife's soulful letters. The authors verify that Mao received a special allowance for professional revolutionaries from the Soviet Union soon after he joined the CCP and that he often said that the money was very useful in improving his standard of living. While establishing his rule in Jiangxi, under the guise of purging spies, he connived with Li Shaojiu to kill any who opposed him. Thousands of people were victimized in this slaughter. On the eve of the Anti-Japanese War (1937–45), Mao gave up the idea of killing Chiang Kai-shek and settled the Xi'an Incident peacefully only because of pressure from Stalin. After the Anti-Japanese War broke out, say Chang and Halliday, Mao frequently accepted additional and substantial financial assistance from Stalin. Mao even gave orders to plant opium to raise money in trade with territory outside communist control. In the later phases of the war, he utilized Kang Sheng, the head of the secret police, to launch the Rescue Campaign (part of the Rectification Movement) and to conduct the Red Terror. He forced communists 'to accept being saved' or 'to save themselves' under the threat of being named a Nationalist Party spy. To win the Battle of Changchun (1946) in the Civil War (1946–49), he created a famine and refused a request from commander Lin Biao to let the common people leave the occupied city, a decision that led to the death by starvation of 170,000 innocent people.

Moreover, Chang and Halliday show that although Mao signed the Sino-Soviet Treaty of Friendship, Alliance, and Mutual Assistance, in doing so he agreed that Northeast China and Xinjiang were to be within the Soviet sphere of influence. In the period of the Korean War (1950–53), he disregarded Kim Il-sung's appeal for peace and refused to concede to America, resulting in the continuation of the war and the slaughter of North Koreans. Only when the Soviets threatened to reveal that the so-called American 'germ warfare' was in fact directed by the CCP was the CCP forced to sign the truce agreement. Chang and Halliday reveal that during the

---

Land Revolution (1950), the Movement to Suppress Anti-Revolutionaries (1950), the Anti-Rightist Movement (1957), the Great Leap Forward (1958–60), and the Cultural Revolution (1966–76), all of which were launched by Mao, millions of people were killed as a result of violence and famine. They emphasize Zhou Enlai's absurd loyalty to Mao. Although Zhou Enlai did not always agree with the policies of Mao, he allowed himself to be utilized by Mao and he himself carried out the great purge of the CCP from 1966 to 1967.

   Most of the details that Chang and Halliday provide about these issues and campaigns are believable. However, most are also generally known and some are very well known, even by some experts outside the Mainland. Possibly for this reason, for the Chinese version, Chang and Halliday changed the book's title from *Mao: The Unknown Story* to *Mao: The Little-Known Story* (*Xian wei renzhi de Mao Zedong*).

   Chang and Halliday also advance some opinions that really are unknown, but their proof is not persuasive. For example, to demonstrate the wickedness of Mao, they point out that he forced Zhou Enlai to abandon the position of military commander soon after Mao learned that Zhou had published a notice in 1932 in Shanghai's *Shenbao* newspaper announcing his intention of quitting the CCP. They even imply that this announcement was invented by Mao himself. They suggest that Mao arrested many people under the guise of purging anti-revolutionaries and then hypocritically appealed to stop the slaughter in order to earn the favour of Liu Zhidan, a northern leader of the CCP. Then, they say, Mao sent Liu to the battle-front and had him assassinated in the disorder. They also charge that Mao asked his private doctor to murder Wang Ming, whose status was equal to Mao's during the period of the Anti-Japanese War, by adding poison to a prescription. They charge that Mao exported a great deal of food to the Soviet Union in the period of the Civil War, resulting in famine in the Northeast and in northern Shaanxi Province. They claim that Mao was a warmonger who persuaded Kim Il-sung to invade South Korea in pursuit of Mao's own aims of extorting a large amount of modern military equipment from the Soviets. According to Chang and Halliday, Mao even rashly launched the artillery war in the Jinmen area off Fujian to force the Soviets to offer him the atomic bomb and the necessary equipment to protect the bomb. They charge that although Mao claimed that the Soviet Union was the leader of the socialist countries, he also implied that the leaders of the Eastern European countries secretly supported him against Stalin. They charge that although Mao knew that food was in short supply on the eve of the Great Leap Forward, he 'deliberately falsified records of the world-record amount of food output' to have an excuse for further exploiting people, an instance of 'catching all the fish by draining a pond'. They maintain that Mao launched the Cultural Revolution for revenge while enriching his own book collection by expropriating good editions and while obtaining foreign currency by selling rare relics (as Stalin had done in the 1930s). Although Deng Xiaoping, Zhou Enlai, and Ye Jianying seized actual power two years before his death in 1976, Mao merely warned them not to launch a coup. He himself did not care whether the Cultural Revolution system continued or not, according to Chang and Halliday.

All of these condemnations lack sufficient proof. Some are totally fictitious. Two startling opinions deserve special attention. One is that the heroic story of the 25,000-*li* Long March is fraudulent. In Chang and Halliday's view, Chiang Kai-shek permitted the Long Marchers to leave Jiangxi so that Stalin would care for his son Jiang Jingguo and to reclaim military and political control in the south-western provinces. Without this context, they argue, Mao could never have led the Red Army to the loess plateau in northern Shaanxi. Another astonishing and unsupported historical claim concerns Mao's planting of four Red spies – Shao Lizi, Zhang Zhizhong, Wei Lihuang, and Hu Zongnan – in Chiang Kai-shek's camp. Further, Chang and Halliday maintain that Mao won the Civil War entirely because of their betrayal of Chiang. Three of them declared themselves and surrendered to the CCP before or after Mao seized the Mainland. Only Hu Zongnan did not expose his true role; he was a lifelong anti-communist who died in Taiwan. It is a pity that these two opinions – never encountered before – are basically conjectural.

For all these reasons, Chang and Halliday's biography of Mao Zedong leaves the impression that they are following the habit common in inner-CCP struggles, especially Mao's own strategy of criticism that focuses on one point but disregards others. Chang and Halliday attack Mao chiefly from the perspective of morality. Like Mao himself, they explain historical facts immoderately, falsely, and with distortion, even with the aid of abundant Soviet, Eastern European and oral materials. Because of their strong prejudice, they can only criticize and condemn Mao rather than present a realistic image of him. Apart from adding to the view that Mao was a Machiavelli with little in the way of morality, they do not add significantly to our understanding of him. On the contrary, they simply embroider their personal feelings. Their description of Mao oversimplifies reality, revealing only a pattern of wickedness.

Jung Chang and Jon Halliday set the tone for their book at the very beginning. They quote three notes written by Mao after reading Friedrich Paulsen's *A System of Ethics* (1899) at the age of twenty-four. Their conclusion is that Mao's life was based wholly on his personal ethics, which advocated absolute selfishness, meaning that he cared only about the satisfaction of personal impulses and was not concerned with social conscience. He calculated only what would benefit him, but took little responsibility for any other person. … As long as there was no punishment, he did anything he liked.

However, Chang and Halliday overlook a totally different Mao that emerges from the full text of which they quote only a part:

> Although pursuing self-interest is human nature, it is not the only nature of human beings. Altruism is another nature of human beings. The key point regarding self-interest rests in benefiting one's spirit rather than one's body. Benefiting one's spirit lies in the satisfaction of one's feelings and mind. If my beloved is in danger, I [would] try my best to save her. If the situation is critical, I [would] sacrifice myself rather than her. Only in this way can I feel comfortable. The reasons that filial children, chaste women, loyal ministers,

and trusting friends throughout history have sacrificed for love, for country, or for ideals is essentially because of the pursuit of self-interest.[1]

I have two opinions about ethics. The first one concerns individualism. All one's behaviour and moral tenets are for self-fulfilment rather than for benefiting others. Since I have such an ideal, I must make it come true. Both Sakyamuni and Mozi were persons who achieved their own goals. If I cannot fulfil the ideal, then my life is pitiful and my objective has not been attained. The second opinion regards realism. I can only take responsibility for my current life. Both the past and the future have no relationship to my subjective or objective existence, so I bear no responsibility for them. It is said that people should bear responsibility for inheriting the past and looking forward to the future. I do not agree with this opinion and will develop only myself.[2]

When Chang and Halliday, advancing their interpretation of moral nihilism, find that Mao tried to exclude everything that restricted his inherent drive, they shudder. However, if they were to research Mao from the perspective of moral practice, they would find that he stressed self-determinism because he wanted to pursue success by taking responsibility for himself and by striving for absolute freedom of action.

The danger in Mao's personal ethics lies not in the lack of morality but in its excessive morality. It is precisely due to this excessive morality that Mao insisted that if he could pursue truth, he would do so even if thousands opposed him. As he said, 'I will not abandon my nature and give up my ideals because they might damage others'. The result was that he inevitably imposed his own ideals on other people. The truth that Mao defined was a subjective understanding of objective facts. Although the truth can be applied at any time and in any place, there is much space for objective explanation. To practise his ideal, Mao was often headstrong and even used foul means. In carrying out his own great and beneficent policy, he did not hesitate to sacrifice other people's beneficent policy. To realize his own great mercy and virtue, he disregarded other people's mercy and virtue, the so-called 'small mercy and virtue'. To achieve his truth, he disregarded the justice of process, did not avoid violence and scheming, and even chose to murder others.

Chang and Halliday notice only the political plots that Mao devised to realize his aim. They see only Mao's ruthlessness and cruelty combined with his use of violence and terror, but do not discuss the three main principles of Mao's struggle: rationality, advantage, and self-control. Mao cared most about the rectitude of struggle, although his so-called rectitude might in fact be sophistry and could bring forth violence, bloodshed, affliction and death. Because they do not understand the exact meaning of the so-called 'rationality' that Mao developed, Chang and Halliday can neither explain how Mao propagandized 'rationality' nor understand why Mao was blindly revered both inside and outside the CCP. Since they do not grasp how Mao subjugated so many Chinese intellectuals, who regarded him as the representative of scientific truth (Marxism-Leninism) and patriotism (nationalism), they also fail to understand how Mao mobilized the impoverished masses. Similarly, they cannot understand why Zhou Enlai was willing to be driven like a slave by Mao or to work himself to death for him. As Ke Qingshi, the former East China Bureau party secretary and vice-premier of the People's Republic of China, once remarked, Peng Dehuai, regarded by Chang and Halliday as 'China's conscience', and Liu Shaoqi and Deng Xiaoping, whom Chang and Halliday consider to have been the 'saviours of the Chinese people', *all* believed in Mao to a fetishistic extent and obeyed him blindly.

Mao Zedong monopolized the legitimacy of morality by claiming the sole right to explain scientific truth and patriotism. The Chinese were driven by him on that basis. If we do not research him from this perspective, we can neither understand his ambiguous and complicated behaviour nor understand why he still has so many adherents. These people believe in Mao's socialist ideal and that the Chinese 'stood up' thanks to his leadership. There is no doubt that we can heavily criticize Mao, but we should not try to do so by denigrating his personal character. We should criticize and deconstruct the Marxism-Leninism and the nationalism he expounded. We should also remind readers that Marxism-Leninism is not a universal truth that can be applied at any time and any place and that its meaning varies greatly according to who is explaining it. When it is combined with political power and goes to extremes, it will be transformed into dogmatic Marxism-Leninism and national chauvinism, the dangers of which are innumerable. If we can understand Mao's Marxism-Leninism and nationalism from this angle, we cannot deny Mao's sincerity. We will also be able to distinguish the correct and false parts of Mao's belief system and admit that it was a double-edged sword. It can bring liberation but can also bring slaughter. It can bring solidarity but can also bring disintegration. It can bring hope but can also bring persecution.

Furthermore, in establishing the supreme status of his ideas, Mao always emphasized the importance of power in real politics. While creating a highly centralized political system, he also established a military machine that could defy the world's two strongest powers – the USSR and the USA – simultaneously. He was able to explain, represent and manipulate the scientific truth and nationalism in which he believed. Moreover, because he developed the techniques of mass mobilization and ideological remoulding and believed deeply in their effects, the Chinese sometimes became the victims of his ideology and nationalism. If we see Mao only as a manipulator, we will not only fail to understand how he conquered a generation of intellectuals; we will also underestimate his talent in making himself *the* representative of ideology and nationalism.

How Mao Zedong gained his status as the sole interpreter and key representative of Chinese Marxism-Leninism and nationalism and how he interpreted Chinese Marxism-Leninism and nationalism are the two main problems in the study of CCP history before and after the establishment of the PRC. It is regrettable that although Chang and Halliday, by dint of their great effort, have discovered the so-called 'unknown' Mao Zedong, they do not help us address these two topics. Mao brought the Chinese both liberation and bondage, both renascence and Red terror, both belief and curse.

When young, Mao dreamed of saving the country and the masses. After embracing Marxism-Leninism, he believed that class struggle was scientific truth and the only way to accelerate the progress of a society. But in order to practise the ideal of Marxism-Leninism, he required the breaking of every form of bondage, whether in opposition to thousands of people or at the price of sacrificing some people's lives. He never avoided violence, terror, coercion, disintegration and machination. He did not have the traditional character of the upright man who avoided wrong-doing. On the contrary, he believed that he could use all kinds of means – foul or fair – to achieve his aims. He considered the realization of his subjective desires as the most important thing.

11 *Mao: The Unknown Story*
An intellectual scandal

Mobo Gao

This contribution comprises edited extracts from Mobo Gao (2008), *The Battle for China's Past: Mao and the Cultural Revolution*, London: Pluto Press.

Hyper-promotion of a book

Mao: The Unknown Story became a number one best-seller soon after it was released in the UK, Australia and New Zealand in 2005. The book was promoted with such media frenzy that a review in the British *Guardian* is titled 'The book that will shake the world'. The BBC's 'Off the Shelf' – more commonly devoted to fiction – gave a 'dramatic' reading of excerpts of the book in a 'voice dripping with cynicism and irony' (Weil 2006). One reviewer called the book 'a work of unanswerable authority. ... Mao is comprehensively discredited from beginning to end in small ways and large; a murderer, a torturer, an untalented orator, a lecher, a destroyer of culture, an opium profiteer, a liar' (Hensher 2005).

The *Australian*, a broadsheet newspaper, collected various trend-setting writers and journalists in Australia and asked them to choose the 2005 Book of the Year. The senior journalist Nicolas Rothwell chose *Mao: The Unknown Story*. This is what he said: reading the book about 'the 20th century's most bloodstained dictator was a litmus event', 'I cannot recall finishing a book that inspired in me such sharp feeling of nausea, horror and despair' (Rothwell 2005, p. R5).

Jonathan Mirsky, a seasoned journalist who writes for the British *Observer* and *The New York Times*, stated that the book proves that Mao 'was as evil as Hitler or Stalin, and did as much damage to mankind as they did'. Montefiore (2005) declared that 'Mao is the greatest monster of them all – the Red Emperor of China'. 'China's Monster, Second to None' is the title of a review in *The New York Times* (Kakutani 2005), whose author said that the book makes 'an impassioned case for Mao as the most monstrous tyrant of all times'. In *The New York Times Book Review* Nicholas D. Kristof (2005) called it a 'magnificent biography' and 'magisterial' work. The last Governor of Hong Kong Chris Pattern and the influential German *Spiegel* endorsed the book. Even Andrew Nathan, though unable to support its blatant violation of scholarly norms, still thought it contains jade (Nathan, in this volume).

'Whether it's the news that Mao never actually marched in long stretches of the Long March but was, instead, carried in a bamboo litter he designed himself, or of the scale of his purges and executions, this is a catalogue of disclosures that overturns almost all our received wisdom. The impact will be substantial. It's an impressive achievement', said Will Hutton (2005), an influential British political commentator. 'Chang's new book is actually a vast work of scholarship rather than an emotionally-charged personal attack' asserts Thorpe (2005). Chang and Halliday cast new and revealing light on nearly every episode in Mao's tumultuous life claimed Yahuda (2005), a veteran scholar of the London School of Economics.

Scholarship, what scholarship?

Of course, anyone can make claims. What is special about *Mao: The Unknown Story* is that its claims are supposed to have been backed up by scholarship and painstaking research. What has impressed journalists, political commentators and some academics is that Jung Chang and Jon Halliday say they consulted something like 1,200 written sources, the majority of them in Chinese, and interviewed 400 people. The book has an impressive display of 68 pages of notes. It took the husband and wife co-authors more than a decade to finish it, we are told.

The interviewees

Let's first start with the impressive list of people the authors claim to have interviewed. They include dignitaries such as András Hegedüs, a prime minister of Hungary, Prince Mikasa, brother of the Japanese Emperor Hirohito, Eugenio Anguiano, a certain Mexican ambassador to Beijing, Frank Corner, a foreign minister of New Zealand, and Lech Walesa, former President of Poland. Of course His Holiness the Dalai Lama is also included on the list. With enormous financial resources and prestige from the success of *Wild Swans*, Chang could get anyone interviewed. But the question is: what does Lech Walesa or a prime minister of Hungary know about Mao, or China?

The list of course also includes many who do or could claim to know about Mao, or China, such as Joseph Needham, Steven Fitzgerald (first Australian ambassador to Beijing), Mao's daughter Li Na, Mao's grandson Mao Xinyu, or Liu Shaoqi's wife Wang Guangmei. It is a clever marketing strategy to approach these people and then claim to have interviewed them. However, whether it is scholarship remains to be proved. To start with, one would like to see whether the interviewees said anything relevant to the content or arguments of the book. I would not list someone as an interviewee for a book on Mao if all they talked about was the weather.

Secondly, we would like to know how Chang and Halliday dealt with information that contradicted what they set out to prove. Professor Frederick Teiwes is a well-known expert on CCP elite politics and is listed in the book's acknowledgements. According to Teiwes, he met Jung Chang a couple of times but could not say anything substantial about the subject on Mao because Chang would not listen unless what he said fitted her predetermined ideas. An indication of what Teiwes thinks of the book is that he declined to participate in *The China Journal*'s special issue of reviews on it.

Yes, Chang interviewed Mao's daughter and a grandson, but do we know what Li Na said about her father and Mao Xinyu about his grandfather? It is standard practice in scholarly writing that you list a source only if it is referred to or cited in the text. If you do not want to tell the reader what an interviewee has said, you cannot include that interviewee as a source of evidence in support of your book.

How evidence is selected: the example of Gong Chu

All writing aims to argue for or against something and therefore has to select its evidence, but the selection must be seen to be reasonable and justifiable in the context of existing knowledge. Scholarship has to engage the existing literature and address opposing views and evidence. Throughout the book Chang and Halliday often write as if there were no scholarship on the subject. If they cite something from a publication, it is to serve the purpose of their agenda – the demonization of Mao.

Here is one of many examples. Gong Chu, a former senior Red Army officer, who worked with Mao during the early period of the communist revolution but gave up and ran away to live in Hong Kong before the communist victory, published his memoirs in Hong Kong. Chang and Halliday cite Gong as an insider, but only to prove that Mao was a cunning power hungry manipulator who was cruel but otherwise good at nothing. When I read Gong's memoirs, I found the image of Mao that emerges is entirely different from the one presented in Chang and Halliday. Gong's book, published in 1978, shows that Mao had ups and downs during the early period of the communist revolution and was vulnerable and emotional, just like any normal person. When he talked with Gong about how he was oppressed and dismissed by Zhou Enlai, Mao even shed tears (Gong 1978, p. 550). Gong says the first clear understanding of the rural nature of the Chinese Revolution came from Mao, so Mao did not become leader of the CCP by luck or accident (Gong 1978: 493). Gong also testifies that land reform in the Jiangxi revolutionary base under Mao was mild and did not victimize rich peasants. However, when the CCP central leadership from Shanghai headed by Zhou Enlai arrived in 1931, they struggled against Mao's *funong luxian* (rich peasant line) and Zhou Enlai wanted to *xiaomie dizhu, zhancao chugen* (liquidate the landlords as if uprooting the grass). When Gong Chu said the policy was too radical and that many so-called landlords were just households with very little land, it was Zhou, not Mao, who expelled him from the party for one year.

Referencing: a clever deception

The 68 pages of notes are designed to impress readers and intimidate them intellectually. A very unusual reference format is adopted, as we shall see below. If the book were meant as fiction, there would be no need for a discussion about the notes. But since it is meant to tell the truth about Mao and what happened in China, its claims should be backed up by evidence. Are they?

In the text itself, there is little evidence of referencing, except for the odd footnote indicated by an asterisk. The reader interested in the referencing needs to go to the Notes section at the end of the book in which references are arranged as follows: book pages are listed, followed by a phrase in bold that is either a direct quote from the book or key words about the topic under discussion. As an example, here are the first few lines of the 'Notes' section on page 677 with references to part of the text in Chapter 1.

Chapter 1 On the Cusp from Ancient to Modern

3–4 Parents: Snow 1973, pp. 130–4: *Mao Clan Chronicle*: Mao's father-in-law Yang Chang-chi's diary, 5 Apr. 1915, in *Mao 1990, p. 636 (E:MRTP Vol. 2, p. 60): Li Xiangwen, pp. 25–51: *Zhao Zhichao, pp. 273–4: visit to Shaoshan and conversations with locals.

Readers want to be assured that what they are being told is an honest presentation of the evidence, that it is presented as accurately as possible and other people's research and arguments are treated fairly and reasonably. References are offered so that the assumption of honesty, integrity, fairness and reasonableness can be checked and confirmed. However, in the case of Chang and Halliday's book, we have a problem. For instance, pages 3–4 say quite a lot about Mao's parents, but there is no indication which reference relates to which bit of information.

There are numerous references in the Notes section for any given page of text. This gives the impression of scholarship and painstaking research. However, if you check, you may find that the references are little more than show. On p. 97, for example, we read:

Once he had tightened his grip on the army, Mao turned his attention to the Jiangxi Communists. On 3 December he sent Lie with a list of his foes to the town of Futian, where the Jiangxi leaders were living. Mao condemned the meeting in August which had expelled his ally Lieu as an 'AB meeting' which 'opposed Mao Tse-tung'. 'Put them all down', he ordered, and then 'slaughter en masse in all counties and all districts'. 'Any place that does not arrest and slaughter members of the Party and government of that area must be AB [*xun-ban*, implying torture and/or liquidation], and you can simply seize and deal with them'.

The references for the above paragraph are

97   Mao order, 3 Dec. 1930: in *Dai & Luo, pp. 94–6, see a follow-up letter on 5 Dec., in Vladimirov, 10 Nov. 1943 (mis-dated 15th). 'AB meeting': Mao to Shanghai, 20 Dec. 1930, *ZDJC vol. 14, p. 636 (E: *MRTP* vol. 3,

pp. 704–5); *Liou Di, letter to Shanghai, 11 Jan. 1931, RGASPI, *cit.*;
*Provincial Action Committee, Emergency Announcement no. 9, 15 Dec.
1930 RGASPI, 514/1/1008. Lie torture: ibid.

The text asserts that Mao ordered the slaughter of his opponents in large numbers.
But how do we know whether this is supported by evidence? The note entry
'Mao order, 3 Dec. 1930' is not exactly the same wording as in the text. Which
reference shows that Mao ordered his opponents to be slaughtered en masse? Is
it Dai & Luo and Vladimirov? These two references would seem to refer to the
section of the text before 'AB meeting', but the 'slaughter' sentence appears only
after 'AB meeting'. Is it 'Mao to Shanghai, 20 Dec. 1930, *ZDJC vol. 14, p. 636
(E: MRTP vol. 3, pp. 704–5); *Liou Di, letter to Shanghai, 11 Jan. 1931, RGASPI,
cit.; *Provincial Action Committee, Emergency Announcement no. 9, 15 Dec.
1930 RGASPI, 514/1/1008' that supports the 'slaughter' statement? Or do these
references actually apply to the 'AB meeting'? The sentence '"Put them all down",
he ordered, and then "slaughter en masse in all counties and all districts"' does not
make sense. Does it mean that Mao ordered his opponents to be put down and then
slaughtered? One would think that the sentence in quotation marks is a translation
from Chinese or Russian. One would understand the first part of the sentence 'put
them all down' as meaning 'to get rid of them by killing them' which is the same
as the second part of the sentence 'slaughter en masse ...'. Perhaps the authors
mean that Mao gave the order ('put them all down') and someone else then carried
it out. If so, why not say so?

Appearance and instant satisfaction

The authors frequently make dubious claims while dressing them up as serious
scholarship backed up by research. The trick is to cite a reference or even references
to a trivial statement or a piece of insignificant information which is then followed
immediately by a substantial or serious claim, sometimes unreferenced. There is
a source cited for the statement that 'On 29 May he had to return to Red Jiangxi'
(p. 118). But immediately after this Chang and Halliday claim that Mao led 'the
tens of thousands of troops' into 'an isolated cul-de-sac' and 'a large number fell
ill and died' (p. 118), a claim without evidence or any supporting source. However,
because there is a reference to the first sentence it seems as if the substantial claim
is also backed by a reference.

   Readers who are not professionals would probably not take the trouble to check
whether the claims made in the book are based on solid evidence. Such is modern
show business: it is difficult to distinguish what is authentic from what is dubious. The Chinese writer Zhang Xianliang once commented, after his first visit to
Singapore and some other modern cities in the West, that in these developed places
real flowers look fake and plastic flowers look real.

Flawed claims and absurd explanations

In trying to explain why Mao turned out to be a decisive leader of the Jiangxi revolutionary base areas during the late 1920s and early 1930s, Chang tries very hard to sell the message that Mao was not good at military affairs and that it was his personal ruthlessness and Stalin's support that helped him to the top. Why did Stalin support Mao instead of someone else? One reason was that 'Mao's drive assumed urgent importance' to Moscow because Russia wanted to invade Manchuria (p. 75). What was this 'drive' that was so appreciated by Moscow? The book claims that another reason for Stalin's support of Mao was that the first General Secretary of the CCP Chen Duxiu was turning Trotskyist and Stalin was afraid that Mao might side with Chen since Chen was Mao's mentor (p. 75). But there is no evidence to back such a claim.

There are more extraordinary claims: 'The Party had handed him [Mao] the biggest Red Army outside the Soviet bloc after he had broken all the rules. Moscow and Shanghai were palpably bribing him, which meant they needed him'. Why would Moscow and CCP in Shanghai want to bribe him if Mao not only 'broke all rules' but was also such a hopeless good-for-nothing? Why would the party and Moscow need Mao? The whole matter is made so mysterious simply because the authors do not want the reader even to contemplate the possibility that it was Mao's military and organizational skills that made him successful.

In order to slander Mao's character, the authors describe him as selfish and greedy, 'consuming plenty of milk (a rarity for the Chinese), as well as a kilo of beef stewed into soup every day, with a whole chicken on top' (p. 75). Regardless of whether or not there was that much beef available in Jiangxi at that time (there could not have been many cows, and water buffaloes were precious farming animals), was it humanly possible to digest a kilo of beef in addition to a whole chicken every day?

A good example of how the authors treat documentary sources is their comment on a report of the death of Mao's first wife, Yang Kaihui. According to them, the day after Yang was executed the local Hunan *Republican Daily* ran a headline 'Wife of Mao Tse-tung executed yesterday – everyone claps and shouts with satisfaction'. Some credulous Western readers might see this as an example of how the authors worked hard to research Chinese sources, including local newspapers from the 1930s. Chang and Halliday go on to comment: 'This undoubtedly reflected more loathing of Mao than of Kai-hui' (p. 83). They do not even contemplate the possibility that one cannot simply take what the local papers said at the time as hard fact, when communist activists were hunted down as 'bandits' by the then Nationalist government.

Regarding Mao's relationship with Yang Kaihui, the authors allege:

> During his [Mao's] assault on Changsha, Mao made no effort to extricate her and their sons, or even to warn her. And he could easily have saved her: her house was on his route to the city; and Mao was there for three weeks. Yet he did not lift a finger.
>
> (p. 91)

There is no evidence to back up this extraordinary charge. There are numerous other claims of this nature made in the book without supporting evidence. The very first sentence reads: 'Mao Tse-tung, who for decades held absolute power over the lives of one-quarter of the world's population, was responsible for well over 70 million deaths in peacetime, more than any other twentieth-century leader'. Later they assert: 'In late September he [Mao] started his slaughter' (p. 91), and 'Moscow also appointed Mao head of the state …' (p. 104). 'Given that escapes were few, this means that altogether some 700,000 people died in the Ruijin base. More than half of these were murdered as "class enemies", or were worked to death, or committed suicide, or died other premature deaths attributable to the regime' (pp. 113–14). The book is filled with similar accusations based on inadequate evidence. How did Chang and Halliday come up with a figure of 700,000 deaths in Ruijin, for instance? They cite two sources referring to a population drop of 20 per cent in Red Jiangxi (p. 113). Even if these figures were true, they do not prove that all these people actually died – they could have migrated to other areas because of the civil war – or that all of them died as 'class enemies' of the revolution; some might have been killed by the Nationalists.

After claiming that Shao Li-tzu, a prominent KMT official, who took Chiang Kai-shek's son to Moscow to study, was a CCP mole, the authors declare that 'Ultimately, the agents played a gigantic role in helping deliver China to Mao …' (p. 139). As if China could just be delivered to Mao with the help of a few KMT agents.

Further flaws

It is true that the *Unknown Story* is not without its critics. James Heartfield (2005) has researched their distortions. Kakutani also points out the lack of reference in the book to Mao's 'mature writings that might shed light on his politics or values', and the absence of historical context, calling the work 'tendentious and one-dimensional'. Even Steve Tsang of Oxford University, a historian who has no love for Mao and the CCP, says the authors used sources dishonestly. Tsang agrees that 'Mao was a monster', but regrets that 'their distortion of history to make their case will in the end make it more difficult to reveal how horrible Mao and the Chinese Communist Party system were, and how much damage they really did to the Chinese people' (quoted in Heartfield 2005).

In approaching the subject of Mao, it is perfectly legitimate to have a point of view. 'You don't feel cold analysis in this book, you feel hatred, which helps make it a wonderful read. But history should not work this way', says Francesco Sisci of Italy's *La Stampa* (McDonald 2005). Teiwes says: 'When someone [Mao] is responsible, and I believe he was, for upwards of 30 million deaths, it's hard to defend him. … But on the other hand to paint him as a totally monstrous personality who just goes out to kill people and protect his power at all cost is not only over the top but a bit crazy in terms of what actually went on'. In order to do that, '[Chang] just had her views so set, and was unwilling to entertain other opinions or inconvenient evidence' (McDonald 2005).

Jung Chang claims to have interviewed the last surviving eyewitness at Luding Bridge, who was said to have confirmed that there was no battle at the bridge during the Long March. When McDonald went to Luding he did not find a trace of Jung Chang's witness. Instead, he found another eyewitness who confirmed that a battle had indeed taken place (McDonald 2005). Davin (in this volume) points out a number of historical errors and speculative assumptions. One concerns the death of Wang Shiwei. *The Unknown Story* asserts that Wang's execution was used by Mao to terrify the young intellectuals at Yan'an during the 'rectification' campaign of 1942. However, Wang's execution did not take place until 1947 (Williems 2005). It happened without Mao's knowledge and Mao was reportedly furious about it.

'There are numerous such accusations in the book. Unfortunately it is not always so evident to expose them as mere fantasy' (Williems 2005). 'Let me make it clear that I fully share the authors' view that Mao was a monster, as were Hitler and Stalin', McLynn (2005) declares, but the book has 'too much hate too little understanding'. Even Nathan, whose published political stand is perhaps close to Chang's, says 'that many of Chang and Halliday's claims are based on distorted, misleading or far-fetched use of evidence' (Nathan, in this volume).

Another good example of how Chang and Halliday distort and misquote is provided by Ball (2007). When discussing the Great Leap Forward, Chang and Halliday say that Mao did not care that people were dying from starvation. Chang and Halliday quote Mao as saying that 'working like this, with all these projects, half of China may well have to die', to support their charge that he 'was ready to dispense with' half of China's population for the sake of Mao's industrialization plan. But as Ball points out, the quote is taken out of the context. Mao actually meant the exact opposite: to warn his audience of the dangers of overwork and over-enthusiasm in the Great Leap Forward.

Questioned about the sensational claim that Chiang Kai-shek intentionally let the Red Army escape on the historic Long March of 1934–35, the authors point to 26 sources for their claim about the Long March. Nathan was compelled to ask: 'Of these 26 items, which one, two or three unequivocally support the improbable claim that Chiang let the Reds escape intentionally?' (Fenby 2005) The answer is: none.

Mao, China's Hitler and Stalin

Many Western commentators tend to agree with Chang and Halliday that Mao was like Hitler and Stalin. However, it was public knowledge that Mao, unlike Stalin and Hitler, did not execute his political rivals. Before Mao came to power in the CCP he was sidelined and demoted by Bo Gu, Zhang Wentian and Zhou Enlai. Bo Gu and Zhang Wentian suffered in their careers and Zhang even underwent humiliation later in life, but they were not executed. Zhou Enlai served as Premier of the PRC until the last day of his life. When Zhang Guotao, another of Mao's rivals, defected to the Nationalists, Mao agreed to let his wife and children join him. During the Sixth Congress of the CCP, Mao worked hard to keep Wang Ming, another of his political opponents, as a member of the CCP's Central Committee.

Wang later migrated to the Soviet Union and died there. Peng Dehuai was demoted in 1959 and sidelined and humiliated and even brutally beaten up by some Red Guards during the Cultural Revolution. But Peng died of bowel cancer in 1974. Liu Shaoqi was persecuted and humiliated, but he died a natural death (though he could have lived longer had he not been persecuted).

Chang and Halliday have to admit that Mao disapproved a report that recommended the execution of Liu Shaoqi's wife. This militates against their thesis that Mao was a Stalin-type of murderer of his opponents. There is much more evidence to show that Mao was not like Stalin or Hitler. When Mao was told of Lin Biao's fleeing in a plane, he apparently ordered that it not be shot down. The story of Deng Xiaoping is well-known: though humiliated and criticized, Deng was never physically harmed. During the most turbulent days of the Cultural Revolution in the second half of 1966, when everyone in the CCP hierarchy was under attack except Mao and Lin Biao, Mao was determined to protect Zhu De and Chen Yi (Wang Li 2001, p. 714), two people who were very critical of him in the 1930s and, together with Zhou Enlai, responsible for stripping him of his leadership of the Red Army.

Fairy tale and how scholarship changes

As Heartfield (2005) points out, it was Chang, in *Wild Swans*, the best-selling family memoir, who told us that Chiang Kai-shek had adopted a policy of non-resistance in the face of the Japanese seizure of Manchuria and Japan's increasing encroachments on China. Chang also said that it was Chiang who, instead of mobilizing forces to fight the Japanese invasion, had concentrated on trying to annihilate the communists. But, in many instances, the *Unknown Story* flatly contradicts *Wild Swans*. In the *Unknown Story*, Mao is said to have engineered Chiang's abduction by his own general Zhang Xueliang in 1936. But, according to *Wild Swans*, Chiang was 'partly saved by the Communists'. If the *Unknown Story* is intended to correct the wrong claims made in *Wild Swans* for the sake of its 10 million readers, then Chang should have indicated these corrections either in the text or in footnotes, says Heartfield.

Chang's co-author Halliday says that being married to Chang is like a fairy tale (Thorpe 2005). In earlier days Halliday condemned the Japanese invasion of Manchuria and China (Halliday 1973). Now, however, he agrees with his fairy-tale wife that the Japanese war in China was more or less the result of a Mao/Stalin conspiracy. How does Halliday compare Chang's and his interpretation of the Korean War now with that in his earlier book *Korea: The Unknown War* (note the familiar title), or his understanding of the Cultural Revolution now with his previous interpretation of the riots in 1967 in Hong Kong – that they were 'anti-colonial' and against an administration where there was 'no democracy' (Halliday 1973)? In those days he wrote about British colonial oppression in China and Hong Kong; now he blames the bloody repression in Hong Kong in 1967 on provocation by Mao. The Korean War (1950–53) is largely blamed on Mao, whereas he previously stressed Truman's role as warmonger (Williems 2005). How times change.

Does it matter?

What is surprising is how few people take the trouble to question the book's methodological flaws. Those who do raise concerns about its scholarship still do not challenge its basic message, even though it is obvious to them – as it is to Phillip Short, whose own biography of Mao was published in 1999 – that the scholarship is flawed. Short says that Chang and Halliday have reduced Mao from a complex historical character to a one-dimensional 'cardboard cut-out of Satan'. And yet almost no reviewers seem to think that this is a problem.

The Unknown Story remains the apple of many an eye, even though the stains on the apple's surface would seem to suggest emptiness within, or even worms. Take the case of Nicholas Kristof. Kristof tells us that 'One of those listed [by Chang and Halliday] as a source is Zhang Hanzhi, Mao's English teacher and close associate; she's also one of my oldest Chinese friends, so I checked with her. Zhang Hanzhi said that she had indeed met informally with Chang two or three times but had declined to be interviewed and never said anything substantial'. Kristof complains that in the book, 'Mao comes across as such a villain that he never really becomes three-dimensional', and that he is 'presented as such a bumbling psychopath that it's hard to comprehend how he bested all his rivals to lead China and emerge as one of the most worshipped figures in history'. Yet Kristof still calls it 'a magisterial work' (Kristof 2005). Perry Link of Princeton, an editor of *The Tiananmen Papers*, feels obliged to say something about the book's methodology but still retains a largely positive view of it (Link 2005).

The media are the book's biggest admirers. Should the academic community take the media seriously? The academic community in general seems critical of the book, whereas the media seem to be generally positive. It is probably naïve even to ask whether the media should be taken seriously. After all, they set the agenda and decide what the majority of the public think about. It will take years, if it ever happens, to deconstruct the Chang and Halliday 'truth' promoted by the media. I agree with Thomas Bernstein (2005), who calls the book 'a major disaster for the contemporary China field. ... [But] [b]ecause of its stupendous research apparatus, its claims will be accepted widely'.

It does not matter as long as the politics are right

To demonize Mao is politically correct, of course. When someone pasted a criticism of the Chang and Halliday book on the Amazon sales website, it was immediately attacked as 'ugly Chinese propaganda' (Jin, in this volume). On the other hand, Jin's critique of the book met with absolute silence by the Western media (no Western media outlet was ready to publish the seventeen questions he raised). When the Chinese version of Jin's critique appeared on the Chinese language website Duowei (blog.chinesenewsnet.com), a lively debate ensued. Jung Chang had to admit, when pressed, that Jin's seventeen questions were good but refused to participate in providing convincing replies to them. For the Western media it does not matter as long as the politics is right, and the right politics is that Mao must be discredited.

Hitler: a favourite European comparison

Instead of discussing Mao, a political figure of such consequence, in his political, social and economic context, Chang and Halliday focus on slaughtering his personality. Naturally, it is legitimate to write a biography that focuses on personality, private life and private thoughts. Such a biography may bring insights and understanding that cannot be found in biographies of a non-personal nature. However, this cannot be combined with an agenda single-mindedly designed to attack the subject's personality. One needs to explore the personality's inner tension and conflicts, his or her complexities, paradoxes, ironies and tragedies – in other words, the unintended consequences of human life, individual or collective.

An exploration of the complexities of character is essential to any good biography. In the case of Mao, his personality has to be examined in the context of Chinese history, tradition and culture. Any non-contextual comparison of Mao with a European figure is either intellectually infantile or politically motivated, or both. In the *Unknown Story* and its media reception, we are constantly urged to compare Mao with Hitler.[1] However, in my understanding, Hitler and Mao belonged to completely different worlds. Mao became a leader in the long process of a popular revolution that transformed the political, social and economic landscape of a large country whereas Hitler was the leader of a regime that invaded other countries out of a desire to conquer. Hitler's regime designed scientific means and methods to physically wipe out other ethnic groups. Hitler and Mao worked for very different causes and were utterly different personalities.

Any Chinese who reads what Hitler said, sees how he made his speeches, and knows what he did would almost certainly conclude that he was clinically insane. A personality like Hitler's could never achieve prominence in China. He would be a laughing stock and treated with contempt. Mao, on the other hand, was and still is considered by many in China (here 'many' really means many) to be a philosopher, a thinker, a military strategist, and a revolutionary statesman. The idea that Hitler had charisma never ceases to baffle me. In fact there is no proper Chinese word for 'charisma', even though Weberian charismatic leadership features prominently in Western political theory (Wang 1995). This shows how misleading it is to use Western theoretical concepts to explain Chinese phenomena.

Chang and others would say that the Chinese people are still suffering thought control, are still brainwashed and therefore incapable of seeing what she sees, as she keeps on telling journalists. Despite a lot of anti-communist Cold War rhetoric, I have yet to see any well-researched evidence to support the judgement that so many Chinese refuse to hate Mao simply because they have been brainwashed. The fact that this elitist attitude towards the masses of Chinese is conceptually antithetical to the idea of democracy and human rights is hardly ever noticed.

Personality of Mao: the known story

In the simple, black and white caricature in *Unknown Story*, Mao is portrayed as a callous monster without feelings even for his own family. However, the literature tells a different story that Chang and Halliday ignore, even though they supposedly interviewed so many people and consulted so many documents. In his memoirs Mao's bodyguard Li Yinqiao described how during the famine year of 1960 Mao's daughter Li Na came home from boarding school to have dinner after three weeks' absence. The cook and her mother Jiang Qing arranged for a special dinner for the whole family. When the meal started, Li Na was so hungry and ate so fast that both Mao and Jiang Qing stopped eating. Eventually, Li Na finished everything on the dinner table. Both the cook and Jiang Qing sobbed and Mao was so moved that he stood up and walked first into his bedroom and then back out to the court-yard, totally lost for words.

Chang and Halliday, like many in the West, would argue that we cannot trust accounts like this since they are officially published in China. One should not forget that though the Chinese authorities do not allow personal attacks on past CCP lead-ers, most of what we know about China (including negative information about Mao) can be found in official Chinese publications. In any case, what motivation would Li Yinqiao have for lying about daily details such as these? What benefit would he get from it? We know that Liu Shaoqi is officially rehabilitated as a victim of Mao's wrongdoing. It is therefore politically correct and rewarding to say good things about Liu. However, any observant researcher could not fail to notice that hardly any personal memoirs by Liu's former bodyguards or those who served him or worked with him had much to say about Liu that is personally warm.

The logic of denial of the known story

The Chinese version of *The Unknown Story* was contracted to be published by Yuanliu, but this Taiwanese publisher abandoned the project after it became clear that the book could not be factually verified, at least for some of its claims. Especially controversial for the Taiwanese publisher is the claim that Hu Zongnan, one of the KMT's most prominent generals, was a CCP agent. Descendants of Hu demanded that the publishers delete such a claim or they would face a law suit. For Chang and Halliday, it is important that such claims be retained. The book sets out to prove that two known stories are untrue: that the CCP triumphed over the KMT because Mao was an excellent military strategist (as opposed to a monstrous murderer and a useless military leader); and that the KMT was defeated because it was led by a corrupt dynasty of four powerful families (Seagrave 1986) and had no socio-economic programme to win over the peasants. How can you explain the success of the CCP when a peasant army defeated the modern KMT army, sup-ported by the most advanced and powerful force in the world, the USA? Chang and Halliday have little choice other than to say that China was delivered into Mao's hands by agents such as Hu Zongnan.

The Chinese version of the *Unknown Story* appeared eventually, thanks to the *Kaifang* magazine in Hong Kong, an anti-communist popular publication that con-stantly spreads rumours about mainland China.

Truth or fabrications

In the Preface to the Chinese version Chang Jung (2006c) claims that she and her husband spent twelve years on the book 'dragging for truth and digging for gold'. One example will show what kind of truth Chang was dragging for. To inform the uninformed about the evils of the Chinese communist regime, Chang (2006a) claims that when she was sent by the Chinese government to study in the UK she had to be accompanied by another student whenever she went out or else she would be sent back to China. She also claims that she was probably the first student from mainland China to enter a public bar and the first to go out alone.

It is a known fact that the Chinese government sent people to study in the UK as early as 1974. I myself went to the UK as a student before Chang, in 1977, along with seventeen others. The Chinese embassy did tell us that we should only go out in groups of two or more for reasons of safety. However, we were never told that if we ventured out alone we would be sent back to China. In the beginning we went in groups to classes and to parties or out shopping. But after a while, once we had got used to our new environment, we would go out alone whenever we wanted. We visited bars and even went alone to the red-light district in Soho. I even dated a local girl. Two of us took a tour trip to the US. Were any of us sent back to China? Of course not.

This is typical of Chang's version of the truth, convincing but unfounded. Chang says, 'As long as China exists people will want to read our book, because this is the real history about modern China. I know I should be making understatements and being self-deprecating, but I think this book will shake the world and will help shape China' (Allardice 2005). For Chang, the truth is that Mao was a psychopath and had a superpower programme to rule the world. She wants the world to know that. Incredibly, many readers believe her.

Why was plastic so appreciated?

One might assume that by the commonly accepted standards of scholarship, the *Unknown Story* should be tossed into the rubbish bin as worthless. We all know that if the methods are unsound the conclusions must be treated with suspicion. It is true that even in natural science researchers start with presumptions and assumptions. We all seek evidence to prove our conceptualizations or explanatory models. However, we also know that if a scientist or a scholar or a writer distorts evidence knowingly the work should be condemned. Nathan may try to appear to be balanced when he titles his review 'Jade and Plastic', but it is an unfortunate fact that plastic and jade do not mix well.

The academic community did make a serious effort to review the book in *The China Journal*. Benton and Tsang criticized Chang and Halliday's 'flawed assertions', for the fact that they 'misread sources' and 'use them selectively' and 'out of context' (Benton and Tsang, in this volume). They repudiate ten major claims made in the book. Timothy Cheek (in this volume) thinks the book is 'a great waste of effort', and its 'TV soap opera – *Dallas*' (Mao a "JR")' offers 'very little that is new'. As Barmé points out, Chang and Halliday's telling of history has a 'callousness' and 'evokes the image of Oriental obliquity' (Barmé, in this volume). Chan, in his *coup d'œil* review (in this volume), shows unequivocally that Chang and Halliday's '[n]ew information is manufactured out of a manipulation of facts to such an extreme that they can no longer be sustained by empirical evidence', that the co-authors 'prioritize entertainment, sensationalism and titillation over historical accuracy'.

In a rare response to the scholarly criticism, Chang claimed, not without reason, that 90 per cent of the reviews are positive and that the reason why some academics are critical is that they have to be critical in order to save face, or they would have to admit that they got it all wrong (Chang 2006b). Right or wrong, by the end of 2006, the *Unknown Story* has already been translated into twelve languages, with thirteen more translations in progress. It is on the best-seller list in every language that it has appeared in so far (Chang 2006b).

Even the supposedly left wing or progressive British *Guardian* took the book very seriously. 'Together, [Chang and Halliday] make a formidable literary partnership, a yin and yang of exotic glamour and scholarly erudition', declared Lisa Allardice (2005), in a review published in its pages. A Western yang with a Chinese yin is really exotic. But scholarly erudition? You must be joking.

Chang starts her biography with an attitude of hatred and the desire to diminish Mao in the scale of history. This can be achieved and perhaps Chang has already done so. People, educated or otherwise (we would hope the latter), seem to like ready-made and easily consumable commodities. Here is one.

Revolution: from farewell to burial

The 'forward' looking neo-Enlightenment Chinese intelligentsia bid their farewell to revolution only a few years after its foremost leader Mao died in 1976. By the early 1990s the intellectual climate internationally was such that a farewell was seen as insufficiently rigorous from an intellectual point of view. Revolutionary ideas and practices not only have to be dead but nailed into the coffin. The Berlin Wall fell, the Soviet Union collapsed, and the Soviet Communist Party was dismantled under Yeltsin. Even the symbols of revolution were dismantled.

Time magazine confidently declares that if the Chinese ever get to read Chang's 'atom bomb of a book', it will cure them of Mao admiration. 'Chang and Halliday have plunged a dagger deep into the heart of the Mao legend, so deep it is hard to imagine anything like a full recovery', declared another reviewer (French 2005). This explains why an intellectual scandal is not treated as such. Yes, Mao has to be brought down. To have the portrait of Mao on the Tiananmen rostrum is offensive to the Cold War warriors, however recently converted. Only a complete uprooting of the CCP can guarantee the End of History. That is why in spite of some acknowledgements that Jung Chang's work is deeply flawed, almost all mainstream reviewers feel compelled to kowtow to the theory that Mao was indeed a mass murderer (Williems 2005).

In the global climate of liberal democracy and neoconservative market capitalism, the fall of the Berlin Wall was not enough. The Chinese still stubbornly remained 'communist' by refusing to dig Mao's grave. Only when the Great Wall of China is brought down can the revolution be finally and permanently buried.

References

Allardice, Lisa (2005) 'This book will shake the world', *Guardian*, 26 May.

Ball, Joseph 'Did Mao Really Kill in the Great Leap Forward', www.monthlyreview.org/0906ball.htm, accessed on 23 May 2007.

Bernstein, Thomas, 'Throwing the Book at Mao', www.theage.com.au, accessed on 10 June 2005.

Chang Jung (2006a) Duowei boke, blog.chinesenewsnet.com/?p=16278, accessed on 3 October.

—— (2006b) Duowei boke, blog.chinesenewsnet.com/?p=13117, accessed on 25 November.

—— (2006c) www.peacehall.com/cgibin/news/gb_display/print_version.cgi?art=/gb/lianzai/2006/11&link=200611220010.shtml, accessed on 15 December.

Fenby, Jonathan, 'Storm Rages over Bestselling Book on Monster Mao: China Experts Attack Biography's "Misleading' Sources"', *The Observer*, http://www.observer.co.uk, accessed on 15 October 2005.

French, Howard W. (2005) 'Putting a Knife into the Heart of the Chairman's Legend', *San Francisco Chronicle*, 23 October.

Gellman, Marc, and Hartman, Tom (2002) *The Reader's Digest*, April, p. 98.

Gong Chu (1978) *Gong Chu jiangjun huiyilu* (General Gong Chu's memoirs), Hong Kong: Mingbao yuekan she.

Halliday, Jon and McCormack, Gavan (1973), *Japanese Imperialism Today*, London: Association for Radical East Asian Studies.

Heartfield, James, 'Mao: The End of the Affair'. http://www.spiked-online.com/Articles/0000000 CAC41.htm, accessed on 4 July 2005.

Hensher, Philip, www.seattlepi.com, accessed on 6 August 2005.

Hutton, Will (2005) 'Complex Legacy of Chairman Mao', *The Observer*, 29 May.

Kakutani, Michiko (2005) 'China's Monster, Second to None', *The New York Times*, 21 October.

Kristof, Nicholas D. (2005) 'Mao, the Real Mao', *The New York Times Book Review*, 23 October.

Link, Perry (2005) 'Mad, Bad Mao', *Times Literary Supplement*, 20 July.

McDonald, Hamish, 'Throwing the Book at Mao', www.theage.com.au, accessed on 10 June 2005.

McLynn, Frank (2005) 'Too Much Haste, Too Little Understanding', *The Independent*, 6 June.

Montefiore, Simon Sebag (2005) *The Sunday Times*, *Books*, 29 May.

Rothwell, Nicholas (2005) 'Books of the Year', *The Australian*, 3–4 December.

Seagrave, Sterling (1986) *The Soong Dynasty*, New York: Harper Perennial.

Thorpe, Vanessa (2005) 'From Swan to Hawk', *The Observer*, 1 May.

Wang Li (2001) *Wang Li fansi lu* (Wang Li's reflections), vol. 2, Hong Kong: Beixing chuban she.

Wang Shaoguang (1995) *Failure of Charisma: The Cultural Revolution in Wuhan*, Hong Kong: Oxford University Press.

Weil, Robert (2006) '"To Be Attacked by the Enemy Is a Good Thing": The Struggle over the Legacy of Mao Zedong and the Chinese Socialist Revolution', *Socialism and Democracy* (New York), vol. 20, no. 2, July.

Williems, Frank (2005) 'Mao, the Untold Story', SF.Indymedia.org, http://sf.indymedia.org/news///.phpandfrank.

Yahuda, Michael (2005) 'Bad Element', *The Guardian*, 4 June.

12 A critique of Jung Chang and Jon Halliday, *Mao: The Unknown Story*

Jin Xiaoding

Introduction

China's economic growth is one of the most significant developments of recent times. It is at least partly the consequence of China's social and political evolution and revolution in the past century. If the West wants to understand modern China, it is essential not to misunderstand its founder, Mao. However, *Mao: The Unknown Story* prevents the Western public from achieving a proper understanding of Mao, China's modern history or China itself.

The book's central theme is that Mao was an evil monster, 'as bad as or worse than Hitler'. The Western media immediately accepted this claim. When the book was first published in the UK in June 2005, it was hailed by all major media with great enthusiasm, including by many well-known China experts from the political sphere (e.g. Chris Patten, the last British governor of Hong Kong), journalists (e.g. Jonathan Mirsky, *The Time*'s East Asia editor) and academics (e.g. Mike Yahuda, the ex-chair of the Department of International Relation at the London School of Economics). According to these experts, any reasonable person should be completely convinced by the book. On this issue there is a rare harmony, in which the voice of *The Guardian* is indistinguishable from that of *The Daily Mail*. Within a week, the book jumped to the top of the non-fiction best-seller list. Jung Chang has become an authority on Chinese history. Anyone asking challenging questions at her seminars was deemed to be 'an obvious Maoist' and was sometimes unable to finish his or her question. Some Western readers condemned a less than complimentary comment on the book on the Amazon web site as 'ugly Chinese propaganda'.

Chang's supporters have such unlimited confidence partly because the book is supposedly the outcome of ten years' intensive research in the archives and hundreds of interviews in many countries. Unfortunately, a careful reader will see that there are big problems with these sensational claims. Moreover, the book's evidence often contradicts rather than supports these claims. This review will point out these contradictions and inconsistencies, which may have escaped most readers' notice and have failed to figure in Western media accounts.

To assess the overall quality of the book, we examine its seventeen major claims, which are evenly distributed across Mao's life. Instead of picking on minor weaknesses, we focus on the following issues, which tarnish Mao's character most and whose treatment in the book is highly regarded in the Western media:

1   The purge in the Ruijin base.
2   Chiang let the Reds go (I).
3   Chiang let the Reds go (II).
4   The 'fake' battle at the Luding Bridge.
5   Mao was carried throughout the Long March.
6   Mao did not fight the Japanese.
7   The New Fourth Army (N4A) trap.
8   Mao sacrificed his brother Tse-min.
9   The Rectification Campaign.
10   Selling opium.
11   Three million deaths in 1950–51.
12   Twenty-seven million deaths in prisons/labour camps.
13   The Superpower Programme.
14   Thirty-eight million deaths in 1958–61.
15   Three million deaths in 1966–76.
16   Mao's aim in the Cultural Revolution.
17   Mao compared with Hitler.

This review has been sent to many Western media outlets since early August 2005, but received no response. However, it is not the only negative review of Jung Chang's book. Four months after its first publication, critical voices began to emerge from outside Europe. In an article in *The New York Review*, Jonathan Spence of Yale University singled out two false stories in the book (in this volume). In *The New York Times*, a former correspondent in Beijing, Nicholas Kristof, reveals that one of the interviewees listed in the book, Zhang Hanzhi, denied she had been interviewed by the authors. Hamish McDonald reveals in *The Age* that a recent visit by reporters to Luding Bridge confirmed the battle 70 years ago, which Jung Chang claims to be a complete invention. He quotes Thomas Bernstein of Columbia University that 'the book is a major disaster for the contemporary China field'. Princeton's Perry Link felt compelled to criticize Jung Chang's 'factual errors and dubious use of sources'. Moreover, 'many scholars point out that much of what Chang and Halliday present as a previously "unknown story" was in fact exposed long ago. ... But no credit is given to these earlier writers'. In *The London Review of Books*, Andrew Nathan of Columbia University provides plenty of evidence to show that 'Chang and Halliday are magpies: every bright piece of evidence goes in, no matter where it comes from or how reliable it is' (in this volume).

This review differs from those of Western academics in two respects. First, it shows that the book is a total fallacy, rather than containing just a few inaccuracies. Second, it demonstrates the book's major flaws simply by using information and references mainly from the book itself. In so doing, the review raises a further question: why did most media and experts in the UK fail to see these obvious inconsistencies and contradictions in the book?

Although this review met with absolute silence in the West, it has attracted some attention from overseas Chinese. One of the websites that published the review, Duowei, interviewed Jung Chang in New York in October 2005 and put my questions to her.[1] This is what Jung Chang said about this review: 'I have read it, and read carefully. Some questions are quite good. I do hope to have opportunities to answer them. I think it is very important. However, there are many issues, I do not know whether he did not understand English, or did not look at the references provided at the back of the book. There are many details, the origins of the figures, all in the back of the book. Among 800 pages, there are 150 pages of references, the sources of the references. One has to read those sources from the references. I think he either did not understand English, or did not read references carefully. I have looked at his questions, and can give easy answers to all of them'.

In the interview, Jung Chang did respond to three of my seventeen questions, namely, (2), (3) and (4). Readers can check the paragraphs below marked with asterisks, to appreciate her 'easy answers'.

After the appearance of this review, Jung Chang's brother, Pu Zhang (a translator of the Chinese version of the book), claimed in October 2005 on the Duowei website that my Chinese translation seriously distorted Jung Chang's words, and said he would post a direct comparison of the original text and my translation on the web so readers could see the difference. However, despite readers repeatedly asking him to keep his promise, his comparison has not yet been seen anywhere.

1 The purge in the Ruijin base

Jung Chang's first major accusation against Mao is that his purge of the Ruijin base, the first Red state in China, caused more than 350,000 deaths, or 10 per cent of the total population. Her figure is grossly exaggerated because she assumes the reduction of 0.7 million in Ruijin's population was the result of people either being killed in battle or dying of persecution under Mao. She ignores civilian deaths and emigration.

From 1931–35, 'the population of Red Jiangxi fell by more than half a million. ... The fall in Red Fujian was comparable. ... Altogether some 700,000 people died in the Ruijin base' (p. 113). Jung Chang apparently deduces this figure from the population ratio of Red Jiangxi to that of Red Fujian. But from her 'half a million' population reduction in Jiangxi we should get a reduction in Ruijin's population of 700,000, not 700,000 deaths.

Since '238,844 people in Jiangxi were counted as "revolutionary martyrs", i.e., people who had been killed in wars and intra-party purges' (p. 114 fn.), Jung Chang again uses the population ratio to get the total number of martyrs in the whole of Ruijin, i.e. 238,884 × 700,000/500,000 = 334,438. The rest of the reduction in population, 700,000 – 334,438, is = 365,562. 'More than half', she concludes, 'were murdered as "class enemies", or were worked to death, or committed suicide, or died other premature deaths attributable to the regime' (pp. 113–14).

This calculation ignores civilian deaths caused by the war, through killing, illness, economic hardship, starvation, etc., which often account for a larger part of the loss of life in long wars. During that period Chiang Kai-shek launched five 'annihilation expeditions' against Ruijin, one of which involved 'half a million troops' (p. 125). At one time the Ruijin base 'had been reduced to a mere several dozen square kilometres' (p. 103) from '50,000 sq. km' (p. 104). Chiang's army had occupied most of the area of the base.

Many people cooperated with the communists, even 'children were used as sentries, and formed into harassment squads, called "humiliation teams" to hound people into joining the army' (p. 110). Chiang's army was not known for treating civilians with mercy. Even before the Red state came into existence, 'tens of thousands of Communists and suspects were slaughtered' during Chiang's campaign in 1927 (p. 47). Given all these factors, civilian deaths must have been significant.

Secondly, Jung Chang's calculation ignores emigration out of the Ruijin area, which would have been natural after five annihilation expeditions in five years. We are told that Mao's policy in the Red base 'was to confiscate every last single thing' (p. 111), and 'China's first Red state was run by terror and guarded like a prison' (p. 113). In that case, people would have escaped Mao's hell on the five occasions Chiang's army liberated them. So the number of refugees must have been significant.

If we assume that the sum of civilian deaths and refugees together is roughly the same as the number of martyrs, far fewer would have been 'murdered as 'class enemies', or were worked to death, or committed suicide, or died other premature deaths attributable to the regime. The number would be 700,000 – 334,438 × 2 = 31,124, less than 10 per cent of Jung Chang's figure.

2   Chiang let the Reds go (I)

Jung Chang's second major innovation is to deny Mao's contribution to the Red Army's survival during the Long March. She argues that Chiang Kai-shek let the Red Army go because he wanted an excuse to send his own army into Guizhou and Sichuan. She gives no evidence for this. Even by her own reasoning, Chiang did not need to use Mao's army as an excuse, since a strong Red Army had already been active in Sichuan for nearly three years before Mao's arrival.

'There can be no doubt that Chiang let the CCP leadership and the main force of the Red Army escape'. 'He wanted to drive the Red Army into these hold-out provinces, so that their warlords would be so frightened of the Reds settling in their territory that they would allow Chiang's army in to drive the Reds out' (p. 137).

Jung Chang's reference does support the well-known fact that Chiang considered his entry into Sichuan as a beneficial by-product of his pursuit of the Red Army. But it does not follow that Chiang let the Red Army escape. On the contrary, in the autumn of 1932, another CCP leader, Chang Kuo-tao, had 'moved to northern

Sichuan, where he built a new and bigger base within a year, and expanded his army to over 80,000. Chang Kuo-tao was undoubtedly the most successful of all the Communists' (pp. 147–8). At the time of Mao's arrival in Sichuan, Chang's 80,000 soldiers 'were well fed, well equipped with machine-guns and mortars and ample ammunition, and superbly trained' (p. 163). On the other hand, Mao's army 'was down to some 10,000. ... The surviving remnant was on the verge of collapse' (p. 163).

It seems odd that Chang Kuo-tao's 'most successful' army of 80,000, after having been in Sichuan for three years, still could not frighten the Sichuan warlords, so that Chiang had to use Mao's army which 'was on the verge of collapse'. Why? Without any further explanation, one must certainly 'doubt that Chiang let the CCP leadership and the main force of the Red Army escape'.

* Dealing with this question in her interview with Duowei, Jung Chang replied: 'This is a good question. But we have studied it already. When Chang Kuo-tao entered Sichuan, he was in the north; Chiang Kai-shek indeed wanted to follow. But Sichuan had a regional defence system then, each region had its own warlord, not together, all divided. Chiang Kai-shek drove the Central Red Army from the south into Sichuan. He wanted to conquer the south, the west, the north, also to conquer the warlord in the east'.

So why did Chiang Kai-shek not drive Chang Kuo-tao from the north to the west, east and south, and instead allegedly drove the Central Red Army far away from Jiangxi? Jung Chang's answer leads once again to almost the same question. It explains nothing. These 'easy answers' are perhaps too easy.

3 Chiang let the Reds go (II)

To deny Mao's contribution to the Long March, Jung Chang offers another theory about why Chiang let the Red Army go: he did it to get his son back from Russia. Jung Chang's evidence shows that Chiang wanted his son back, but does not show that he let the Reds go. On the contrary, she shows that for his same beloved son, Chiang was not even willing to release two unknown spies.

According to Jung Chang, for Chiang Kai-shek's decision to let the Reds go 'there was another, more secret and totally private reason. Chiang's son Ching-kuo had been a hostage in Russia' (p. 138). 'Chiang had devised a carefully crafted swap: the survival of the CCP for Ching-kuo. It was not an offer that could be spelt out. He executed his plan in subtle ways' (p. 140).

It was so subtle that no record was left for Jung Chang to prove that Chiang did this, or even intended to do it. The only evidence is that Chiang was worried about his son and asked Moscow to let him go. No swap was mentioned anywhere, not even in Chiang's diary. But another swap was certainly spelt out. According to Jung Chang, Chiang's 'sister-in-law, Mme Sun Yat-sen (née Soong Ching-ling), who was another Soviet agent', 'speaking for Moscow', spelt out a proposal for 'swapping Ching-kuo for two top Russian agents who had recently been arrested in Shanghai. Chiang turned the swap down' (pp. 139–40).

Since Chiang was unwilling to let two Russian agents go in exchange for his son's release, it is unlikely that he would have let the Red Army of tens of thousands of armed men escape. If he did, one might wonder what kind of agents could be so important. Actually, the 'two top Russian agents' are the Chinese couple Niu Lan and his wife. Jung Chang does not even mention their names, though a dozen other named Russian agents feature in her book. Why? Maybe Jung Chang has some 'more secret and totally private reason'.

* In her interview with Duowei, Jung Chang said: Chiang Kai-shek 'wanted to trade the Reds' survival for his son's return. How did we get the references? There are many, many references. The first comes from the Russian Archive, how Chiang Kai-shek negotiated with the Russians. There are also many records in Chiang Kai-shek's diary. Chiang Ching-kuo had an own account of the event; it contains such information as well. Moreover, as for how Chiang Kai-shek let the Red Army go, there are many historical materials regarding the Long March, the telegraphs between the Kuomintang armies. We have given detailed explanations for all of them in the book'.

Naturally, I have read all these detailed explanations. Precisely for that reason, I wrote: 'Jung Chang's evidence only shows that Chiang wanted his son back, not that he let the Reds go'. Jung Chang simply repeats what she wrote in the book, but still fails to provide any evidence for how Chiang let the Reds go. Why didn't she simply quote a sentence from her 'many, many references' that indicate that Chiang let or wanted to let the Reds go? Wouldn't this be easier than to list many, many circumstantial references?

4 The 'fake' battle at the Luding Bridge

Jung Chang's claim that the battle at the Luding Bridge did not happen has been widely publicized in the West as a fatal blow to the Red Army legend. In the official account, the CCP and Red Army were close to destruction when they reached the Dadu River. If they had failed to secure the Luding Bridge, they would have been eliminated. The Luding Bridge battle is famous for its historic significance, not its scale.

Instead of disproving existing accounts, Jung Chang bases her claim mainly on an interview with a 93-year-old woman. But even according to that account, the Red Army did fire heavy weapons at the bridge. Jung Chang does not explain why. Given the Reds' limited ammunition, it is unlikely they would have wasted it with no enemy in sight.

According to Jung Chang, the battle at the Luding Bridge 'is complete invention. There was no battle at the Dadu Bridge'. 'There were no Nationalist troops at the bridge when the Reds arrived' (p. 159). A 93-year-old woman lived there at the time. 'She remembered the Communists firing as "only Yin a shell, and Yang a shot" – a Chinese expression for sporadic. She did not remember her side of the river being fired on at all' (p. 159).

Jung Chang does not clarify whether her definition of 'Nationalist troops' includes the troops of Sichuan warlords that did not belong to the Nationalist regular army. Her source suggests it does not. If so, her proof is flawed, because according to the official story, it was exactly the warlord's army that defended the bridge.

On the other hand, Jung Chang acknowledges that the Red Army 'shelled and fired across the river at Luding on the opposite side' (p. 159), and 'there was a fire in the town itself, caused, most likely, by Red Army shelling' (p. 160). The Red Army could not have used their gunfire simply as fireworks because their ammunition was very scarce. Just a month later, without any serious battle, it had 'lost all its heavy weapons, leaving it only with rifles, with an average of five bullets each' (p. 163). Its heavy weapons would have been used only if absolutely necessary. Jung Chang does not explain why the Reds shelled Luding.

It is unlikely that the shelling was due to a reconnaissance failure. As 'the bridge was not reduced to bare chains' (p. 160), sending a man over could have been done in a few minutes, probably more quickly than setting up a firing position.

The only possible explanation left for the shelling is that it was to fake a battle for propaganda purposes, as suggested by Jung Chang. In this case, the Reds did not need to fire at all, unless they had a camera to record the scene. Moreover, they would not have undertaken extra efforts that might have exposed the sham. But they held 'a celebration immediately afterwards', presenting each of twenty-two 'fake' heroes with 'a Lenin suit, a fountain pen, a bowl and a pair of chopsticks' (p. 160). The myth could have been easily exposed by any one of these explicitly identified 'fake heroes'.

Furthermore, Jung Chang does not explain why the Nationalists did not expose this lie for seventy years. Their propagandists, unaware of Chiang's plan to set the Reds free, would have no reason to keep the sham an 'unknown story'.

Who would benefit from this lie? According to Jung Chang, as Mao had just led the Red Army along a disastrous '2,000-kilometre detour' (p. 162), 'a deep resentment grew towards Mao. … Everyone was furious with Mao' (p. 155). If Mao could have let the Red Army cross the Dadu River without firing a bullet, his image as a military genius and his popularity would have shot up. A fabricated battle could only have reduced his reputation. Anyone who made up such a battle is more likely to have been Mao's enemy than his friend, let alone Mao himself.

* In her interview with Duowei, Jung Chang answered my question in this way: 'Many of his arguments are because he did not read our references, even not our texts'. She said that her main evidence is not from the 93-year-old woman, 'the main references are written documents, one of them shows that the 22 Red Army soldiers crossed the bridge first, these 22 men did not suffer any injury, and held a ceremony after crossing. Each of them got a bowl and a pair of chopsticks, and a pen. … He did not read our references, not even the text, but made comments, I do not know why. We also conducted a lot of research on which Kuomintang army defended the bridge, and explain in detail in the book. We find that this army was moved away from here before the Red Army arrived. There was a telegraph from that time. Our references contain the origin of the telegraph. He does not mention

this at all, it is not reasonable. Answering such questions would waste too much time'.

Sorry, it is exactly because I read her text and reference sources that I wrote: '*Jung Chang does not clarify* whether her definition of "Nationalist troops" includes the troops of Sichuan warlords *that did not belong to the Nationalist regular army. Her source suggests it does not. If so, her proof is flawed, because according to the official story, it was exactly the warlord's army that defended the bridge*'. From Jung Chang's reply, we still cannot see 'whether her definition of "Nationalist troops" includes the troops of Sichuan warlords'. Apparently, she does not want to waste her time reading my question, she just wants to 'give easy answers'.

Jung Chang emphasizes that her main evidence that no battle existed is that no deaths happened. It is true that I did 'not mention this at all', but simply because it is not evidence. Even if 'these 22 men did not suffer any injury', we can only doubt the intensity of the battle, we cannot rule out the possibility of its occurrence. The warlord army that defended the bridge was composed of 'double gunners', one rifle and one opium gun, with a lack of basic training and experience. The mere fact that no Red Army men died cannot prove that the battle 'is complete invention'.

5 Mao was carried throughout the Long March

Another of Jung Chang's sensational allegations is that Mao was carried on a litter throughout the Long March. But none of her references suggests that Mao was carried regularly. The only real 'evidence' is a statement by Mao himself that was published in one of the most authoritative and tightly controlled Chinese official presses.

According to Jung Chang, at the start of the Long March, Mao, Lo Fu and Wang Jia-xiang formed a trio. 'The trio travelled together, usually reclining on litters. ... For much of the Long March, including the most gruelling part of the trek, most of them were carried' (p. 144).

Oddly, for such a sensational accusation, Jung Chang provides no reference to support this particular sentence. Several questions arise. The first question is whether Mao's trio had the power to obtain such a privilege. 'Lo Fu, the only member of the trio who was in the Secretariat' (p. 145), said, 'I felt I was put in a position completely without power' (p. 144). It was even worse for Mao, who 'was isolated and miserable' (p. 132). Before the Long March he was worried that he might be abandoned, and went everywhere he thought the Red Army might go, hoping to be picked up mercifully as he stood on the side of the road (p. 128). Given his position, Mao's riding in a litter was probably not for his own comfort, but due to the fact that 'days before the planned departure, his temperature shot up to 41°C and he grew delirious with malaria' (p. 132).

Another question is whether Mao desired to be carried. Since the trio were plotting a coup in the Red Army (pp. 144–46), they would have been keen to boost their popularity. 'Aversion to privilege was particularly strong in the army because many had originally been attracted to join by the lure of equality, which was the

Party's main appeal' (p. 77). It is unlikely that the trio would have been able to grab the leadership while lying in litters. Why didn't their opponents complain? Perhaps they too were being carried? But in that case, how could the Red Army have stuck together and endured hardship, e.g. in the swamplands, as Jung Chang herself describes (pp. 167–9)?

Jung Chang's other evidence is the existence of a charge that 'Mao and the other leaders had "sat in sedan chairs" all through the March' (p. 165). The only quoted part of this charge is 'sat in sedan chairs', without a subject. This reference comes from Mao's arch rival Chang Kuo-tao, writing long after he defected to the Nationalists. Chang and Mao met in late June 1935 and parted in early August (p. 166). As indicated on the map in Jung Chang's book, they shared a common path only from Fubian to Maoergai, just a fraction of the March. Chang's charge that Mao sat '"in sedan chairs" all through the March', even if true, must have derived from others' testimony. Whose testimony? Neither Chang Kuo-tao nor Jung Chang gives any clue.

The best 'evidence' that Mao was carried is: 'Mao himself told his staff decades later: "On the March, I was lying in a litter. So what did I do? I read. I read a lot"' (p. 144). Mao's words do not necessarily imply that he was carried regularly. They appear in his personal secretary Ye Zilong's memoirs, published by the Press of the Central Archive (2000), one of the most authoritative and tightly controlled government publishing houses. Jung Chang accuses the Chinese government of covering up Mao's secrets. But a crucial part of her story comes from an official press. Even if Mao's loyal follower Ye Zilong betrayed him and the government pioneered Jung Chang's denunciation of him, it is hard to believe that such an accusation, as Jung Chang implies, generated no awareness in China and remained an 'unknown story'.

6 Mao did not fight the Japanese

To discredit Mao in the eyes of Chinese people, Jung Chang claims he had no interest in fighting Japan, but only in starting a civil war against Chiang Kai-shek. But the evidence that she herself presents shows that Mao's strategy was the only feasible way for the Reds to fight Japan effectively.

In a chapter titled 'Fight Rivals and Chiang – Not Japan' (p. 218), Jung Chang writes: 'Mao had no strategy to drive the Japanese out of China' (p. 211). 'He bombarded his military commanders with telegrams such as "Focus on creating base areas. ... Not on fighting battles" ... all the time, Mao was urging them to stop fighting the Japanese and concentrate on taking over territory' (pp. 212–13).

What if the Reds had followed an opposite strategy, i.e. fighting the Japanese head on? In August 1937 a war between the Japanese and Chiang's armies broke out. 'In Shanghai, 73 of China's 180 divisions – and the best one-third – over 400,000 men, were thrown in, and all but wiped out. ... The Japanese suffered much fewer, though still heavy, casualties: about 40,000' (p. 209).

'At this time, the Chinese Red Army had some 60,000 regular troops' (p. 211). Let's assume they were as efficient as the best part of Chiang's troops (although their equipment, supply and training were actually far inferior). If they had challenged the Japanese head on, they could hardly have inflicted more than 6,000 Japanese casualties before being 'all but wiped out'. That is less than one sixth of what Chiang achieved in Shanghai, certainly insufficient to defeat Japan. If Japan had secured its rear, Chiang's force would probably soon have given up resisting.

Fortunately, the Reds followed Mao's strategy. The result: 'By mid-November (1937), the first new Communist base in the Japanese rear was formed, near Peking, called Jinchaji, with a population of some 12 million' (p. 213). 'By January 1940, the 8RA [Eighth Route Army], under Zhu De and Peng, had grown to at least 240,000 (from 46,000 at the beginning of the war). And the N4A, operating under Liu Shaoqi near Shanghai and Nanking, had tripled, to 30,000. A score of sizeable bases sprang up in the Japanese rear. The base of Jinchaji alone, only some 80 km from Peking, expanded to control a population of 25 million' (p. 225). This evidence suggests Mao indeed had a 'strategy to drive the Japanese out of China'.

7 The New Fourth Army trap

According to Jung Chang, Mao not only avoided fighting the Japanese but set up his own troops, the N4A with 9,000 men, to be killed by Chiang Kai-shek in order to start a civil war. Instead of offering any evidence for this accusation, Jung Chang provides facts that suggest Mao had neither an incentive nor the ability to do so.

During the Sino-Japanese war, Chiang's army destroyed the headquarters of the N4A. Jung Chang explains that Mao wanted this to happen. In July 1940, Chiang called 'the Red N4A to move out of the Yangtze region' (p. 233). 'By December 1940, Xiang Ying's group was the only part of the N4A south of the Yangtze. ... That month Mao set Xiang Ying's group up to be killed by the Nationalist army, in the hope that the massacre would persuade Stalin to let him off the leash against Chiang' (p. 236). 'Mao was asking Moscow to endorse him starting a full-scale civil war, in the thick of the Sino-Japanese War' (p. 234). According to Jung Chang, Mao achieved his plan by telling the N4A to take a path vetoed by Chiang earlier, but did not inform Chiang of his order. 'A much larger Nationalist force' did not know the N4A 'was only passing through, and thought this was an attack. Fighting broke out. ... During the most critical period of bloody fighting, the four days from 6 to 9 January, Mao claimed he received no communication' (p. 237). Thus, the N4A's plea to call off the Nationalist encirclement did not reach Chiang before it was wiped out (p. 238).

Let's first look at whether Mao really wanted 'a full-scale civil war'. His main force, the 240,000-strong 8RA, 'only some 80 km from Peking', and the 30,000-strong N4A, 'near Shanghai and Nanking', were both 'in the Japanese rear' (p. 225). Where was Chiang Kai-shek? He had 'moved his capital to Chongqing, further inland' (p. 223). If the Reds were let off the leash to attack Chiang, they would have to deal with the Japanese before reaching Chiang. In terms of arms, they were no match for Chiang. At the beginning of the war, Chiang had received '1,000 planes, plus tanks and artillery' from the Russians alone (p. 209), while 'the Communist

8th Route Army had had only 154 pieces of heavy artillery' even towards the end of the war (p. 295).

Secondly, let's see if Mao's alleged disruption of communications might have accomplished his plan. Anyone with military training can tell whether a detachment of 9,000 troops is moving somewhere or attacking someone. Jung Chang implies that the Nationalist generals were unable to do so. Moreover, Mao's plan would have failed if the Nationalist generals had transmitted an inquiry to the N4A before destroying it, or during 'the four days' of 'bloody fighting'. Even if Chiang's generals really were that dumb, they must have informed the Generalissimo and asked his permission to slaughter this huge army of fellow Chinese, unless their own communications had also broken down. Since 'the Generalissimo had vetoed' the N4A's route earlier (p. 236), he would have realized what was going on immediately. If 'Chiang was desperate to avoid a total civil war in the middle of the war against Japan' (p. 240), he could have cabled the N4A, as he had done three days earlier (p. 237), and ordered them to stop, return or switch to another route, etc., instead of authorizing his generals to 'exterminate the Reds' (p. 237). Then Mao's plan would definitely have failed.

After the event, Chiang was criticized by the governments of the US (Jung Chang blames President Roosevelt's informant, marine officer Evans Carlson, for this) and the UK (Jung Chang blames British ambassador Clark Kerr), as well as by the Soviet Union (p. 241). Jung Chang argues that this was because Chiang 'presented his case poorly' (p. 241). But most of the information Jung Chang now presents was available at the time. This included the N4A's allegedly unauthorized route and the alleged fact that Chiang did not receive their request, etc. (though it almost certainly excluded the dubious story about Mao's radio breakdown). But Mao's radio problem only concerns which group of Reds was to blame, Mao or the N4A, not the broader issue between the Reds and the Nationalists. Even if Chiang had used Jung Chang's argument in his defence at the time, he would still have 'presented his case poorly'.

8 Mao sacrificed his brother Tse-min

Even Hitler did not kill his relatives. But Mao did, according to Jung Chang. She claims that Mao let his brother Tse-min be killed by Chiang Kai-shek in order to start a civil war. Her sole evidence is Mao's failure to repeat his instruction to Zhou Enlai to ask Chiang for Tse-min's release within two days during Tse-min's nine months of imprisonment. This accusation typifies Jung Chang's contradictory style.

'To stir up anti-Chiang fervour in the CCP, Mao cogitated another "massacre" by the Nationalists. … This time the sacrificial victims included his only surviving brother, Tse-min. Tse-min had been working in Xinjiang. … In early 1943, Tse-min and more than 140 other Communists and their families … were imprisoned' (p. 259). 'The CCP leadership collectively (in the name of the Secretariat)' (p. 260) told 'the CCP liaison, Zhou Enlai, to ask for their release' (p. 259). 'Two days later, on the 12th (February), Mao sent Chou a separate cable. … The release of the Xinjiang group was not on it. Chou, by now taking orders from Mao alone, did not raise the matter. … Tse-min and two other senior CCP figures were executed on 27 September on charges of plotting a coup. But with so few deaths – only three – Mao was unable to cry "Massacre". He did not make any announcement condemning the executions, either, as this might raise questions about whether the Communists were indeed guilty as charged' (p. 260).

This is too funny to be treated seriously. Let's consider an imagined conversation in a court:

PROSECUTOR: Sir, I find Mao guilty of cogitating a massacre, sacrificing his brother T.

JUDGE: What was his motivation?

PROSECUTOR: He wanted to stir up anti-Chiang fervour.

JUDGE: How did he do it?

PROSECUTOR: He did it by not telling Chou to plead for T's release.

JUDGE: But he had done so two days earlier. How did his failure to repeat his instruction kill T?

PROSECUTOR: Chou then knew Mao wanted T dead, so he did not raise the matter with Chiang.

JUDGE: I don't understand Chou's thinking. Did Mao condemn the killing of T?

PROSECUTOR: No, because this would reveal that T was indeed guilty.

JUDGE: If so, how could Mao use T's death to stir up anti-Chiang fervour?

PROSECUTOR: He expected Chiang to kill many more.

JUDGE: But only three were killed. I don't see how Mao could have expected that.

PROSECUTOR: Because another 140 communists were also guilty of plotting a coup.

JUDGE: Do you mean that Chiang not only killed T legitimately but was entitled to kill many more?

PROSECUTOR: Yes, sir.

JUDGE: Then, why are you so sure that Mao could have saved T by his second order?

If you believe in fair trials, the judge would most probably have 'raise[d] questions about whether' Mao was 'indeed guilty as charged'.

9 The Rectification Campaign

During the Sino-Japanese war, many young and radical students flocked to Mao's base in Yan'an. To consolidate his political control and purge this new blood from Nationalist or Japanese territories, Mao launched the Rectification Campaign, in 1942–43. Jung Chang claims thousands died, as suspected Nationalist agents or spies. But she offers no evidence to support her claim. The most famous victim, described by Jung Chang as Mao's personal target, did not even die during the Campaign itself. It is unlikely that many suffered more than he.

During the Rectification Campaign, according to Jung Chang, 'the number who perished was in the thousands, at least' (p. 257). No reference supporting this statement can be found in the book. To make a reasonable guess about the extent of the loss of life, we can look at the case of the most famous victim, Wang Shi-wei, personally targeted by Mao as 'the champion of the young volunteers' (p. 250). After reading Wang's article in *Liberation Daily*, Mao 'slammed the newspaper on the desk and demanded angrily: "Who is in charge here? Wang Shi-wei or Marxism?"' (p. 251). It became more personal when Mao saw 'Shi-wei's enormous popularity. He said at once: "I now have a target." He later complained: "Many people rushed from far away to ... read his article. But no one wants to read mine!" Wang Shi-wei was the king and lord master ... he was in command in Yenan ... and we were defeated ... He denounced him as a Trotskyist .... Trotsky, Shi-wei had said, was "a genius", while Stalin was "an unlovable person" who had "created untold countless evils"' (p. 252).

Hardly anyone could have faced a more serious threat to his life than Wang. Yet he survived for a full four years after the campaign, and was killed only in 1947, when the Nationalist army led by General Hu Zongnan forced the Reds to evacuate Yan'an. He was not killed by Mao's order. Given this example, one really requires evidence to believe that 'the number who perished was in the thousands'.

Moreover, the Rectification Campaign must be seen in its historical context. As Jung Chang tells us, Mao's moles played decisive roles in all the major ensuing military campaigns, including Hu Zongnan in Yan'an (pp. 312–18), Wei Li-huang in Manchuria (pp. 318–19), associates of Fu Tso-yi in Peking-Tianjin (pp. 319–20), and Liu Fei and Kuo Ju-kui in Huai-Hai (pp. 320–21). In strong contrast, 'during the civil war, while the Nationalists were penetrated like sieves, they had virtually zero success infiltrating the Communists' (p. 258). The difference meant millions of lives or deaths. This probably could not have happened without the Rectification Campaign.

By the way, Jung Chang's provides no evidence for her allegation that General Hu Zongnan was a communist agent, except for his apparent military blunders and earlier links to some communists in 1920s. This led to a strong protest by Hu's son, Hu Wei-zhen, a Taiwanese representative in Singapore. According to Jung Chang's brother Pu Zhang, Jung Chang's response was to ask Hu Junior to 'provide the relevant evidence to show his father is not a red spy'.[2] What kind of evidence can prove someone is NOT a spy?

10 Selling opium

Jung Chang accuses Mao of selling opium worth $60 million in 1943 alone. The Western media are delighted to see Mao condemned as a drug baron. However, if Jung Chang's figures and her accounts of Mao's heavy taxation in Yan'an were true, Mao's opium market would have reached most of China or beyond. Unfortunately, there is no evidence that Yan'an sold opium on such a scale.

'In 1943 the Russians estimated Mao's opium sales at 44,760 kg, worth an astronomical 2.4 billion fabi (roughly US$60 million at then current exchange rates, or some US$640 million today)' (p. 287).

In that year, Yan'an 'had accumulated savings ... worth 250 million fabi ... This sum was six times the official Yenan region budget for 1942' (p. 287). Hence, opium sales in 1943 were almost 58 times (2.4 billion × 6/250 million) the Yan'an budget for 1942. Since tax revenue should not greatly exceed the budget, we must conclude that opium sales were 58 times the annual tax revenue from Yan'an region.

At the time, according to Jung Chang, the Reds levied very heavy taxes in Yan'an. 'Sometimes ... "almost equals the entire year's harvest"; ... For many, "there was no food left after paying the tax"' (p. 284). Hence, the region's taxes must have accounted for almost its entire disposable income. So Mao's opium sales were equal to 58 times the Yan'an people's entire disposable income. But Mao did not sell opium in the Yan'an region, because 'a drug-addicted peasantry was no use to him' (p. 290). So the money had to come from outside Yan'an.

If the area around Yan'an had a similar population density and income level, to get opium sales of 2.4 billion fabi Mao would have had to suck in the entire disposable income from an area 58 times of Yan'an, 'which was roughly the size of France' (p. 284). If Yan'an's average income was just one third of that of China as a whole, every Chinese would have to spend his or her entire disposable income on Mao's opium. Yan'an must have been China's Golden Triangle. This could not have remained an 'unknown story' at the time, let alone today, sixty years on.

11 Three millions deaths in 1950–51

At the beginning of her book, Jung Chang writes: 'Mao Tse-tung ... was responsible for well over 70 million deaths in peacetime' (p. 3). This is her main justification for likening Mao to Hitler. The first of these 70 million deaths are the three million that she says happened in 1950–51. In fact, this figure is inflated from an initial 0.7 million by Jung Chang's arbitrary multiplication. These 0.7 million deaths, although a big loss of human life, resulted from the final stage of the civil war and the Korean War.

During the 'campaign to suppress counter-revolutionaries' in 1950–51, 'some 3 million perished either by execution, mob violence, or suicide' (p. 337). The calculation is explained in the footnote: 700,000 were executed, 'those beaten or tortured to death ... would at the very least be as many again. Then there were suicides, which, based on several local inquiries, were very probably about equal to the number of those killed' (p. 337 fn.). Hence 700,000 × 2 × 2 = 2.8 million, roughly 3 million, as Jung Chang claims. There is no explanation for why 'those beaten or tortured to death ... would at the very least be as many' as those executed. Her claim that suicides 'were very probably about equal to the number of those killed' is based on 'several local inquiries', with no detailed information.

To generalize an execution/killing ratio or a suicide/killing ratio from 'several local inquiries' to the whole nation is hardly professional. The results can be unreliable. For instance, if we apply 700,000 executions out of a total population of 550 million to a 'major target of Mao's – the Roman Catholic Church' (p. 340) (apparently, 'China had about 3.3 million Catholics at the time' [p. 340]), we would expect the total number of execution to be 700,000 × 3.3m/550m, i.e., 4,200. But Jung Chang assures us that only 'hundreds of Chinese Catholics were executed' (p. 340).

It is also questionable whether these 700,000 deaths should count as 'deaths in peacetime'. When the People's Republic was established in October 1949, almost half its territory had yet to be liberated. Military campaigns continued into 1950 and even 1951 in certain parts of China. The Campaign to Suppress Counter-Revolutionaries and 'the land reform in the newly occupied areas, where some two-thirds of China's population lived' (p. 337), were closely related to the last stage of the bloody civil war. Many if not most of the 700,000 people were executed for their military actions during the war, and cannot accurately be described as victims in peacetime. In a large part of China, bandits had existed since time immemorial. Mao's army cleaned them up almost instantly. Killing, unfortunately, was necessary to achieve 'peacetime' in China.

Moreover, 'China was hurled into the inferno of the Korean War on 19 October 1950' (p. 380). The war lasted three years until 'an armistice was finally signed on 27 July 1953' (p. 394). During this period, especially in the early stage, Chiang Kai-shek in Taiwan called on his loyalists on the mainland to rebel against the communists in every way possible and to welcome their forthcoming liberation by the US army and his own army. Many responded with acts of subversion, propaganda, espionage, explosions, poisonings, arson, murder and even armed risings. These acts accounted for a significant part of the 700,000 executions.

12 Twenty-seven million deaths in prisons and labour camps

Jung Chang's second large group of Mao's peacetime victims is those who died in Chinese government custody. The number is actually produced by magic formula. Mao's responsibility is not discussed, merely assumed.

During Mao's 27 years of rule, 'the number who died in prisons and labour camps could well amount to 27 million' (p. 338). The proof: 'China's prison and labour camp population was roughly 10 million in any one year under Mao. Descriptions of camp life by inmates, which point to high mortality rates, indicate a probable annual death rate of at least 10 per cent' (p. 338 fn.). So 10m × 10% × 27 = 27 million.

Jung Chang accuses Mao of killing $x = a \times b \times c$ number of people, where a = 'China's prison and labour camp population', b = 'annual death rate', and c = the years of his rule. She does not explain why a = 10 million. Her justification of b = 10 per cent is based on 'descriptions of camp life by inmates'. If we applied this magic formula to Deng Xiao-ping's reign from 1978 to 1989, we get the figure of 12 million deaths, and 14 million for his successor Jiang Ze-min (1990–2003). Jung Chang does not show why Mao was responsible. Apparently she simply blames Mao for every Chinese death of whatever kind.

13 The Superpower Programme

Throughout much of her book, Jung Chang repeats allegations that Mao started a secret 'Superpower Programme' in 1953 and continued up to his death to pursue his dream of world dominance. This sounds very alarming to the Western world, and echoes the theory of the 'China threat'. But she provides no evidence that any such programme ever existed. The word *programme* should mean an explicit plan, not a hidden ambition. The word superpower did not even exist in the Chinese language in 1953.

In Ch. 36, titled 'Launching the Secret Superpower Programme', we read: '[I]n May 1953, Stalin's successors in the Kremlin agreed to sell China ninety-one large industrial enterprises. … It was in effect Mao's Superpower Programme. Its utterly military nature was concealed, and is little known in China today' (p. 396). Right after that, Mao forced through 'collectivisation of agriculture' and 'ordered the nationalisation of industry and commerce in urban areas, to channel every single resource into the Superpower Programme' (p. 412). During the Suez crisis in 1956, Mao realized that the only thing he could offer Egypt were 'small arms such as rifles', and hence became 'more impatient to speed up his Superpower Programme' (p. 425). Later he silenced dissent through the Anti-Rightist Campaign and launched the Great Leap Forward 'to accelerate his Superpower Programme' (p. 444). In spite of a setback during the famine, 'becoming a superpower had remained Mao's dearest dream. This was partly why he had carried out the Purge – to install new enforcers who were more in tune with his demands. After this process was complete, he started to accelerate the Programme' (p. 573). 'Mao began seeking relations with America, in order to gain access to Western technology for his Superpower Programme' (p. 601).

Mao's superpower ambition, even if it really existed, is not the same as a programme. According to *Webster's New World Dictionary*, a programme is (i) 'a proclamation', which means 'something that is proclaimed, or announced officially'; (ii) 'a prospectus', which means 'a statement outlining the main features of a new work or business enterprise'; or (iii) 'a plan or procedure for dealing with some matter'. A programme is something proclaimed, announced or stated explicitly about concrete features, objectives or procedures of a given undertaking. It is not something hidden in a person's head but never expressed on paper or in words.

Throughout the book, there is no record, written or spoken by Mao or his colleagues, of a Superpower Programme. Even the name is dubious, for Mao maintained that China belonged to the Third World (p. 650) and would never seek to be a superpower (as Deng Xiaoping declared at the UN in 1974). Even if he had planned to become a superpower, he would hardly have used the word 'superpower', which did not exist in Chinese until the 1970s. How could Mao have 'first outlined his Superpower Programme' in 1953 (p. 432)? If Mao used another name or just a code, what was it? Without a name or even a code, how could Mao and his colleagues discuss and implement it?

Although she lacks evidence of its existence, Jung Chang gives two examples of components of Mao's supposed Superpower Programme. One is the 'ninety-one large industrial enterprises' sold to China by the Soviet Union in 1953. She does not explain the 'utterly military nature [that] was concealed' in these hydro-power plants, dams, tractor factories, mines, steel mills, truck factories, oil refineries, machine-tool factories, etc.

Her other example is the atom bomb. Several countries have possessed such weapons before and after China acquired them. Jung Chang does not explain why China's possession of them is necessarily part of a Superpower Programme. However, she does remind us that '[i]n March 1955 the US said it would use nuclear weapons under certain circumstances. Eisenhower very deliberately told a press conference on the 16th that he could see no reason why they should not be used "just exactly as you would use a bullet or anything else" … China seemed to be in real danger of a US nuclear strike' (p. 414). She does not mention that even before that, during the Korean War, General McArthur requested permission to drop more than twenty atom bombs on Beijing and other Chinese cities, and that his plan was only vetoed by President Truman after a long and hotly contested discussion. Nor does she mention that, after Eisenhower and before China had its atom bomb, 'JFK was ready to use a nuclear bomb on China' too (*The Independent*, 27 August 2005). However, she is aware that 'China seemed to be in real danger of a US nuclear strike' as a result of Mao's 'bombing and strafing more Nationalists-held islands' contained within China's own territory (p. 414). Jung Chang probably knows whether or not other nuclear nations faced the same nuclear threat. When its first bomb exploded, China pledged never to be the first to use nuclear weapons. Jung Chang probably knows whether or not other nuclear countries did the same. Does she think they all had Superpower Programmes?

14 Thirty-eight million deaths in 1958–61

The famine of 1958–61 was no doubt the biggest disaster ever to hit the Chinese people under the CCP and Mao in particular. Jung Chang has every right to choose the highest estimated death toll in order to condemn Mao. But her claim that Mao intentionally made this famine cannot be substantiated: her evidence suggests the opposite.

Jung Chang writes: 'Close to 38 million people died of starvation and overwork in the Great Leap Forward and the famine. … Mao knowingly starved and worked these tens of millions of people to death' (pp. 456–7).

The number of deaths given in the book is not Jung Chang's finding, but the accusation that Mao 'knowingly' allowed them is definitely her contribution. She provides no evidence to show that Mao knew that millions were dying and did nothing to stop it. Her strongest argument is: 'During the two critical years 1958–9, grain exports alone, almost exactly 7m tons, would have provided the equivalent of over 840 calories per day for 38 million people – the difference between life and death' (p. 457).

The Chinese government had to make its export plans for 1958 and 1959 about one year earlier, mainly on the basis of grain production in 1957 and 1958, when the bad news had not yet emerged. Mao could not know that millions would die. The scales of grain exports in 1959 reflected Mao's false estimate of grain production a year earlier, which led him to 'announce that the harvest figure for 1958 was more than double 1957's' (p. 461), an estimate he apparently believed. This estimate was based on nationwide misreporting. For example (as Jung Chang reports), 'in September (1958), *People's Daily* reported that "the biggest rice sputnik" yet had produced over 70 tons from less than 1/5th of an acre, which was hundreds of times the norm' (p. 446). Mao can be condemned for his bad judgement and the role he played in creating the political atmosphere conducive to such misinformation. He can also be blamed for not abolishing grain export contracts earlier, possibly in part because he thought China's national pride was at stake. But bad judgement is not the same as 'knowingly starv[ing] ... tens of millions of people to death'.

In judging whether or not 'knowingly' is the right word, we should bear in mind the difficulty of gaining accurate information at that time. According to *Wild Swans*, Jung Chang's father was the minister of Sichuan's Department of Propaganda (she coined a special name for her father's unit, 'Department of Public Affairs'). His main job was to visit peasants and provide help when needed. According to Jung Chang, seven million people died in Sichuan during the famine. No one would have known this better than her father. Had he reported what he saw, it is extremely unlikely that he could have hidden it from his wife (another 'Public Affairs' official, or propagandist) for more than a decade. It is even more unlikely that his wife could have hidden it from Jung Chang for the next three decades. However, neither *Wild Swans* nor this book reveals that Jung Chang's father knew about the famine in Sichuan. Even the figure of seven million deaths was not revealed to Jung Chang until more than a decade after her departure from China. If the top 'Public Affairs' official in the province did not know it, how could Mao in Beijing 'knowingly [have] starved ... tens of millions of people to death'?

In fact, it should not be so difficult for Jung Chang to prove her point. She could simply show that the Sichuan government had reported to Beijing that people were starving to death and asked for urgent food relief but received no immediate response. If Jung Chang thinks that the absence of evidence to that effect was due to the impact of Mao's terror, she could at least try to show with just one or two examples that Mao had punished people for requesting food relief. Her story of Peng Dehuai (pp. 468–70) does not fit here, because he did many other things, e.g. he 'contemplated something akin to a military coup' (p. 464).

Why does Jung Chang fail to provide such evidence? In fact, the Sichuan party leadership concealed millions of death in Sichuan. When news of the mass starvation reached Beijing, the party bosses of most famine-stricken provinces were sacked for not reporting it in time (Wu Zhifu in Henan, Zeng Xisheng in Anhui, Shu Tong in Shandong, Zhang Zhongliang in Gansu, etc.). The only exception is the Sichuan party boss Li Jingquan, who was instead promoted. Li put all the blame on his subordinates, at county or commune level, accusing them of having 'knowingly starved ... people to death'. Most people in Sichuan believe that Li used them as scapegoats. The issue may be debatable. But if we use the word 'knowingly' about Li, the same must apply to the local officials, unless their pleas for help were ignored by the provincial authorities. By the same token, if Jung Chang accuses

Mao of having 'knowingly starved ... people to death', the same charge must apply to Li and his colleagues, unless their pleas for help were ignored by Beijing.

For Li to conceal starvation and his own responsibility there was a crucial and necessary condition: the full cooperation of the Sichuan media, which were under the absolute control of the Department of 'Public Affairs', led by Jung Chang's father. Let's stop here.

Readers should know that the death toll of 38 million is the highest of many widely varying estimates. It is, astonishingly, as high as the estimated total Chinese deaths during the Sino-Japanese war of 1937–45. To convince her readers of its validity, Jung Chang provides death rates and population numbers, backed up by references to *China Statistics Yearbook 1983*. However, her data do not agree with those published in the *Yearbook*. Without alerting readers to this fact, Jung Chang argues that '[t]he official statistics published in 1983 are recognised as partly defective, because local policemen understated the number of deaths in the years 1959–61' (p. 457 fn.). Chinese statisticians would surely have corrected such obvious defects in the *Yearbook*. Jung Chang does not explain the source of her 'corrected' data, although the corrections are not minor. For instance, the death rate in 1960 was 4.34 per cent according to her, while the official one was 2.54 per cent. This alone generates an extra 12 million deaths, almost one third of her total death toll.

Whatever the true figures may be, the abnormal deaths, as explained by Jung Chang (pp. 456–7 fn.), include all those related to but not directly caused by starvation or overwork, such as deaths caused by illness partially due to malnutrition, and those caused by various injuries and problems due to poor medical and social care. These deaths may account for the greater part of the 'abnormal deaths' shown in statistics, though they were not considered to result from starvation and did not attract the immediate attention of society and government. This is probably why there is no widespread evidence of starvation on a level compatible with Jung Chang's claim. If we applied Jung Chang's method to the Russian population data after Yeltsin's shock therapy, the rate of abnormal deaths would be higher than those during China's famine. Yeltsin could be blamed for genocide, as some Russians did (unfairly, however).

Finally, let us look at Jung Chang's 'proof' that Mao intended to let tens of millions of people die. She wrote: 'We can now say with assurance how many people Mao was ready to dispense with ... On 21 November 1958, talking to his inner circle about the labour-intensive projects like waterworks and making "steel", and tacitly, almost casually, assuming a context where peasants had too little to eat and were being worked to exhaustion, Mao said: "Working like this, with all these projects, half of China may well have to die. If not half, one-third, or one-tenth – 50 million – die." Aware that these remarks might sound too shocking, he tried to shirk his own responsibility. "Fifty million deaths", he went on, "I could be fired, and I might even lose my head ... but if you insist, I'll let you do it, and you can't blame me when people die"' (pp. 457–8).

In her BBC interview, Jung Chang uses this quotation to show that Mao knew that half of the population would die under his policy and 'deliberately' starved tens of millions of people to death. It is worth checking its source.

The words are taken from Mao's speech at a politburo meeting in Wuchang on 21 November 1958. The translation, including the context, should actually run as follows:

> Do not pursue vanity, and get a disaster. We should reduce the amount of our task. On the waterworks, the whole nation accomplished 50 billion cubic metres of earth last winter and this spring, but for this winter and next spring, the plan is 190 billion, three times more. There are various other tasks, steel, iron, copper, aluminium, coal, transport, machinery, chemicals, how much labour and financial resource are needed? Working like this, I am afraid that half of China may well have to die. If not half, one-third, or one-tenth – 50 million deaths. 50 million deaths, if you are not fired, at least I will be. Should we do so much? It is OK if you really want to, but the principle is no death. If you insist, I cannot stop you, but I should not be killed when people die. Next year's plan is to produce 30 million tons of steel, should we plan so much? Can we do it? How many people must work for it? Will people die? We should lower our tone in this meeting, cool the air down. The string of the Huchin [a Chinese instrument] should not be pulled too tightly. There is a risk of breaking down.

In the light of his actual words, 'we can now say with assurance how many people Mao was ready to dispense with'.

15   Three million deaths in 1966–76

The final time large numbers of people died under Mao was during the Cultural Revolution. Jung Chang adds three million to Mao's record for this period. This figure is not based on professional research. Her evidence points to Mao's general responsibility for launching the Cultural Revolution, but not his direct involvement in or encouragement of violence and brutality, which caused most deaths in some (mostly remote) provinces.

'In the ten years from when Mao started the Purge until his death in 1976, at least 3 million people died violent deaths. ... The killings were sponsored by the state' (p. 569).

The figure of three million is much higher than the official estimate. Jung Chang's main source for it is an article published in *China Spring*, a fervently anti-Chinese government magazine published in the US, and not known for its neutrality and objectiveness.

China had 29 provinces or regions at the time. The worst case on Jung Chang's list is Guangxi, where 'killing claimed some 100,000 lives' (p. 566). To reach a total of three million nationwide, proportionately the same number must have died in all the other provinces. In Jung Chang's second and third positions, however, we find Yunnan, where some 'seventeen thousand of them were executed or beaten to death, or driven to suicide', and Inner Mongolia, where '16,222 died' (p. 567). If we assume that 20,000 people died in every province except Guangxi, the total number would be 0.66 million. The rest of the 2.34 million claimed by Jung Chang have to remain her 'unknown story'.

Now let us consider Mao's responsibility. According to Jung Chang, Guangxi offers 'the clearest illustration' of a situation in which 'one faction refused to recognise the authority of Mao's point man, General (Wei) Guo-qing' (p. 565). So the killing was mainly due to faction fighting. Jung Chang provides the following evidence for Mao's attitude towards such violence. At the beginning of the Cultural Revolution, 'Mao had Zhou Enlai announce to a Red Guard rally on Tiananmen on 31 August (1966): "Denounce by words, and not by violence"' (p. 540). 'In 1968, factional clashes with firearms had shown little sign of abating, despite a flood of commands from Peking. One man who was being conspicuously unruly was Kuai Da-fu, the Qinghua University student whom Mao had used to torment Liu Shaoqi and his wife. Kuai had by now become the most famous "leftist" in the country, and he was determined to bring his opponents in the university to their knees. He ignored repeated orders to stop. ... Mao had to step in personally to get him to toe the line, and simultaneously made an example of him to send a warning to the whole country that faction wars had to stop' (pp. 564–5). Since Mao personally stopped his favourite 'leftist' using violence in faction fighting, it is unlikely that he would have supported factional violence by other provincial leftists. The real story was probably what Jung Chang tells us: 'Mao had unleashed a dynamic that was undermining his own power. He had to abandon his attempt to identify factions as Left and Conservative, and called for all groups to unite. But his orders were ignored' (p. 564).

According to Jung Chang's evidence, Mao was guilty of miscalculation, but not of evil intent.

16 Mao's aim in the Cultural Revolution

Mao saw the Cultural Revolution as one of his two major achievements. Jung Chang claims that Mao 'had intended the Great Purge to install much more merciless enforcers' for his Superpower Programme (p. 558), that his real target 'was the old enforcers who had shown distaste for Mao's extremist policies. Mao aimed to get rid of them en masse' (p. 543). However, her evidence not only contradicts her claim but supports the view that Mao's aim in the Cultural Revolution was 'a move to rid China of Soviet-style "revisionists"' (p. 570).

Her evidence leads to four main conclusions. (1) Mao did not need to replace merciful officials to enforce his plan for what Jung Chang called his Superpower Programme. (2) Mao neither targeted merciful officials nor promoted merciless ones during the Cultural Revolution. (3) Mao's mobilizing of the masses to topple officials would seriously have damaged any such enforcement, and was completely unnecessary if his goal was 'to install much more merciless enforcers'. (4) Jung Chang believes that there was a pro-Russian faction within the Chinese government before the Cultural Revolution. We will explain each of these points in detail below.

(1) Jung Chang shows that Mao did not need the Cultural Revolution to 'install

much more merciless enforcers', since there was no serious resistance to his so-called Superpower Programme at the top level. In 1964 Mao started his biggest project after the Great Leap Forward, the Third Front. 'It cost an astronomical 200 billion-plus yuan, and at its peak it sucked in at least two-thirds of the entire nation's investment. The waste it created was more than the total material losses caused by the Great Leap Forward' (p. 503). In spite of that, 'Liu Shaoqi and Mao's other colleagues put up no resistance to this lunacy. ... For Mao to forgo deaths and political victimisation seems to have been the best his colleagues thought they could expect – and enough to make them feel they might as well go along with him' (p. 504).

(2) If Mao's aim was to replace merciful enforcers with merciless ones, he would have targeted the former and promoted the latter during the Cultural Revolution. But Jung Chang's evidence is to the contrary. She first gives an example: one of the Cultural Revolution's outspoken opponents was 'Mao's old follower Tan Zhen-lin, who had been in charge of agriculture during the famine (showing how far he was prepared to go along with Mao)' (p. 546). Later, Jung Chang puts it more flatly: 'Mao did not differentiate between disaffected officials and those who were actually totally loyal to him and had not wavered even during the famine. In fact, there was no way he could tell who was which. So he resolved to overthrow them all first, and then have them investigated by his new enforcers' (p. 543). This is not the way to get merciless enforcers. If Mao could not 'tell who was which' among his old followers after years of scrutiny, how could he trust the party's totally unknown rebels? In fact, merciless enforcers were more likely to be thrown out by the rebels, who might have suffered under them for years. For instance, this time the Sichuan boss Li Jingquan and his associates (including 'Public Affairs' officials), who cooperated quite well to cover up the famine, were unable to escape.

(3) Mao's mobilizing of the masses to plunge the party apparatus into chaos contradicts Jung Chang's theory. If Mao's goal was merciless enforcement, he would hardly have wanted to destroy the very basis for any such enforcement, the authority of his government. Mao's approach can only be made to chime with Jung Chang's theory if it can be shown that it was necessary 'to install much more merciless enforcers'. Unfortunately, Jung Chang's evidence rules this out.

Jung Chang shows that Mao could get rid of his enemies without mobilizing the masses. Let's consider, for example, 'the first list of victims of the Great Purge, four big names described as an "anti-Party clique": Mayor Peng, Chief of Staff Luo, Yang Shang-kun, the liaison with Russia and the tape-recording suspect, and old media chief Lu Ding-yi. Mao did not bother to come to the occasion'. The meeting 'was actually chaired by Liu Shao-chi, who knew he was chairing an event that was ultimately going to bring him to ruin'. 'Liu then asked all in favour to raise their hands. All did, including Mayor Peng and Liu' (p. 531).

The Red Guards were involved in toppling President Liu Shaoqi, but Jung Chang shows their contribution was nominal. After quoting Kuai Da-fu, the Rebel leader who condemned Liu, Jung Chang writes: 'This is a good self-confession of how the Rebels really worked; they were tools, and cowards, and they knew it' (p. 550). To formally purge Liu, 'Mao had Zhou Enlai telephone Liu and tell him to stop meeting foreigners, or appearing in public, unless told to do so. That day, Mao wrote a tirade against Liu which he himself read out to the Central Committee two days later, in Liu's presence, breaking the news of Liu's downfall' (p. 548).

'Out of his remaining top echelon, there came only one burst of defiance. In February 1967, some of the Politburo members who had not fallen spoke up, voicing rage at what was happening to their fellow Party cadres' (p. 546). 'But these elite survivors were either devoted veteran followers of Mao's, or men already broken by him. Faced with his wrath, they folded. … The mini-revolt was easily quelled' (p. 547). The masses were not needed to face down the challenge by a group that included some of the country's top military leaders. Clearly, Jung Chang cannot explain the essence of the Cultural Revolution.

(4) Actually, Jung Chang's evidence supports a totally different view of the Cultural Revolution, one proclaimed by Mao himself, who 'had presented the Cultural Revolution as a move to rid China of Soviet-style "revisionists"' (p. 570).

'On 14 October 1964, Khrushchev was ousted in a palace coup. … Within days, Chou was telling Soviet ambassador Chervonenko that it was Mao's "utmost wish" to have a better relationship. Chou requested an invitation to the anniversary of the Bolshevik Revolution in Moscow on 7 November' (p. 510). 'At the reception in the Kremlin on 7 November … Soviet defence minister Rodion Malinovsky approached Chou. … Out of the blue, Malinovsky said to Chou: "We don't want any Mao, or any Khrushchev, to stand in the way of our relationship." … Malinovsky then turned to Marshal Ho Lung, China's acting army chief: "We've got rid of our fool Khrushchev, now you get rid of yours, Mao"' (p. 511).

Moreover, Jung Chang reveals secret moves within the Chinese leadership. In 'February [1966], with the backing of Liu Shao-chi, Mayor Peng issued a "national guideline" forbidding the use of political accusations to trample on culture and the custodians of culture. Moreover, he went further, and actually suppressed Mao's instructions aimed at starting a persecution campaign. … As soon as he issued the guideline, Mayor Peng flew to Sichuan, ostensibly to inspect arms industries relocated in this mountainous province. There he did something truly astonishing. He had a secret tête-à-tête with Marshal Peng. … [J]udging from the timing, and the colossal risk Mayor Peng took in visiting a major foe of Mao's, without permission, in secret, it is highly likely that they discussed the feasibility of using the army to stop Mao. … Marshal Ho Lung, the man to whom Soviet defence minister Malinovsky had said "Get rid of Mao", soon also went to Sichuan, also in the name of inspecting the arms industries. … And there was more that was gnawing at Mao's mind. It seems that Mayor Peng was contemplating getting in touch with the Russians, and may have thought of seeking Russian help to avert Mao's Purge' (p. 528).

After reading Jung Chang's evidence, one has little choice other than to view Mao's 'Cultural Revolution as a move to rid China of Soviet-style "revisionists"'.

(5) The mass mobilization not only contradicts Jung Chang's theory but fits Mao's declaration of 'denouncing those power-holders inside the Party pursuing a capitalist road'. Mao believed that capitalism would benefit officials at the expense of ordinary people. His proclaimed goal is also consistent with China's reality today. Few people doubt that China is now capitalist, at least from an economic

point of view. The transformation happens to have been guided by the then No. 2 capitalist-roader Deng Xiao-ping (p. 553). Since Mao foresaw the arrival of capitalism, and even anticipated its top campaigner, it seems logical that he would have launched the Cultural Revolution to prevent that happening.

17 Mao compared with Hitler

Jung Chang's central theme is that Mao was at least as bad as Hitler. Based on her book, we will show (1) that Mao did not invade lots of other nations and kill their people en masse, like Hitler; (2) that there is no evidence that he intentionally killed millions of civilians under his rule, like Hitler; and (3) that he had more serious political opponents than Hitler but killed none, while Hitler killed all of his. So any reasonable person would disagree with Jung Chang's likening of Mao to Hitler.

(1) Hitler invaded the greater part of Europe in World War Two, in which tens of millions perished. Mao sent Chinese troops to Korea in the 1950s and Vietnam in the 1960s, invited by the North Korean and North Vietnamese governments to join in fighting a superpower. In 1962, China fought a brief war with India, because 'China had refused to recognise the boundary that had been delineated by the British in colonial times' (p. 486). 'As border clashes worsened' (p. 486), Mao sent troops into India. After a quick victory, he ordered the troops to return home in days. Jung Chang's words imply that China was adjacent to British India (the boundary 'had been delineated by the British in' 1903) well before Mao sent troops to Tibet in 1950. So Mao's troops did not invade Tibet (it was the Qing Dynasty's army that made Tibet a part of China, two hundred years earlier). In 1969, China clashed with the Soviet Union. On 'a small uninhabited island … Chinese laid an ambush that left 32 Russians dead', while 'Russia's claim to the island was far from established' (p. 570). During his reign Mao never annexed a single piece of land into Chinese territory.

(2) Hitler intentionally killed millions of Jews, communists and leftists, homosexuals, Jehovah's witnesses, Gypsies, and others. The last mass killing under Mao took place in 1950–51 and led to 700,000 executions. However, this was at the end of a civil war and during the Korean War. Many if not most victims were executed for the military roles they had played (see section 11). During Mao's reign, many must have died in prisons, but there is no evidence that Mao's prisons were anywhere near as bad as the Gulag in the Soviet Union (see section 12). Millions of people died during the famine because of Mao's mismanagement, but there is no proof that he intended to let people die or was indifferent to their deaths (see section 14). Several political campaigns, for example, the Cultural Revolution, caused many deaths as a result of persecution or maltreatment, but not on Mao's direct orders (see section 15).

(3) Probably the most relevant comparison relates to the way in which the two dictators treated political challengers, since here their personal responsibilities are irrefutable. There are few examples of how Hitler treated his political rivals, since he hardly had any. But we do know that he ordered the killing of his fellow Nazi leader Röhn for alleged homosexual behaviour and forced Germany's best general,

Rommel, to commit suicide for his role in a suspected coup. He also executed von Stauffenberg and his co-conspirators for trying to assassinate him.

As for Mao, his first challenger was Chang Kuo-tao, who defected to the Nationalists in 1938 (pp. 220–1). His second rival, Wang Ming, stayed in the CCP and even praised Mao after being defeated (p. 357), and later died in Russia (in 1974). The third victim was Gao Gang, who committed suicide in 1954 (p. 405). The fourth, Peng De-huai, 'was put under house arrest' (p. 470) after his fight with Mao in 1959 and died of rectal cancer in 1974 (p. 557). The fifth was Liu Shaoqi, who died in neglected circumstances in 1969 due to persecution (p. 556). The sixth, Lin Biao, died in an air crash in Mongolia in 1971 (p. 582). His seventh and final rival was Deng Xiao-ping, to whom 'Mao had had to give in and let him live in the comfort of his own home, among his family' (pp. 649–50) until Mao's own death in 1976. None of his political challengers was executed. Nor were any of their co-conspirators. In the case of Lin Biao, who mounted the most deadly and militant coup attempt, 'incredibly, given that an attempted assassination – of Mao, no less – was involved, not a single person was executed' (p. 586).

Among those cases, let's look at 'Mao's persecution of the man he hated most' (p. 548), Liu Shaoqi. The 'report, which was delivered to the Central Committee by Mao's faithful slave, Zhou Enlai, called Liu a "traitor, enemy agent and scab", and recommended the death sentence. But Mao rejected it, as he did for Mme Liu. He preferred a slow, lingering death' (pp. 555–6). In April 1969, 'the Ninth Congress convened', and Liu's 'death came … on 12 November 1969' (p. 556). It was hardly slow. On the other hand, the 'slow, lingering death' of Liu's wife, Wang Guang-mei, not only outlasted Mao but has still not been completed today, nearly forty years on.

Let's see how Mao obtained his evidence against Liu. 'Mao had told it (Liu's case team) he wanted a spy charge. … A large number of other people were imprisoned and interrogated, to try to turn up evidence against him. … Shi Zhe, who had interpreted for Liu with Stalin … was pressed to say that Liu was a Russian spy. … American Sidney Rittenberg … had known Mme Liu in the 1940s. Pressure was put on him to say that he had recruited her, and Liu, for American intelligence' (p. 555). Jung Chang does not mention any torture being used. 'The team … found itself in a Catch-22 situation, as concocting evidence could be as dangerous as failing to unearth it. On one occasion, the team claimed that Liu had wanted American troops to invade China in 1946, and that Liu had wanted to see President Truman about this. "Making such a claim", Mao said, "is … to treat us like fools. America sending in troops en masse: even the Nationalists did not want that"' (p. 555). The result: Liu was not charged as a spy.

Jung Chang does not show at any point that Mao allowed his team to use torture to obtain evidence or imposed charges without evidence, although his evidence was often proved to be faulty.

The points made in this section are sufficient to refute Jung Chang's likening of Mao to Hitler. In fact, it is easy to find counter-arguments to most, if not all, of Jung Chang's claims throughout the book. It simply requires a careful reading and the application of reason.

To expose the numerous contradictions and inconsistencies in Jung Chang's book, no specific knowledge or information about China is necessary. The question is: why cannot the Western journalists and China experts see this? It is hard to believe that they are incapable of logical thinking, or have not read the book carefully. The most plausible explanation? Their profound anti-Chinese prejudice.

Appendix A: Jung Chang, the well-known story

According to *Wild Swans*, Jung Chang was sent to a rural area in western Sichuan after graduating from high school in 1969, a fate shared by millions of Chinese youths at the time. What made Jung Chang special is that she stayed there for only 26 days. She was then transferred to the suburbs of Chengdu as a result of the forging of a number of documents, an act most Chinese youths would not have even contemplated, especially those whose families were allegedly under 'persecution'. Although officially resident in the Chengdu suburbs, Jung Chang actually stayed there for only about one third of the time, and seldom joined other city youths and peasants in farm work. In 1971, Jung Chang's mother used her connections to get her a job in a state-owned firm in Chengdu, the best option a Sichuan youth could have hoped for at the time. After the universities reopened, in 1973 Jung Chang's mother arranged a place for her in Sichuan University's Department of Foreign Language, an ideal place, especially for those not good at science. This sort of 'going through back doors' marked the beginning of communist corruption in China. After Jung Chang's graduation, her mother helped her get a job at the university by blocking her return to the company that had sent her to study, to which under normal circumstances she would have been expected to revert. The chance to study abroad came in 1978, when Jung Chang's mother used her influence to secure it for her daughter, who would otherwise not have been qualified.

Appendix B: Miscarriage of the Chinese version of *Mao: The Unknown Story*

Quoted from Wanwei website, 23 April 2006.[3]

- The Yuanliu Publishing House in Taiwan has decided to abandon its original plan to publish a Chinese version of Jung Chang's *Mao: The Unknown Story*.
- The president of Yuanliu, Wang Rongwen, says that the editor and authors cannot reach an agreement to modify the book to make its descriptions more neutral. He expects the evidence in the book to be reliable, while the evidence in Jung Chang's book is insufficient to convince him.
- The publication was originally planned for around the end of 2005, later postponed to April and to May 2006.
- The historian Li Yongzhong from Taiwan and the bibliographer Hu Zhiwei from Hong Kong claim that the failure of the book's publication 'represents a victory for true history over false history'.

- A fellow of the Academy of Social Science in Taiwan, Xu Zhuoyun, says the book is not academic, although it was unfortunately regarded as such. He even considers the book to be basically garbage, and believes that it is not necessary to publish garbage to protect the freedom of the press.
- The director of the History Institute of the Academy, Chen Yung-fa, says the relation between Jung Chang's conclusions and her evidence is weak, so the book cannot be treated as an academic work. He sees it as 'a popular book with an academic background'.

Part V
Other reviews

13 Mao lives

Arthur Waldron

First published in *Commentary*, October 2005.

The twentieth century was remarkable not only for the number and scale of the atrocities it witnessed but also for the slowness with which these frightful events were recognized for what they were, let alone condemned. Of these crimes, which began with the mass murders by Lenin and Stalin in the USSR (costing over 20 million lives) and continued through the Nazi Holocaust and the democides in China and Cambodia, only the Nazi horror is regularly acknowledged and truly well known. The others are still primarily the province of specialists.

This is particularly the case with the crimes of Mao Zedong, the founder in 1949 of the People's Republic of China and, until his death in 1976, its supreme ruler. China has never repudiated Mao as Khrushchev did Stalin at the party congress of 1956. Embalmed in Tiananmen Square, he remains today the final source of legitimacy for the government in Beijing. Nor, with honourable exceptions, have Western scholars ever dealt with Mao as at least some did with Lenin and Stalin. Today, no one in his right mind would put a portrait of Hitler in his house. Yet, in many places in the West, Mao kitsch – posters, badges, busts, and so forth – is still considered not only acceptable but even fashionable. One reason, perhaps, is that Mao Zedong was introduced to the world stage as a hero. He made his first appearance – as a genial and modest man who happened also to be a dedicated social revolutionary – in a long interview with the American journalist Edgar Snow. The interview, which took place at the communist party's headquarters in a remote corner of northwest China, formed the core of Snow's book, *Red Star Over China*, which has been continuously in print ever since its first appearance in 1936.[1] Nearly all subsequent accounts descend, in one way or another, from his.

Mao was forty-two when he met Snow. As he told the American journalist, he had been born to a farming family in the south-central province of Hunan, spent a rebellious childhood and youth, attended a teachers' college, and helped to found the Chinese Communist Party.

What Mao grasped, in this account, was that communism could succeed in China only if it stood with the hundreds of millions of impoverished rural dwellers rather than (as the party's real leadership in Moscow had insisted) with the relative handful of China's industrial workers. So, from the start, Mao's communism contained a strong admixture of indigenous elements. This remarkable and, as it seemed, durable blending of traditional elements with modernity (in its communist form) held a powerful appeal for many Chinese whose sense of identity had been shattered by the ending of the old order when the last dynasty abdicated in 1912.

Naturally, Mao's liberationist intentions also alarmed the class of rural landlords and 'gentry' who supported the then central government of Chiang Kai-shek at Nanjing. Chiang and his allies mounted five 'extermination campaigns' against the base areas of the communists. The fifth, planned with German assistance, would have finished them (so the standard story goes) had not Mao led a brilliant break-out, the celebrated 'Long March', that moved through the most remote areas a step ahead of the pursuing Nationalists, fighting valiantly when attacked and eventually escaping to the security of the northwest, where Snow recorded Mao's stirring account.

Then came World War II, when – according to the received version – the communists were the only Chinese really willing to fight the Japanese. (Chiang Kai-shek himself was supposedly much more interested in fighting Mao.) It was then that Mao led a great revolutionary upsurge that, translated into a mighty military force, helped not only to drive the Japanese back but to sweep him and his followers to power in the ensuing civil war of 1945–49. Snow later told this story, too, though its most eloquent and influential version came from the pen of the late Barbara Tuchman.

In *Stilwell and the American Experience in China, 1911–1945* (1971) and other writings, Tuchman argued that, in supporting Chiang's Nationalists, the United States had backed the wrong horse in China. This is the so-called 'Lost Chance in China' school, whose adherents believe to this day that a different US policy would not only have spared us future conflicts with China over Korea, Vietnam and the Taiwan Strait but would have changed Mao himself. Aligned with the US (as he wished) instead of with the USSR (as we forced him to become), he would have ruled China in a far more democratic and pro-Western fashion.

Even aligned with the USSR, however, Mao in power continued to be viewed favourably by most Western scholars and commentators. To be sure, confiscating and redistributing land from the rich to the poor involved bloodshed, as did the cleaning-up of such notoriously lawless cities as Shanghai. Mao also attacked the educated, even some who had supported him, as in the Hundred Flowers campaign of the mid-1950s when criticism of the regime was invited but then crushed as soon as it crossed certain boundaries. Later, in the Great Leap Forward (1959–61), he attempted to substitute China's abundant manpower for its limited capital in order to make possible a rapid growth of the economy, unfortunately causing widespread death by starvation in the process. Towards the end of his life, worried by the near-extinction of the revolutionary flame in the Soviet Union, he launched the Great Proletarian Cultural Revolution (1965–76) in which marginalized groups, above all students and young people, were encouraged to run riot against entrenched authority. These blemishes were duly noted, though never the scale of death and destruction they entailed. Always, Mao was seen as searching for new ways to build socialism, and on these grounds much if not everything could be forgiven him.² In 1955, Simone de Beauvoir judged that 'the power [Mao] exercises is no more dictatorial than, say, Roosevelt's was'; in 1972, Jean-Paul Sartre hailed his 'revolutionary violence'.

In the academic world, Mao's achievements were extolled while the alternatives offered by the rival Nationalists, or by parties calling for parliamentary democracy, or by refugee critics were dismissed as hopeless dead ends. Scholars who dissented often paid with their careers. Certainly, it was concluded, Mao had shed blood as he 'reformed' the system, and he had often shown a hard, authoritarian hand. But given the results, who could cavil? As the influential Harvard professor John K. Fairbank observed in 1972 on returning from a visit, 'The Maoist revolution is on the whole the best thing that has happened to the Chinese people in centuries'.

Something like this view is still very widespread, among both specialists and the broader public. No American textbook of Chinese history classes Mao with Stalin, or with Hitler. Nor has any foreign leader since the 1960s ever spoken out against the evils of Chinese communism with anything like the forthrightness showed by some towards the Soviet Union. Today, though Mao's legacy is still very much in evidence in China, the European Union is eager to end the trade embargo put in place after the Tiananmen Square massacre of 1989 and to begin selling advanced weapons systems to the communist regime. Israel has long been a supplier of weaponry to Beijing (though this may be changing). American companies, including Loral, Boeing and Microsoft, have provided important assistance to China's military programmes and to its suppression of free speech and access to information on the Internet. Although the overwhelming majority of the world's unfree people live in China, ordinary visitors, cocooned in its luxurious new hotels, are largely unaware of the brutality around them, or, if they are aware, console themselves with the thought that, repressive trends notwithstanding, commerce and trade will eventually transform things for the better.

They need to think again. Luckily, to aid their thinking, they can now turn to *Mao: The Unknown Story*, a bombshell of a book that quickly soared to first place on the best-seller lists of Britain and has recently been released here. Its author is Jung Chang (born in China in 1952), writing in collaboration with her husband Jon Halliday (born in Ireland in 1939). Halliday, an excellent stylist, is proficient in Russian and other languages and was for a brief time the editor of the British *New Left Review*. Chang, who lives in England, has been known till now mainly for *Wild Swans* (1991), a brilliantly fictionalized story of three generations of women in her own family: her grandmother, a concubine whose feet were bound; her mother, initially an enthusiastic communist but later disillusioned; and herself, who grew up in the violence and anarchy of the Cultural Revolution, during which she worked as a 'barefoot doctor' in the poverty-stricken countryside while her mother was sent to a detention camp and her father was driven mad. *Mao: The Unknown Story* is no ordinary book. Reaching for comparisons, one looks inescapably to Alexander Solzhenitsyn's *Gulag Archipelago*. His was not the first negative account of Soviet communism, and *Mao* is not the first book to present Mao and his collaborators as criminals. But like the *Gulag*, *Mao*, while factual, is much more than that; resting on a mass of evidence, overwhelmingly accurate and well-supported, it conveys its story in the voice not of the bloodless scholar but of the novelist and the moralist. Already Beijing is terrified of this book, going so far as to ban an issue of the *Far Eastern Economic Review* that contained an account of it. But we can be certain that pirated copies will soon be circulating in China, if they are not doing so already. Chang and Halliday may not be the first to expose Mao's crimes, but their work, even with its limitations (of which more below), cannot be ignored. Like Solzhenitsyn's *Gulag Archipelago*, it delivers a death blow to an entire way of thinking.

The Mao who emerges from the pages of Chang and Halliday's book is in every way repellent. He is an ignorant, power-obsessed, manipulative and cruel mass murderer.

To begin with, the authors show, Mao was an ignoramus, hostile to learning and to intellectuals. A drifter as a youth, he evinced talent but refused the discipline of study, including the 'classics of Marxism-Leninism' that his contemporaries mastered as their fathers had mastered classical Chinese literature. Unlike many of those who rose to the top of the communist hierarchy, he never studied abroad, nor did he travel outside China until after he had taken power – and then only to Moscow, which formed his idea of 'the West'. The antique editions of Chinese classics shelved at the head of his enormous bed, which so impressed visitors to his inner sanctum and photographs of which were studied by Western intelligence agencies for clues to his 'thought', were mostly plundered from the libraries of doomed scholars and arranged for show.

Mao's hatred of learning was coupled with a passion to destroy China's cultural heritage. In 1949, when he came to power, the Mongol-Ming-Qing capital of Beijing was still intact, with its massive dressed stone walls and gates, its hundreds of temples, its traditional courtyard houses with their exquisite tile roofs, its memorial arches or *pailou*, and its distinct drama, cuisine, customs and traditions. Everything had survived the war with Japan; were it extant today, it would constitute one of the world's most magnificent historical sites.

But Mao decreed its obliteration. In 1958, on the eve of his campaign, roughly 8,000 historical monuments were listed as still standing in the capital. Mao planned to keep only 78 of them; most were destroyed.

Ignorant himself, Mao saw to it that others were kept ignorant as well. Contrary to widespread Western belief, he spent less on the education of his countrymen than had his predecessors. He also ruthlessly limited access to learning. His policy, write Chang and Halliday, 'was not to raise the general standard of education in society as a whole, but to focus on a small elite, predominantly in science and other "useful" subjects.' All other Chinese were to remain 'illiterate or semi-literate slave labourers'. As for Mao's obsession with power, from his earliest days in the communist party he sought control for himself and the physical elimination of those who opposed him. Already in the 1920s he was murdering his colleagues and driving his subordinates to death, gradually consolidating his own position by a series of conspiracies and betrayals. The most important of these took place on the Long March. As Chang and Halliday demonstrate, the received version of this hegira is a myth. Whole episodes, including the great battle at the flaming bridge at Dadu, are inventions. Mao's main purpose, as the authors see it, was less to save the communist party than to cripple the far more numerous and effective forces of Zhang Guotao, a gifted communist general whom Mao was supposed to relieve but whom he left utterly exposed and weakened, thus enabling his own takeover.

By far the most interesting revelation in this section of the book is the authors' account of the paramountcy of Soviet influence in the establishment and growth of the Chinese communist movement. Traditionally, this movement has been portrayed as an indigenous force, and one whose alignment with Moscow was a matter only of expediency. In fact, according to Chang and Halliday, from its foundation (by a Comintern agent) to its financing, communications system, leadership and strategy, the party was an agent of Soviet policy – even when that policy conflicted with the Chinese national interest. Stalin early on recognised in Mao the combination of ambition, intelligence and ruthlessness that would, so he imagined, serve the USSR better than the slavishly orthodox Marxism of many of Mao's Chinese rivals.

The subordination of Chinese to Soviet interests was clearest in the conflict with Japan during World War II. Like Chiang Kai-shek, Mao recognized that war with Japan would be a disaster for China. But Stalin, fearing a Japanese invasion of the USSR from the east, wanted it, and Mao quickly grasped how it would serve his own purposes. By permitting the Japanese to destroy Chiang's forces while simultaneously helping to keep the USSR strong, he would be well placed to supplant Chiang as Chinese leader. Hence, according to Chang and Halliday, the successful effort by communists in the military to start such a war, and hence Mao's decision – again utterly contrary to received myth – to sit it out.

Of course some patriotic Chinese communists could not swallow this, but Mao saw to them, too. At his redoubt in Yan'an, and helped by the ghoulish secret-police expert Kang Sheng, he carried out purges of a number who threatened his will, dispatching them to a state-of-the-art torture facility called the 'Date Garden'. (Well-known to locals, this place is not mentioned by any of the Westerners who visited Mao and his wartime capital.) Over the following decades, he systematically eliminated others, with many finally perishing in the Cultural Revolution three decades later.

Mao was a consummate manipulator. With solid documentation, Chang and Halliday argue that the Hundred Flowers campaign, in which critics of the regime spoke out only to be arrested, was not a product of miscalculation (as it is presented in accounts by Mao's sympathizers) but a carefully laid trap. Similarly, the disastrous Great Leap Forward grew not out of a Marxist fascination with industrialization but out of Mao's determination to extract food from the Chinese people to pay for weapons imports and gifts to foreign leaders. The Cultural Revolution, finally, which the authors rightly call 'the great purge', had nothing to do with renewing an ossified party and everything to do with simple revenge. One of the most striking examples of Mao's manipulative skills was on display in the early 1970s in connection with the Nixon administration's 'opening' to China. This, too, we learn here, was a carefully baited trap, and entirely Mao's idea rather than Washington's. By the time Nixon arrived for his famous visit in February 1972, he was convinced that, as between himself and Mao, 'he was the keener of the two'. But by then Henry Kissinger had already made his own secret visit in July 1971 as Nixon's national security adviser, bearing 'many and weighty gifts and ask[ing] for nothing in return'. Not only did Kissinger offer Taiwan on a platter, write Chang and Halliday, but he promised an American withdrawal from both Vietnam and Korea.

The Mao of *The Unknown Story* is also, like many a tyrant, deeply insecure and fearful. Arriving outside Beijing in 1949, he fell into a crisis of anxiety before daring to enter the city and seize power. A superstitious man, he never once set foot in the Forbidden City where the emperors had lived, even though his residence adjoined it. Wherever he went, bombproof villas were built and staffed. He kept himself far from the public, making use later in his career of a system of tunnels linking his residence, the Great Hall of the People, with military headquarters in the western suburbs.

Mao delighted in personal cruelty. He tortured the women around him, including his four successive wives. When Zhou Enlai, the most popular member of the regime, was diagnosed with bladder cancer, Mao ordered that he be neither told of the condition nor treated for it; even as Zhou was engaged in vital negotiations with the United States, Mao toyed with his loyal servant to ensure that he would die painfully.[3]

Most importantly, Mao was the greatest mass murderer of the twentieth century. Much of the killing was direct, as in the torture and purges at Yan'an. After the communist seizure of power in 1949, the practice became countrywide. Mao set his numerical targets openly, and stressed the 'revolutionary' importance of killing. In 1954, citing the 'softness' of his counterparts in communist Eastern Europe when it came to the need to 'eliminate all those counterrevolutionaries', he urged his inner circle: 'We must kill. ... And we say it's good to kill'.

He was as good as his word. Millions were liquidated in the first years of his tyranny alone. Later, during the famine of 1959–61, which the authors blame above all on Mao's confiscation of crops from the countryside, something on the order of 50 million people died – men, women, children, infants. Cannibalism was not uncommon. Yet Mao continued to enjoy Lucullan repasts, served by his half-starved staff.

And so it went. Chang and Halliday's careful estimate is that by the time of his death in 1976, Mao had been responsible all in all for the death of some 70 million Chinese.

No reader can be unmoved by this book's passion, or unimpressed by the mountain of evidence upon which it rests. The Chinese say that it takes 'ten years to hone a sword', which understates by two years the amount of time Chang and Halliday have laboured over this work. Halliday spent a decade in non-Chinese archives, including those of the Comintern in Moscow and the East-European communist parties; from this has come much new factual information, as well as a clearer view of the control exercised by the Soviet Union over both the Nationalist and the communist parties in China in the first half of the century. The unadorned and readable English prose is evidently also Halliday's, though one can sense his wife's mind behind much of it. As for Chang, she did all the Chinese research and carried out the hundreds of interviews with people in China and around the world who were personally acquainted with Mao or had knowledge of him. Specialists, of course, will have criticisms to make, some of them justified. Neither author is trained in Sinology. This is an advantage – unburdened by the inheritance of the field, they offer a new and fresh look, naïve in the best sense of the word. But it is also a disadvantage. One searches in vain for certain staples of the mainstream literature about Mao, which, whatever its flaws, has established facts and raised issues that must be addressed.[4]

Perhaps surprisingly in light of their own previous immersion in Marxist categories (compulsory, in Chang's case), we find in *Mao* no real discussion of social or cultural forces. Instead, the human actor is everything. There is only conspiracy after conspiracy, each turning, as in the traditional Chinese novels of which Mao was so fond, on deception, betrayal, espionage and a cold assessment of the strengths and weaknesses of other individuals.

This stress on conspiracy and personal politics to the exclusion of nearly everything else is a weakness, perhaps the greatest weakness, of Chang and Halliday's account. Many men, after all, are evil and want power, but only a handful are successful in gaining and holding it and in somehow making their people collude with them in their crimes. In mitigation, one can say that the stress on personal action and conspiracy provides a useful counterweight to the opposite, Western tendency to impose social-science theory onto a Chinese reality that it does not fit and where it does not belong. Nevertheless, there is more to the story.

Specialists will also be puzzled by specific aspects of Chang and Halliday's account (for instance, of the 1945–49 civil war, or of Mao's struggle with Nikita Khrushchev over the Taiwan Strait). And both specialists and general readers will wonder how the authors always know what Mao is thinking – even during the Long March, or on his deathbed (when his mind 'stirred with just one thought: himself and his power').

But none of this should distract us from the basic fact: this is the book that will wreck Mao's reputation beyond salvage. Taken whole, the indictment is too formidable to be dismissed, and any attempt at detailed refutation will inevitably pose even more awkward questions and disclose even more unsavoury facts, thus dragging Mao ever more deeply into the mud.

That it is long past time for such an airing should go without saying. As I indicated early on, Chang and Halliday are not the first to expose Mao Zedong as one of the greatest criminals in human history: a few non-Chinese scholars and journalists had the courage in decades past to follow the facts where they led. More recently, their work has been vindicated (and the work of their 'mainstream' colleagues discredited) by Chinese scholars like Chen Jian, who in *Mao's China and the Cold War* (2001) has given an authoritative account of Chinese foreign policy that matches Chang and Halliday's, and by eyewitnesses like Mao's personal physician, Dr Li Zhisui, whose *Private Life of Chairman Mao* (1994) presented the human, or more accurately the inhuman, Mao for the first time. The many dissidents within today's China have likewise kept up a steady flow of documents and news in spite of the government's best efforts to silence them.

But this brings us back to the question of Western attitudes. Evidence to indict Mao has always been adequate, if not abundant. Shamefully, however, many China specialists and others with access to information actively protected themselves from this evidence, lest it undermine the fantasy of a humane, caring leader. As with early word of the Holocaust, reports of the desperate situation in China during the 1959–61 famine caused by Mao were ignored or buried. When Mao died on 9 September 1976, *The New York Times* ran a triple banner headline and a two-page obituary that drew on much received wisdom, neglecting or dismissing the mounting evidence that contradicted it.

So *Mao: The Unknown Story* is not only a formidable but a necessary achievement: a full and convincing portrait of the destruction of tens of millions of innocent lives and the near-destruction of a civilization by a consummately evil man. Nevertheless, something is still missing, and that something has to do with what comes next. Does this atrocity, from which we can no longer turn away, have any significance beyond its own sheer horror, and does it call for any action on our part and on the part of the Chinese themselves? On this the book is silent, but of course the answer is yes.

The first action that is called for is to discover the names of the dead, locate their remains, and honour them – as has been done in exemplary fashion for the victims of the Holocaust and as is beginning to be done for the victims of communism in Russia and elsewhere in Eastern Europe. China, however, is not only far from having initiated such a process, it completely forbids any activity of the kind. No books published in China acknowledge Mao's evil; no monuments commemorate the dead. Letters to the authorities from the mothers of students killed by the Chinese army in Tiananmen Square on 4 June 1989 are never answered.

Having honoured the dead, we must then seek to understand. Chang and Halliday describe the evil man, but never attempt to probe the origins of his evil or to explain why it spread through Chinese society. Not that this is an easy task. Writing in criticism of Hannah Arendt's interpretation of the Holocaust, for example, Hillel Halkin has recently observed that although the Holocaust may have been, as she stipulated, 'the work of bureaucrats', these were bureaucrats whose 'minds were formed by the Germany of the Weimar Republic, and of the Kaiser, and of the Christian churches. If they were easily persuaded that the Jews deserved to die, this persuasion came from an older Germany'.[5] Here in other words is an effort to get beyond Arendt's mechanistic approach to some appreciation of a living human society, and to understand Hitler as something more than a devil who mysteriously parachuted in to bewitch the German people.

Proposing an analogous social or intellectual explanation for the willingness of the Chinese people to serve as Mao's slaves, to kill and to denounce one another, is an even more difficult task – and Chang and Halliday do not address it. Where in late-Qing or Republican Chinese society would one find the roots of democide? Where in traditional Chinese philosophy is the justification for mass murder? Some of the necessary ingredients were surely imported with Marxism, but that simply begs the question of how Marxism acquired its authority and why so many Chinese accepted it. These problems cry out for pondering.

Nor is that the end of it. Given the bloody morass through which Chang and her husband lead us, it would be comforting in the extreme to know that the evil in Mao died with his body, and that China has been freed from it. But that is emphatically not the case. Mao died in 1976. Thirty years on, there is still no happy ending. To be sure, China has changed – in appearance, feel, atmosphere, economic condition, and so forth. Maoist and post-Maoist China are admittedly very different. But they are also profoundly similar.

And that is the final point. Mao's atrocities are not simply of historical interest, but remain central to today's China – and to our dealings with it. As the authors write in a two-sentence 'Epilogue', 'Today, Mao's portrait and his corpse still dominate Tiananmen Square in the heart of the Chinese capital. The current communist regime declares itself to be Mao's heir and fiercely perpetuates the myth of Mao'.

Mao is, indeed, still revered in China as the wise and heroic founder of the People's Republic. There has never been any public criticism of him remotely comparable to Khrushchev's 1956 speech condemning Stalin. Not only does Mao's embalmed corpse, with its guard of honour, lie in the midst of Tiananmen Square, visited daily by throngs of Chinese who form long lines to pay their respects. Not only does his portrait continue to hang at the Gate of Heavenly Peace a few steps from the Forbidden City, the traditional centre of the Chinese cosmos. In addition, the deep structure of today's China remains as Mao made it.

Rule in China is as arbitrary and capricious as ever under Mao. The only difference is that a single man is no longer in total charge; what is theoretically still the absolute power of the party is now divided among perhaps twenty people, all lacking Mao's intelligence and skill and most working at cross purposes with each other. China is not ruled by its constitution or by its laws, nor do courts actually resolve disputes, even in the realm of commerce with foreign countries.

None of today's Chinese leaders has been chosen according to the rules of the constitution, or even according to the rules of the communist party. Hu Jintao is in charge because Deng Xiaoping named him to follow Jiang Zemin, himself selected after the 4 June 1989 massacre to replace Zhao Ziyang, who was illegally removed and placed under strict house arrest (lasting until his death earlier this year). And how did Deng become leader? By means of a military conspiracy that ousted Mao's designated and party-approved successors.

Like Mao, today's rulers are hypocrites, proclaiming concern for the poor and disenfranchized even as they steal state assets and live lives of luxury. But now the parasitical class of Chinese communists is much larger than in Mao's day, and so is the gap between their lives and the lives of ordinary Chinese, whether rural or urban. While desperate poverty and exploitation remain widespread, party members enjoy a privileged existence comparable only to Mao's, even as they send their children and grandchildren, along with their ill-gotten assets, overseas for safekeeping. What of the formation of government policy? Again, it would be pleasant to report that decision-making in China has become more rational since the demise of Mao, who regularly ordered up insane projects like the destruction of the old city of Peking, or the backyard 'steel' furnaces of the Great Leap Forward, or, in the days of the Sino-Soviet split, the building of immense and useless barriers outside the capital to defend against Soviet tanks. Have Mao's followers done any better with the Three Gorges Dam, or the huge concrete aqueducts intended to divert water from the south to the parched north, or the slash-and-burn industrialization (as it has been called) with its profligate waste of resources and its utter neglect of sustainability?

When it comes to China's dynamic economy, moreover, it is by no means clear that the current, export-driven approach to growth will lift China's poor, let alone help to create a society in which they will be able freely to exercise their talents and energies. Foreign markets now take the place of domestic demand (as they must, for most Chinese have little buying power), and foreign companies are invited not to enrich but to exploit a disciplined labour force under conditions in which any talk of unions or complaints about working conditions are dealt with by the secret police. Labour is kept cheap in China by the government's manipulation of the currency, and capital, the precious savings of the wretchedly poor, is wasted by state-directed bank loans to money-losing state enterprises. Chinese entrepreneurs are being squeezed out by privileged state firms on one side and privileged foreign investors on the other. Water is scarce and polluted, and the air in many places is unbreathable.

Nor does China's foreign policy make more sense now than it did under Mao, at least in terms of the Chinese national interest. To the contrary, post-Mao China has, exactly like Mao's China, poured billions into weapons procurement while ignoring the plight of its people, especially in the countryside. The difference is that the jets and rockets and tanks produced by Mao's militarization did not work. The ones that contemporary China is purchasing, or is building with extensive foreign help, do, threatening the rest of Asia as it never was threatened even under Mao.

Violence continues in today's China: everyday killings by police and untold numbers of deaths in prisons and camps, the victims rarely named and never officially mourned. Censorship, too, remains very tight, with newspapers, radio and television owned and operated exclusively by the government and the party. Vast sums have been spent on advanced equipment to read and track Internet traffic and block sites of which the dictators do not approve. Surveillance by closed-circuit television and the tapping of telephones is blanket in Beijing. Overseas, extensive networks of secret police monitor not only dissidents, students and others but also Internet and telephone traffic in North America and elsewhere. Indoctrination, now stressing xenophobic nationalism rather than Mao's version of communism, is still rampant.

Sadly, we are not soon likely to witness in China anything like the moral clarity of Alexander Yakovlev, once a servant of the Soviet regime, then the 'godfather of perestroika', and now the man entrusted with the task of memorializing the great Soviet purges and the Gulag archipelago. Yakovlev's succinct (and radically understated) verdict on both Lenin and Stalin is this: 'By every norm of international law, posthumously indictable for crimes against humanity'. As Chang and Halliday demonstrate, that fits Mao, too – in spades.

Unfortunately, however, the world is just beginning an honest reconsideration of

Mao Zedong and his poisonous legacy, and China, still Maoist at the root, shows no inclination of moving in that direction at all. The government remains in absolute denial, and, as best as it can, it keeps its people ignorant. Chang and Halliday have given a mighty push, but there are still many to mourn, and many to punish, and much to fear.

14 From *Wild Swans* to *Mao: The Unknown Story*

Bill Willmott

Chang Jung was born and grew up in my hometown, Chengdu, Sichuan. Her first book, *Wild Swans*, was universally acclaimed and widely read. The biography of three generations of women, it provided an excellent social history of the Chinese Revolution through six decades of the twentieth century. A friend from Chengdu told me that Chang, as the daughter of a high communist party official, suffered far less than ordinary people during the 'three bad years' after Mao proclaimed the Great Leap Forward, but that privilege did not carry through to the Cultural Revolution. Chang joined the Red Guards as a fervent disciple of Mao, but when her parents were destroyed so unjustly, her worship changed to hate, and for her Mao became a monster. That is where her biography of Mao starts and finishes.

There are many biographies of Mao, and a list of some is attached. My favourites are Jonathan Spence's *Mao*, written in elegant prose, as are all his books, and Jerome Ch'ên's *Mao and the Chinese Revolution*, not merely because my father taught him English in Chengdu but because it received such excellent reviews when it was published in 1965. Stuart Schram, the top Western authority on Mao and his thought, has written several books on Mao, the most useful of which is *The Political Thought of Mao Tse-tung*, which puts all Mao's writings into their historical and biographical context.

The worst of the biographies, in my opinion, are those that set out to prove a thesis. The first two books of Han Suyin's trilogy, for example, are almost hagiographic in their praise of Mao, while in contrast the very title of Horvath's *Emperor of the Blue Ants* suggests that it's written with a very negative thesis. Similarly, Chang and Halliday are intent on showing Mao to be a psychopathic monster, and their book is full of venomous demonstration of this central idea. When the authors were asked in a public meeting in Christchurch last year if there was anything positive they found about Mao, Chang replied, 'Not one single thing'. Anyone who has visited China recently will find it hard to believe that among the 200 interviews they conducted in China, no one mentioned a single thing positive about Mao!

This is not an easy book to read. It's very long: 655 pages plus bibliographies, index and 67 pages of notes. Checking notes and sources for each fact can be exasperating, as there are no footnotes and one must find the note for each statement and then refer to the bibliography. Having done all that, I conclude that this book represents very bad scholarship, for three reasons:

1   The authors start from a firm conviction that Mao is evil, and they select sources and interpret them from that point of view.
2   The book lacks basic scholarly judgement in that the authors did not test their sources by triangulation. Those supporting the thesis are reproduced as fact, while those opposing it are ignored.
3   The book lacks historical perspective in not providing the social and politi-cal context of the events it chronicles. This reduces the history of the Chinese Revolution to the evil motivations of a single man. In my opinion, this is the most serious fault of this book, given that both authors have some familiarity with China.

I do not want to underestimate the importance of this book. It is the first to use the Soviet archives, opened to scholars only recently and carefully studied by Jon Halliday, an expert on Eastern European languages (he is a linguist, not an historian). Furthermore, it represents a huge amount of research, so it brings together just about everything there is to know about Mao, perhaps even more than one would wish to know (do we really need to read that Mao suffered from under-arm odour and constipation?). Professor Jeffrey Wasserstrom, after damning the authors for 'crossing the line between biography and fiction', suggests that the book should not be ignored but read in tandem with other accounts of Mao's life.

1 Negative thesis

It is certainly not surprising that the authors began their research with such a neg-ative view of Mao. As we learned from *Wild Swans*, Chang began the Cultural Revolution as an enthusiastic Red Guard who worshipped Mao and became disillusioned when it destroyed her parents, both of whom were exemplary com-munist leaders, and then almost ruined her own life. In her mind, Mao shifted from demi-god to devil, and she believed him personally responsible for all the dreadful aspects of the Cultural Revolution.

Similarly, Halliday supported the Cultural Revolution and publicly praised Mao as late as 1973. He later married Chang and adopted her views on China.

Francesco Sisci, veteran China reporter for *La Stampa*, was quoted in the *Melbourne Age* (8 October 2005) as saying, 'You don't feel cold analysis in the book, you feel hatred'. Fred Teiwes, professor of Chinese history at Sydney University and no friend of Mao, said when he met Chang, 'She just had her views so set and was unwilling to entertain other opinions or inconvenient evidence. ... [T]o paint him as a totally monstrous personality who just goes out to kill people and protect his power at all costs is not only over the top but a bit crazy in terms of what actually went on' (ibid.).

For Chang and Halliday, Mao was 'absolute selfishness and irresponsibility', without conscience, whose only motivation was personal power. His actions are explained by his love of killing and destruction, and his wide support was gained entirely through blackmail and manipulation.

There are, of course, many accounts from people who met him that contradict this view of Mao. Edgar Snow described him as shrewd and ruthless but 'quite free from symptoms of megalomania' with a lively sense of humour and boyish laughter (1938, p. 74 f.). *The Far Eastern Economic Review*'s Beijing correspondent Susan Lawrence describes her Chinese grandmother's memories of meeting Mao in Yan'an during the Sino-Japanese war: 'She remembers how approachable he was, and how genuinely he inquired about their strenuous two-month-long journey there. She was particularly grateful at the way he effortlessly charmed my mother, then a restless 17-month-old baby, by turning his full attention to her and gently teasing her in his Hunan brogue' (*Far Eastern Economic Review*, 20 January 2000).

Selective sources

Starting their research with this strongly negative view, the authors have selected their sources to ignore those that would contradict it. For example, Jerome Ch'ên's detailed account of Mao's childhood includes five sources not cited by Chang and Halliday. In particular, a book by Li Jui that Ch'ên identifies as 'extremely important' and 'well documented' is also used by Stuart Schram in his biography of Mao. It contains positive stories of Mao's youth, including an incident when he collected some debts owed his father and then gave the money to a poor peasant. At another time, when bad weather threatened the harvest, Mao helped poor tenants reap their grain instead of working in his father's fields.

Chang and Halliday state (pp. 8–9) that there is 'no evidence' that Mao had any concern for the poor peasants. Since most of his programmes were specifically aimed at improving the lot of the poor peasants, from land reform through to collectivization, this is surprising to say the least. In supporting this claim, they ignore key sources and reject Mao's own words. Indeed, throughout the book they discount anything Mao has said or written himself.

Incredibly, the authors even ignore their own writings when they contradict their thesis in this book. Chang's negative assessment in *Wild Swans* of Chiang Kai-shek's role in the civil war is not mentioned here, nor is Halliday's earlier and careful analysis of the Korean War.

Interpreting sources

Their characterization of Mao as a psychopathic brute affects how they interpret the sources they do cite. A key example is their use of Mao's marginalia in a philosophy book he read and annotated as a young man. This source has been quoted by other biographers, but Chang and Halliday's choice of quotations and interpretation of them is crucial to their attempt to prove Mao a monster.

While a student at Changsha Teachers' College in 1917–18, Mao (then aged 24) read (in translation) *A System of Ethics*, by Friedrich Paulsen, an obscure German philosopher. Mao's reaction to its Prussian values, as evident in the notes he wrote in the margin of the book (which are still extant), demonstrate his youthful commitment to individual freedom. Without mentioning Paulsen's ethical position as a disciplinarian who emphasized self-control and strong will, Chang and Halliday conclude from the notes that 'Absolute selfishness and irresponsibility lay at the heart of Mao's outlook' (p. 14).

In reading the same notes, both Ch'ên and Schram came to the conclusion that Mao was expressing a rejection of authority, the authority of both tradition and family. Mao wrote:

> Wherever there is repression of the individual, wherever there are acts contrary to the nature of the individual, there can be no greater crime. That is why our country's three bonds must go, and constitute, with religion, capitalism and autocracy, the four evil demons of the empire.
>
> (Schram 1963, p. 13)

'There is, perhaps, in ... Mao's marginal notes something of the activism of the revolutionary who wishes to transform the world'. Schram suggests (1963, p. 13).

Chang and Halliday use Mao's notes on Paulsen to support their view that Mao loved destruction and death. They make this a crucial part of Mao's motivation throughout his life. Where Mao's notes state the revolutionary view that the old must be destroyed to bring in the new, they conclude that 'Mao laid the utmost emphasis on destruction', and they go on to quote Mao as writing that '[p]eople like me long for [the country's, the nation's, mankind's, the universe's] destruction' (p. 15).

Jerome Ch'ên gives a quotation from the same marginalia that puts quite a different slant on Mao's views:

> In the past I worried over the coming destruction of our country, but now I know that fear was unnecessary. I have no doubt that the political system, the characteristics of our people, and the society will change; what I am not yet clear on are the ways in which the changes can be successfully brought about. I incline to believe that a [complete] reconstruction is needed. Let destruction play the role of a mother in giving birth to a new country. The great revolutions of other countries in the past centuries swept away the old and brought forth the new. They were the great changes which resurrected the dead and reconstructed the decayed.
>
> (Ch'ên 1965, p. 44 ff.)

In other words, Mao was a revolutionary whose aim was a new society and who sought the destruction of the old society to bring it in. To describe this as a fixation on destruction is to miss the point of Mao's revolutionary politics.

Chang and Halliday point to the great emphasis in Mao's writing on military matters to demonstrate his cruel and destructive nature. However, Schram shows that this was a preoccupation of all Chinese intellectuals in Mao's day during the

'100 Years of Shame' China suffered at the hands of Western powers and Japan because of its military weakness.

Another example of how this book interprets sources to suit its thesis is Chang and Halliday's treatment of Mao's attitudes towards women. His personal relations with women were appalling, but he early on put women's equality high on the political agenda. In an early article titled 'On Women's Independence', he emphasized the need for women to become economically independent, even that 'women should stockpile necessities for the period of childbirth themselves'. Rather than see this as a materialist view of the foundation of women's equality, Chang and Halliday conclude that 'Mao did not want to have to look after women. He wanted no responsibility towards them' (p. 18). The monster could not see beyond his own selfish needs.

2 Lack of scholarly judgement

Andrew Nathan wrote a long review of this book (republished in this volume) that carefully examines the scholarship it manifests. Nathan is familiar with most of the author's sources including those in Chinese. He shows that at times they have misused sources, misquoted sources, sometimes provided no source for crucial statements, and cited 'anonymous sources' that no one else can check. 'It is clear', he writes, 'that many of Chang and Halliday's claims are based on distorted, misleading or far-fetched use of evidence'.

Several other reviews, some of which I have listed at the end of this article, are equally strong in their attack on the book's poor scholarship. My own assessment of the scholarship is much milder, per force, because I cannot check the sources with such care. Nevertheless, even a casual reader can see that some of their sourcing is dubious. Many statements are accepted without any evident checking for veracity – if and only if they fit the author's thesis. For example, Chiang Kai-shek's statements are accepted without question, while Mao's are rejected. Statements from some of Mao's opponents are quoted without qualification, for example, Zhang Guotao's accounts of inner-party struggles. (Zhang Guotao was a rival leader of the CCP in 1935 and left China for Canada some time later.) Similarly, Liu Shaoqi's widow Wang Guangmei, who lost her husband and suffered humiliation at Maoist hands, is the only source for Mao's motivation in founding the people's communes, suggesting that he 'even toyed with the idea of getting rid of people's names and replacing them with numbers' (p. 453). Their evidence that Mao organized a slaughter within his own ranks at the start of the Long March is a gruesome and uncorroborated account by a deserter living in Hong Kong who had obvious reasons for wanting to put the best light on his own defection.

Some sources appear at first sight to be qualified, but turn out to be rather thin. For example, we seem to have a first-hand account from Sergei Polevoy of an event in 1920 when Mao gave up learning Russian because 'According to Polevoy the other students teased Mao when he could not even master the alphabet' (p. 16). But the notes at the back of the book show that the account came in a telephone conversation with Polevoy's son eighty years after the event.

So poor is the scholarship that Thomas Bernstein, Professor at Columbia University in New York, concluded that 'the book is a major disaster for the contemporary China field' (*Melbourne Age*, 6 October 2005). Most China scholars agree.

3 Lack of historical perspective

According to this book, all twentieth-century Chinese history is simply a monster satisfying his lust for power and destruction. The Chinese Revolution is reduced to a conspiracy without political or social context. This seriously denigrates the Chinese people and their revolution and makes the book a poor source for those wanting to learn some Chinese history. Below, a few examples demonstrate this point.

a) *Soviet conspiracy*

The first is the founding of the Chinese Communist Party (CCP), which Chang and Halliday claim is a Soviet creation (p. 19). This account ignores the political situation in China at the time. A ferment of ideas emerged in the May Fourth Movement that followed the demonstrations in 1919 against the Treaty of Versailles, and Chinese intellectuals across the spectrum were discussing ideas for new organizations. Li Dazhao and Chen Duxiu had organized a Marxist study group at Peking University in 1918, and Cai Hesen proposed in 1920 that a communist party be established independent of the Soviet-led Comintern. In this context, the agents of the Comintern worked with Li and Chen and others on the left.

The conspiracy theory goes so far as to suggest that Mme Sun Yat-sen (Soong Ching-ling), who led the Gung Ho Cooperative movement Rewi Alley worked in, was a Soviet agent (p. 140), that Roosevelt's envoy Lauchlin Currie in 1942 was a Soviet agent (p. 142), and even the British Ambassador, Sir Archibald Clark-Kerr, who enthusiastically supported Rewi Alley's Gung Ho movement during the war, 'had Soviet connections' (p. 141). They quote Clark-Kerr as telling the British government that Zhou Enlai was 'worth all the Nationalists rolled into one', evidence to them that he was pro-Soviet.

b) *1927*

My second example is the events of 1927, when Chiang Kai-shek betrayed the united front and slaughtered some three thousand communists in Shanghai with the help of his colleagues in the criminal Green Gang on the night of 12 April. The best account of these events I have found is in Seagrave's *The Soong Dynasty* (Harper and Row, 1985). Chang and Halliday's account completely ignores the treachery of Chiang's actions, which led to an important redirection of the Chinese Communist Party towards the countryside and Mao's leadership.

Incidentally, Chang and Halliday describe Mao at this time as 'ascend[ing] a beautiful pavilion on the bank of the Yangtze in Wuhan … the Yellow Crane Pavilion' and writing a poem while 'leaning on its carved balustrade' (p. 46). But the Yellow Crane Pavilion burned down in 1884 and was not rebuilt until 1985.

This was the year Mao wrote his report on the peasants in Hunan province, which described the struggles in the countryside and urged communists to support the peasants rather than condemn them as anti-revolutionary. He argued in the report that peasant violence was the only way to break the traditional rural hierarchy that oppressed them. He praised the peasant association for accomplishing in forty days what Sun Yat-sen had never accomplished. Chang and Halliday's summary of this report concentrates entirely on the violence, utterly ignoring the politics, in order to make their point that sadistic Mao 'discovered in himself a love for bloodthirsty thuggery' (p. 41). That this was a crucial turning point in communist policy and focus is not even mentioned.

c) The soviet period

A third example of the authors' lack of historical perspective is their account of the period of the soviets established by the communists in the countryside, 1927–34. In concentrating their entire attention on Mao himself, they miss the complicated political struggles that were going on both in the chaotic country and within the communist party. While a civil war raged between Chiang Kai-shek's army and the communist-led forces, the CCP itself was divided between its underground urban headquarters, which were calling for military assaults on cities, and the rural bases, where Mao and others opposed this policy. Chang and Halliday describe all these events in terms of Mao's self-aggrandisement. That the leadership criticized Mao 'for leaning to the right' and 'not having done enough burning and killing' (Ch'ên 1965, p. 139) is absent from their account, because this point would contradict their view that Mao was a bloodthirsty thug. They even denigrate his efforts to democratize the peasant army through soldiers' committees, describing them as 'a means to curry favour with the troops' by giving them 'a say in the proceeds of looting' (p. 59).

d) The Long March

In describing the four-thousand-mile retreat of Mao's forces from south-eastern China to Yan'an in the north-west in 1935, the authors' aim is to discredit the Long March and particularly Mao's role in it. They write that Mao was carried in a litter the whole way, making light of the fact that he was ill much of the time and too feverish to walk (Ch'ên 1965, p. 192).

Two incidents on the Long March in particular are used to demonstrate their thesis. The first was in Guizhou, when Mao's armies moved in different directions over several weeks, abandoning their direct route into Sichuan and eventually moving west into Yunnan before turning north again. Chang and Halliday explain these manoeuvres entirely in terms of Mao's rivalry with Zhang Guotao, who led a soviet in the eastern hills of Sichuan. According to them, Mao feared linking up with Zhang because he realized Zhang might well wrest the leadership of the party from him, so he waited until Zhang's forces were destroyed and didn't join him until some months later in north-western Sichuan, by which time Mao could control the merger of forces.

Whatever Mao's personal ambitions, there were, in fact, two substantial reasons not to cross into eastern Sichuan. One was that Chiang Kai-shek's armies controlled the north bank of the Yangtze, and crossing its wide waters under Chiang's fire from the high bank would have decimated his forces. The other was that, as he headed north, he learned that Zhang Guotao's soviet had been destroyed and Zhang was already on the move westward himself.

The second incident, most famous of all, is the crossing of the Dadu River at Luding, what Edgar Snow called 'the most critical single incident' of the Long March. With Chiang's forces racing westward to cut them off, Mao's army had to cross a chain bridge guarded by a small force on the other side. With few casualties, they managed to secure the bridge and get their army across before Chiang's main force could reach them. This incident has been glorified into a legend of heroism, which Chang and Halliday wish to destroy. They call the story 'complete invention. There was no battle at the Dadu Bridge' (p. 159). Their key source is an eyewitness: a 93-year-old woman they interviewed in 1997 who told them hardly a shot was fired. Chang and Halliday claim that Chiang Kai-shek deliberately held back his troops to let Mao's army cross.

In October 2005, the *Melbourne Age* sent reporters to Luding to investigate this remarkable revision, and although they could find no one who remembered a woman fitting the description, they did find a Mrs Li, whom other locals said was the last surviving eyewitness in Luding. Mrs Li told the *Age* that there was indeed a battle for the bridge. Furthermore, Oxford University's Steve Tsang says that the Chiang Kai-shek archives show that Chiang 'did in fact order the senior warlord in the area to hold the crossing on pain of court martial' (*Age*, 8 October 2005). Nathan agrees and adds that none of the other sources Chang and Halliday used for their story can be verified by other scholars.

Two new books on the Long March were published in 2006, both of which quote eyewitnesses of the battle who confirm that it took place, although all accounts differ on the details. They are Andrew McEwen and Ed Jocelyn, *The Long March: The True Story Behind the Legendary March that Made Mao's China*, Constable and Robinson; and Sun Shuyun, *The Long March*, Harper Collins.

e) *The Sino-Japanese War*

Contrary to all other historians, Chang and Halliday claim that the united front between Chiang Kai-shek and the communists was Chiang's idea, initially opposed by the communists. This ignores the fact, not mentioned in their book, that the communist-led 'Soviet Republic' in south-eastern China declared war on Japan in 1932. It also ignores Chang Jung's own statement in *Wild Swans* that Chiang Kai-shek said '[t]he Japanese are a disease of the skin, the communists are a disease of the heart'. It took the Xi'an Incident of 1936, when Chiang was kidnapped by one of his own generals and threatened with death, to convince Chiang to join with the communists to fight the Japanese.

The authors' claim also ignores the fact that Chiang did little to oppose the Japanese throughout the war, keeping his crack troops in the rear to blockade the communist areas and prepare for the civil war he expected once the Americans had defeated the Japanese for him. Western military and diplomatic representatives in wartime Chungking, such as British Ambassador Clark-Kerr and American General Stillwell, were scathing in their criticism of Chiang's war efforts. When I told my brother what Chang and Halliday had written about Chiang, he laughed out loud. He was in the American OSS in Chungking during the war and was privy to American intelligence, including the fact that Chiang had secreted large amounts of American military aid to be used later against the communists.

f) *Korean War*

Among their unusual claims, one of the strangest is their insistence that the Korean War was all a plot by Stalin and Mao. John Foster Dulles, President Truman, General MacArthur – they don't even have bit parts in Chang and Halliday's drama, for it was cooked up by these two twentieth-century monsters between them. Halliday's own important book on the Korean War (Jon Halliday and Bruce Cumings, *Korea: The Unknown War*, 1988) does not even appear in the bibliography, because it contradicts the one-sided thesis presented.

g) *Cambodia*

I add a final, if trivial, example to this list because I know something about it first-hand. On p. 650, the authors say that 'Mao sent Prince Sihanouk ... back to Cambodia' to join Pol Pot in 1972. I interviewed Prince Sihanouk in Beijing in November 1971, when he told me that he had decided to return to Cambodia because he believed that the Khmer Rouge (no one had heard of Pol Pot at that time) were true patriots and would protect his beloved country from Vietnamese domination. Having followed Sihanouk's political life for a decade already, I could see the consistency of his decision, and the suggestion that Mao 'sent him' is preposterous.

From all this, I conclude that this is a bad book. It is not useful for those interested in understanding the Chinese Revolution because of its narrow focus on Mao himself. It is not useful for those who wish to understand Mao because it is too unreliable. As Professor Nathan has demonstrated, the authors' 'white-hot fury' led them to select, misquote and misinterpret sources to such an extent that none of their conclusions can be taken at face value. There are many, far better biographies to deserve our time and money.

Incidentally, Dr Anne-Marie Brady's review in the *Christchurch Press* provides a quite different slant on this book. She argues that the authors could not have gained access to the many sources and interviews unless they were being 'used' by the current Chinese leaders for their own campaign to discredit Mao. I find this difficult to believe, any more than I believe I myself am a 'stooge' of the Chinese communists. Nevertheless, in the book's concerted attempt to exonerate Chiang Kai-shek we can see a fit with current Chinese government statements, closely associated with their policy of wooing the Kuomintang on Taiwan.

The worst aspect of this book, for me, is how it reinforces a negative attitude towards China and the Chinese people. So many people are keen to believe the worst about China, and this book will reinforce their beliefs. Already prejudiced readers will see the Chinese Revolution as nothing more than megalomaniacs killing each other and millions of others. It completely ignores the genuine progress China has made from the backward, poverty-stricken society rife with inhuman exploitation that I knew as a child, one that was described by most Westerners as 'the sick man of Asia', where the standard expression was *meiyou banfa* ('there's no way').

Much of that progress took place under Mao's leadership. Deng Xiaoping, one of Mao's political victims, made this assessment: *Meiyou Mao zhuxi jiu meiyou xin Zhongguo* (Without Chairman Mao, there would be no New China). When my brother visited China in September 2005, he asked an old man in Chengdu what he thought of Mao. His reply: *Ren buhao. Sixiang hao* (Man not good. Thoughts good).

Mao Zedong 1893–1976, a bibliography

Ch'ên, Jerome (1965) *Mao and the Chinese Revolution*, Oxford University Press.
Han Suyin (1972) *The Morning Deluge, Mao Tse-tung and the Chinese Revolution, 1893–1953*, London: Jonathan Cape.
—— (1976) *Wind in the Tower, Mao Tse-tung and the Chinese Revolution, 1949–1975*, London: Jonathan Cape.
—— (1982) *My House Has Two Doors*, London: Triad/Granada.
Hsiao Yu (1959) *Mao and I Were Beggars*, Syracuse NY: Syracuse University Press.
Lawrence, Alan (1991) *Mao Zedong, a Bibliography*, New York: Greenwood Press.
Li Zhisui (1994), *The Private Life of Chairman Mao: The Memoirs of Mao's Private Physician*, London: Chatto and Windus.
Paloczi Horvath, Gyorgy (1973) *Mao Tse-tung: Emperor of the Blue Ants*, Westport Conn.: Greenwood Press.
Payne, Robert (1969) *Mao Tse-tung*, New York: Weybridge and Talley.
Pye, Lucien (1976) *Mao Tse-tung, the Man in the Leader*, New York: Basic Books.
Schram, Stuart R. (1963) *The Political Thought of Mao Tse-tung*, London and New York: Frederick A. Praeger.
—— (1966) *Mao Tse-tung*, Harmondsworth: Penguin.
Snow, Edgar (1938) *Red Star over China*, New York: Random House.
Spence, Jonathan (1999) *Mao*, London: Weidenfeld and Nicolson.
Terrill, Ross (*c.*1980) *Mao: A Biography*, New York: Harper and Row.
Wilson, Dick (1980) *The People's Emperor, Mao: A Biography of Mao Tse-tung*, Garden City, New York: Doubleday.
—— ed. (1977) *Mao Tse-tung in the Scales of History*, Cambridge: Cambridge University Press.

Reviews of Mao: The Unknown Story

Anne-Marie Brady, 'Privileged Revision', *Christchurch Press*, 25 June 2005.

Delia Davin, in this volume.

James Heartfield, 'Mao: The End of the Affair', Spiked Essays, available at: http://www.spiked-online.com/articles/0000000-CAC41.htm

Hamish McDonald, 'Throwing the Book at Mao', *Melbourne Age*, 8 October 2005, available at: http://www.theage.com.au/news/books/throwing-the-book-at-mao/2005/10/06/1128562936768.html

Andrew Nathan, in this volume.

Jonathan Spence, in this volume.

Arthur Waldron, in this volume.

Jeffrey N. Wasserstrom (2005) 'Mao as Monster, 1-sided book about the Chinese leader sometimes blurs the line between biography and fiction', *Chicago Tribune*, 6 November.

Notes

Introduction

1 Lisa Allardice, 'This book will shake the world', *The Guardian*, 26 May 2005.
2 Nicholas D. Kristof, '"Mao": The Real Mao', *The New York Times*, 23 October 2005.
3 Simon Sebag Montefiore, 'History: Mao by Jung Chang and Jon Halliday', *The Sunday Times*, 29 May 2005.
4 Donald Morrison, 'Taking Aim at Mao', *Time*, 6 June 2005.
5 Michiko Kakutani, 'China's Monster, Second to None', *The New York Times*, 21 October 2005.
6 George Walden, 'The True Colour of Monster Mao', *Daily Mail*, 27 May 2005.
7 Hu Weizhen, Hu Zongnan's son, is said to have planned to sue the publisher and was supported by the Taiwan alumni of the Whampoa Military School's Seventh Branch, who followed Hu in the war years. At the same time, unspecified scholars are reported as saying that Chang and Halliday's materials 'cannot be said to be complete or reliable'. Under these pressures, Yuanliu invited the academician Chen Yung-fa to assess the matter. Chen declared that 'opinions can be publicized so that people can make their own assessments and criticisms'. However, he also said that Jung Chang's work contained too many preconceived opinions about Mao and that 'the relationship between the evidence and the conclusions is not tight, so this cannot be treated as a scholarly work'. See Huang Kun, Chinesenewsnet, 21 April 2006; http://zonaeuropa.com/20060506_1. htm; and comments by Jung Chang herself, *TalkAsia* interview, 27 July 2005, and by her brother Zhang Pu in *Kaifang* (Hong Kong), May 2006.
8 The book, published in February 1938, went under the title *Xixing manji* (Random notes on a journey to the West), in an attempt to avoid provoking the authorities.
9 In Marxism Research Net, 25 May 2006; available at http://www.chinaelections.org/ NewsInfo.asp?NewsID=87796.
10 'Mao Zedong: Bixu zhidao de gushi' (Mao: The story that must be known), *Kaifang* (Hong Kong), no. 239, November 2006, pp. 61–3.
11 'The Chinese Revolution and Conspiracy Historiography', 30 March 2006, http://tieba. baidu.com/f?ct=335675392&tn=baiduPostBrowser&sc=707331071&z=9
12 Examples include comments entered into BBCChina.com and the website 'Chinese in Britain'. Chinese students also challenged Chang at her many promotion tours and talks in the UK and other countries. Examples of such reactions include Jin Bi's blog of 16 October 2005, at http://blog.wenxuecity.com/myblog.php?blogID=6642 and Qin Ge in www.boxun.com, 29 May 2005.
13 The Mao book also contradicts various assertions in Chang's *Wild Swans*, as Delia Davin shows in her review.
14 Kong Dongmei, 'Mao Zedong Liu Shaoqi houren de yi ci juhui' (A gathering of the families of Mao Zedong and Liu Shaoqi) *Zhongguo qingnian bao* (China Youth Daily),

13 October 2004. Kong Dongmei is Mao's granddaughter. The report was proofread by Liu Yuan, Liu Shaoqi's son, who was also present at the gathering.

15 Geremie Barmé, in this volume.

16 Timothy Cheek, in this volume.

17 Cited in Allardice, 'This book will shake the world'.

18 Jeffrey N. Wasserstrom, 'Review of *Mao: The Unknown Story*', *The Chicago Tribune*, 6 November 2005.

19 'Too Much Hate, Too Little Understanding', *The Sunday Independent*, 5 June 2005, the first critical review of the book to appear in the UK.

20 Li Zhisui, *The Private Life of Chairman Mao: The Memoirs of Mao's Personal Physician*, New York: Random House, 1994.

21 The best recent general book that makes this point is Peter Zarrow, *China in War and Revolution, 1895–1949*, London: Routledge, 2005.

22 Chen Duxiu, 'Zhi Zhonggong zhongyang (guanyu Zhongguo geming wenti)' (To the Central Committee of the Chinese Communist Party [on the question of the Chinese Revolution]), in *Chen Duxiu shuxin ji* (Chen Duxiu's letters), edited by Shui Ru, Beijing: Xinhua chuban she, 1987, pp. 434–54, at p. 449.

23 Cf. Tong Shijun, 'Zhongguo xiandai sixiang shi shang de minzhu guannian: Yige yi Li Dazhao wei zhuyao wen ben de taolun' (The concept of 'democracy' in China's modern thought: A discussion of Li Dazhao's texts), in Yang Guorong, ed., *Zhongguo xiandaihua jincheng de renwen xiangdu* (The human dimension of China's moderniza-tion process) Shanghai: Huadong Normal University Press, 2006, chapter 8.

24 Stuart R. Schram, 'Mao Zedong a Hundred Years On: The Legacy of a Ruler', in *Mao Zedong and the Chinese Revolution*, edited by Gregor Benton, 4 vols, London: Routledge, 2008, vol. 4, pp. 384–403, at p. 397.

25 Maurice Meisner, 'The Significance of the Chinese Revolution in World History', *London: LSE Asia Research Centre Working Papers* 1, 1999, p. 1 and 12.

26 Barry Naughton, 'The Third Front: Defence Industrialisation in the Chinese Interior', *China Quarterly*, no. 115 (September 1988), pp. 351–86. Chris Bramall notes that 'con-sumption grew slowly in Maoist China primarily because of the American threat … China could only have avoided this fate by surrendering her sovereignty'. *In Praise of Maoist Economic Planning: Living Standards and Economic Development in Sichuan since 1931*, Oxford: Clarendon, 1993, p. 336.

27 'A Great Leap Backward', *The Guardian*, 23 July 2005.

28 Lu Aiguo and Manuel Montes, eds, *Poverty, Income Distribution and Well-Being in Asia During the Transition*, Basingstoke: Palgrave, 2002, pp. 8–9. See also Amartya Sen on 'China's excellent achievements' in raising the quality of life for women in education, health, employment and other aspects of gender equality in *Development as Freedom*, New York: Knopf, 2000, p. 17.

29 Anonymous, 'Mao Zedong Forever Our Leader! A Statement in Commemoration of the 28th Anniversary of the Passing of Mao Zedong,' in *Mao Zedong and the Chinese Revolution*, vol. 4, pp. 180–2.

30 This is a theme of Mobo Gao, *The Battle for China's Past: Mao and the Cultural Revolution*, London: Pluto Press, 2008.

31 '*Wild Swans* and Mao's Agrarian Strategy', *China Review*, August 1995; quoted in Henry C. K. Liu, 'Mao and Lincoln', *Asia Times online*, http://www.atimes.com/atimes/China/FD01Ad04.html, accessed 17 October 2008. See also Carl Riskin, 'Seven Questions about the Chinese Famine of 1959–61', *Chinese Economic Review*, vol. 9, no. 2 (autumn 1998), pp. 111–24.

32 See, for examples, Penny Kane, *Famine in China, 1959–61*, London: Macmillan, 1988; Justin Yifu Lin and Dennis Tao Yang, 'Food Availability, Entitlement and the Chinese Famine', *Economic Journal*, vol. 110 (460), January 2000, pp. 136–58; and Li Chengrui, 'Da yuejin yinqi de renkou biandong' (Demographic change caused by the Great Leap)', *Dangshi yanjiu* (Communist Party history research), no. 2, 1997, pp. 97–110.

33 Jack Gray, 'Mao in Perspective', in *Mao Zedong and the Chinese Revolution*, vol. 4, pp. 425–5, at p. 431.
34 Quoted in Amartya Sen, 'Nobody Need Starve', *Granta*, no. 52 (winter 1995), pp. 213–10.
35 In an interview about the book broadcast on 24 June 2005, on the BBC's Hardtalk Extra, Chang told Mishal Husain that Mao was as evil as Hitler and Stalin.
36 Chang and Halliday did briefly respond to Andrew Nathan's review in *The London Review of Books*, but they refused permission for their response to be reprinted alongside the review in vol. 4 of *Mao Zedong and the Chinese Revolution*.

3 Portrait of a monster

1 See S. Bernard Thomas, *Season of High Adventure: Edgar Snow in China* (University of California Press, 1996), pp. 132–9.
2 Ibid., p. 147.
3 Zhang Zhizhong, *Huiyilu* (Beijing: Literary and Historical Source Publishing House, 1985), in two volumes, especially p. 109, 111, 116–17, 123, 139.
4 See Jonathan Mirsky's review, *The New York Review*, 17 November 1994.
5 Xiao Sike, *Chaoji shenpan* (Jinan Publishing House, 1992), two volumes, 'three-hour transcript', pp. 87–91.

4 The portrayal of opportunism, betrayal and manipulation in Mao's rise to power

1 Mao Zedong, 'Marginal Notes to: Friedrich Paulsen, A System of Ethics', in Stuart R. Schram, ed., *Mao's Road to Power: Revolutionary Writings, 1912–1949*, vol. 1, *The Pre-Marxist Period, 1912–1920*, New York: M. E. Sharpe, 1992, pp. 175–313, at pp. 201–5, 209, 211 and 257.
2 For Borodin's views, see Warren Kuo, *Analytical History of the Chinese Communist Party*, Taipei: Institute of International Relations, 4 vols, 1968–1971, vol. 1, p. 323.
3 Chen Duxiu, *et al.*, 'An Outline of Our Political Views', 15 December 1929, in *The Rise to Power of the Chinese Communist Party: Documents and Analysis*, edited by Tony Saich, Armonk: M. E. Sharpe, 1994, pp. 414–28.
4 Mao Zedong, 'Evening School Journal, Volume One', pp. 145–56, at p. 156; 'Notice from the *Xiang River Review*', p. 354; 'Letter to Li Jinxi' and 'Business Regulations', p. 538 and 414–15 (all in Stuart R. Schram, *Mao's Road to Power*, vol. 1).
5 Otto Braun, *Chinesische Aufzeichnungen, 1932–1939*, Berlin: Dietz Verlag, 1973, pp. 118–21.
6 These points are argued in Gregor Benton, *Mountain Fires: The Red Army's Three-Year War in South China, 1934–1938*, Berkeley: University of California Press, 1992, pp. 20–5.
7 Warren Kuo, *Analytical History*, vol. 3, pp. 13–16.
8 Peng Dehuai, *Memoirs of a Chinese Marshal: The Autobiographical Notes of Peng Dehuai, 1898–1974*, translated by Zheng Longpu, Beijing: Foreign Languages Press, 1984, p. 360.
9 Otto Braun, *Chinesische Aufzeichnungen*, pp. 124–25.
10 Qin Xiaoyi, Chen Jingzhi, Wu Baiqing, Xu Zhaorui, Deng Yaoqiu and Zeng Baiyun, compilers, *Zongtong Jiang gong dashi changbian zuogao* (First draft of a detailed record of important events in the life of President Chiang), Taibei: No publisher listed, 1978, vol. 2, p. 293.
11 Academia Historica, Chiang Kai-shek Papers, *Tejiao dang'an* (Archive of specially assigned work), 080102–068, 08A-00697 and 080102–068, 08A-00670, provide details of military reforms being examined in 1934, the year the Long March started. Other entries have details of earlier and later reforms.
12 Academia Historica, Chiang Kai-shek Papers, *Shilüe gaoben* (Official diary), entries for 10 and 30 May 1935.

13 Qin Xiaoyi, Chen Jingzhi, Wu Baiqing, Xu Zhaorui, Deng Yaoqiu and Zeng Baiyun, compilers, *Jiang gong dashi changbian*, vol. 3, p. 119.
14 Personal communication from Hamish MacDonald to Steve Tsang, 21 September 2005.
15 Otto Braun, *Chinesische Aufzeichnungen*, pp. 165–6.
16 Peng Dehuai, *Memoirs*, pp. 371–2.
17 These publications are cited in Li Anbao, *Changzheng shi* (History of the Long March), Beijing: Zhongguo qingnian chuban she, 1986, p. 188; Guofang daxue dangshi zhenggong jiaoyanshi, eds, *Changzheng xin tan* (New explorations in the Long March), Beijing: Jiefang jun chuban she, 1986, pp. 259–60; and Wang Tingke, *Hongjun changzheng yanjiu* (Research on the Red Army's Long March), Chengdu: Sichuan sheng shehui kexue yuan chuban she, 1985, p. 131.
18 Cited in Wang Tingke, *Hongjun*, p. 97 and 113.
19 Qin Xiaoyi, Chen Jingzhi, Wu Baiqing, Xu Zhaorui, Deng Yaoqiu and Zeng Baiyun, compilers, *Jiang gong dashi changbian*, vol. 3, p. 195.
20 'Chengdu zhuandian' (Special Chengdu telegram), in *Gongfei xi cuan ji* (A record of the communist bandits' flight to the west), vol. 13, p. 464, cited in Li, *Changzheng shi*, p. 178.
21 Chiang's telegram cited in Zhang Boyan, Yang Xueduan, Zhu Jiewu and Zhang Huaiyou, 'Ershisi jun zai Chuankang bianqu zujie hongjun de shikuang' (The actual situation in which the 24th Army intercepted the Red Army in the Chuankang border region), in Zhongguo renmin zhengzhi xieshang huiyi quanguo weiyuanhui ziliao yanjiu weiyuanhui, eds, *Wenshi ziliao xuanji* (Historical Materials), Beijing: Zhongguo wenshi chuban she, 1979, vol. 62, p. 149.
22 Zhang Boyan, Yang Xueduan, Zhu Jiewu and Zhang Huaiyou, 'Ershisi jun', p. 166. Li Quanshan is written Li Jinshan in some sources. The characters jin and quan are similar and easily confused.
23 Ibid., pp. 167–8.
24 Zheng Guangjin and Fang Shike, *Zhongguo hongjun changzheng ji* (A record of the Chinese Red Army's Long March), No place given: Henan renmin chuban she, 1987, pp. 454–7.
25 Wang Tingke, *Hongjun*, p. 133, citing Nationalist military archives.
26 Liu Bingrong, *Hong yi fangmian jun jishi* (Record of the First Front Red Army), 4 vols, Beijing: Renmin chuban she, 2003, vol. 4, p. 2039. That no casualties among the twenty-two were admitted at the time was clearly a case of wartime propaganda.
27 Chiang Kai-shek, *Shilüe gaoben*, entry for 25 December 1935.
28 Ibid., entries for 14, 24 and 25 December 1935.
29 Ibid., entry for 15 December 1935. This is confirmed by Zhang in his personal account dictated after his release from house arrest, in Zhang Xueliang and Wang Shujun, *Zhang Xueliang koushu zizhuan* (Zhang Xueliang's oral autobiography), Hong Kong: Xiangjiang shidai chuban she, 2004, pp. 310–20.
30 For the sources on which this N4A section is based, see Gregor Benton, *New Fourth Army: Communist Resistance along the Yangtze and the Huai, 1938–1941*, Berkeley: University of California Press, 1999, chapters 13–15.
31 Chiang Kai-shek, *Shilüe gaoben*, entries for 8 August 1940, and 13 and 17 January 1941.
32 Ibid., entry for 23 January 1941.
33 Ibid., entry for 4 November 1940.
34 Ibid., entry for 10 October 1940.
35 Ibid., entries for 9, 14, 18, and 30 November 1943. The launch of the campaign, to be spearheaded by Wei-kuo's unit, the New First Corps, was later deferred.
36 Chiang Ching-kuo, *Fengyu zhong de ningqing* (Calm in the midst of a storm), Taibei: Zhengzhong shuju, 1988, p. 55.
37 Chiang Kai-shek, *Shilüe gaoben*, entry for 19 April 1937. This source is full of outbursts reflecting what Chiang thought of key events and individuals.

38 Fudan daxue lishixi, eds and trans., *Riben diguo zhuyi duiwai qinlüe shiliao xuanbian* (Selected historical materials on Japanese imperialist aggression), Shanghai: Renmin chuban she, 1983, pp. 240–1.

39 Wang Fu, *Rijun qin Hua zhanzheng, 1931–1945* (The Japanese war of aggression against China, 1931–1945), Shenyang: Liaoning renmin chuban she, 1990, vol. 1, pp. 577–8.

40 Ma Zhendu, *Cansheng: Kangzhan zhengmian zhanchang da xieyi* (Horrendous victory: A big picture of the main battles of the War of Resistance), Guilin: Guangxi shifan daxue chuban she, 1993, p. 111 (citing a Japanese Defence Ministry account). A standard Japanese division had about 18,000 men.

41 Qin Xiaoyi, Chen Jingzhi, Wu Baiqing, Xu Zhaorui, Deng Yaoqiu and Zeng Baiyun, compilers, *Jiang gong dashi changbian*, vol. 4, pt 1, p. 74. Six months of military supplies was the maximum the Chinese could manage at the time.

42 Wang Fu, *Rijun qin Hua zhanzheng*, p. 574.

43 Jiang Yongqing, *Kangzhan shilun* (On the history of the War of Resistance), Taibei: Dongda tushu gongsi, 1995, p. 272, quoting the 7 August entry of the diary of Wang Shijie.

44 Hsi-sheng Ch'i, *Nationalist China at War*, Ann Arbor: University of Michigan Press, 1982, p. 42.

45 Chiang Kai-shek, *Shilüe gaoben*, entries for 9 and 30 July 1935 (including a summary of a defence plan) and 14 March 1936.

46 Zhang Zhizhong, *Zhizhong huiyilu* (Memoirs of Zhang Zhizhong), Beijing: Wenshi ziliao chuban she, 1985. Chang and Halliday cite p. 117, which does not deal with the incident. Zhang recalls the incident on p. 120, where he merely says: 'On August 9, 1997, the Japanese officer Oyama clashed with our forces at Hongqiao Airport and was killed; an emergency descended on Shanghai'.

47 Ibid., pp. 121–5.

48 Lu Yang, 'Yunchou weiwo, jinglun tianxia: Zhou Enlai lingdao yishu tanwei' (Devising strategies within a command tent, applying statecraft throughout the world: exploring Zhou Enlai's art of leadership), http://www.people.com.cn/BIG5/shizheng/8198/9403/34150/ 2543612.html, accessed November 22, 2005.

49 Xiong's autobiography is Xiong Xianghui, *Wo de qingbao yu waijiao shengya* (My career in spying and diplomacy), Beijing: Zhonggong dangshi chuban she, 1999.

50 Chiang Ching-kuo, *Fengyu zhong de ningqing*, pp. 275–82. Hu's conduct contrasts with the CCP's efforts to capture Chiang while he was in Chengdu in December 1949. See Chen Yu, *Jiang Jieshi zai dalu zuihou yibai tian* (Chiang Kai-shek's last hundred days on the mainland), Taibei: Babilun chuban she, 1995, pp. 310–17.

5 The new number one counter-revolutionary inside the party

1 One could say that a standard, academic version of these stories appears in John King Fairbank and Denis Twitchett, eds, *The Cambridge History of China*, vol. 12 *Republican China, 1912–1949*, Part 1, Cambridge: Cambridge University Press, 1983, and John King Fairbank, Albert Feuerwerker and Denis Twitchett, eds, *The Cambridge History of China*, vol. 13: *Republican China, 1912–1949*, Part 2, Cambridge: Cambridge University Press, 1986.

2 Personal communication with Dr Teiwes, 8 August 2005; used with permission.

3 Noriyuki Tokuda, 'Yenan Rectification Movement: Mao Tse-tung's Big Push Towards Charismatic Leadership', *Developing Economies*, vol. 9, no. 1 (1971), and Timothy Cheek, 'The Fading of Wild Lilies: Wang Shiwei and Mao Zedong's Yan'an Talks in the First CPC Rectification Movement', *The Australian Journal of Chinese Affairs*, no. 11 (1984), esp. pp. 44–6. See also Merle Goldman, *Literary Dissent in Communist China*, Cambridge MA: Harvard University Press, 1967 and Dai Qing, *Wang Shiwei and 'Wild Lilies': Rectification and Purges in the Chinese Communist Party, 1942–1944*, Armonk: M. E. Sharpe, 1994.

4 H. C. Chuang makes a careful study of this campaign language in 'The Great Proletarian Cultural Revolution: A Terminological Study', *Studies in Chinese Communist Terminology*, no. 12, Center for Chinese Studies, University of California, Berkeley, 1970.

5 Which, as with most names, Chang and Halliday give in modified Wade-Giles romanization as Chang Kuo-tao.

6 Sima Lu, *Douzheng shiba nian* (Eighteen years of struggle), Hong Kong: Yazhou chuban she, 1952.

7 John King Fairbank, Albert Feuerwerker and Denis Twitchett, eds, *The Cambridge History of China*, vol. 13, Part 2, p. 576.

8 Joshua A. Fogel, 'Mendacity and Veracity in the Recent Chinese Communist Memoir Literature', in Timothy Cheek and Tony Saich, eds, *New Perspectives on State Socialism in China*, Armonk: M. E. Sharpe, 1997, pp. 354–57; quote from p. 357.

9 As Jonathan Spence has shown in the instance of Chang and Halliday's use of Super Trial (Chaoji shenpan) concerning the case Ye Qun (Lin Biao's wife), see Jonathan Spence, in this volume.

10 For example, see John King Fairbank and Denis Twitchett, *The Cambridge History of China*, and the companion volume.

11 For thoughtful examples of the questions recent scholarship has addressed when researching Mao, see Jeffrey Wasserstrom, 'Mao Matters: A Review Essay', *China Review International*, vol. 3, no. 1 (Spring 1996), pp. 1–21, and Brantly Womack, 'Mao Before Maoism', *The China Journal*, no. 46 (July 2001), pp. 95–117.

12 *Mao's Road to Power*, Armonk: M. E. Sharpe, vol. 1 (1992) and following; vol. 7 of this title, covering texts from 1939 to 1941, came out in 2005.

13 David E. Apter and Tony Saich, *Revolutionary Discourse in Mao's Republic*, Cambridge: Harvard University Press, 1994; see also Saich's own documentary collection, *The Rise to Power of the Chinese Communist Party: Documents and Analysis*, Armonk: M. E. Sharpe, 1996, and his key assessment of the party history issue in Yan'an, 'Writing or Rewriting History: The Construction of the Maoist Resolution on Party History', in Tony Saich and Hans van de Ven, eds, *New Perspectives on the Chinese Communist Revolution*, Armonk: M. E. Sharpe, 1995, pp. 299–338.

14 See Frederick Teiwes and Warren Sun, 'From a Leninist to a Charismatic Party: The CCP's Changing Leadership, 1937–1945', in Tony Saich and Hans van de Ven, *New Perspectives*, pp. 339–87, and their fuller treatment in their book, *The Formation of the Maoist Leadership: From the Return of Wang Ming to the Seventh Party Congress*, London: Contemporary China Institute, 1994.

15 See Dai Qing, *Wang Shiwei and 'Wild Lilies'*.

16 See Frederick Teiwes and Warren Sun, 'From a Leninist to a Charismatic Party'; Roderick MacFarquhar, *Origins of the Cultural Revolution*, 3 vols, New York: Columbia University Press, 1974, 1983, 1997; Roderick MacFarquhar and Michael Schoenhals, *Mao's Last Revolution*, Cambridge: Harvard University Press, 2006; Frederick Teiwes and Warren Sun, *The Politics of Transition in China, 1972–1982*, vol. 1, Armonk: M. E. Sharpe, 2006.

17 Philip Short, *Mao: A Life*, New York: Henry Holt, 2000.

6 Pitfalls of charisma

1 Li Zhisui, *The Private Life of Chairman Mao*, London: Chatto and Windus, 1994. Chinese readers are also privy to Li's text in a Hong Kong translation (traditional characters) as well as to several other books of this ilk, usually published in Greater China and smuggled in – cf. Jing Fuzi, *Mao Zedong he tade nürenmen* (Mao Zedong and his women), Taipei: Lianjing chuban she, 1990, and Shan Shaojie, *Mao Zedong zhizheng chun qiu, 1949–1976* (Mao Zedong in power), Hong Kong: Mingjing chuban she, 2000. *The China Journal* devoted a review section to Li's book (no. 35 [January 1996], pp. 97–127).

2 See, *inter alia*, Jonathan Spence, Andrew Nathan and Delia Davin, all in this volume, and numerous perceptive reviews by capable journalists. Thus far, the critical controversy has been sharp, due no doubt not only to the massive scholarly apparatus but to authorial assertions of certainty, particularly in the imputation of motives, sometimes inspiring some equally assertive put-downs.

3 Chen Jian, *Mao's China and the Cold War*, Chapel Hill: The University of North Carolina Press, 2001.

4 See Barry Naughton, 'The Third Front', *The China Quarterly*, no. 115 (September 1988), pp. 351–86.

5 See Brahma Chellaney's review, available at http://www.japantimes.co.jp/cgi-bio/makepriV.pl57.htm, accessed 17 October 2005.

6 Cf. Frederick C. Teiwes, *Politics at Mao's Court: Gao Gang and Party Factionalism in the Early 1950s*, Armonk: M. E. Sharpe, 1990; also Jing Huang, *Factionalism in Chinese Communist Politics*, New York: Cambridge University Press, 2000.

7 See also Paul Wingrove, 'Mao's Conversations with the Soviet Ambassador, 1953–55', Cold War International History Project, Woodrow Wilson International Center for Scholars, Washington DC, *Working Paper* no. 36, April 2002.

8 Li Rui, *Lushan huiyi shilu* (A true record of the Lushan Conference), Beijing: Chunqiu chuban she, 1989.

9 Delia Davin, in this volume.

10 For example, cf. Jing Huang, *Factionalism*, pp. 173–97.

11 The complete text of Mao's self-criticism, in which he accepted personal responsibility for the Leap and promised to promote greater democratic centralism within the Party, is in Shan Shaojie, *Mao Zedong*, pp. 231–5.

12 Roderick MacFarquhar, *The Origins of the Cultural Revolution*, London: Oxford University Press, 1997, vol. III.

13 Cf. Helmut Martin, *Cult and Canon: The Origins and Development of State Maoism*, Armonk: M. E. Sharpe, 1982.

14 Anita M. Andrew and John A. Rapp, *Autocracy and China's Rebel Founding Emperors: Comparing Chairman Mao and Ming Taizu*, Lanham: Rowman and Littlefield, 2000.

7 'I'm So Ronree'

1 Geremie R. Barmé, *Shades of Mao, The Posthumous Cult of the Great Leader*, Armonk, NY: M. E. Sharpe, 1996.

2 Jiang Zemin, 'Zai Mao Zedong tongzhi danchen 100 zhounian jinian dahuishang de jianghua (1993 nian 12 yue 26 ri)' (Speech on the occasion of the centenary of Comrade Mao Zedong's birth), *Renmin ribao*, 27 December 1993; and Barmé, *Shades of Mao*, p. 259.

3 Hu as reported in a Xinhua News Agency release dated 26 December 2003, 'Zhonggong zhongyang juxing jinian Mao Zedong tongzhi danchen 110 zhounian zuotanhui' (Symposium held on the occasion of the 110th anniversary of Comrade Mao Zedong's birth).

4 Li Jie, 'The Mao Phenomenon: A Survivor's Critique', in *Shades of Mao*, p. 141.

5 Li Jie, op. cit., p. 143.

6 I would note in passing, however, that given the use of powerful 'moral-evaluative' terminology in Chinese historiography, the Chang-Halliday book reads more 'naturally' in Chinese translation. On the importance of moral-evaluative language in modern Chinese, see my *In the Red: On Contemporary Chinese Culture*, New York: Columbia University Press, 1999, pp. 326–8.

7 *Morning Sun*, Boston: Long Bow Group, 2003. For the related website, see www.morning sun.org

8 See also Linda Jaivin's '"Wild History," A Review of *Mao: The Unknown Story*', *The Bulletin*, 9 August 2005.

9 See Lo Hui-min, 'The *Ching-shan Diary*: A Clue to its Forgery', *East Asian History*, no. 1 (June 1991), pp. 98–124. The diary and its notoriety resonate with the advent and influence in the early years of the new century of *The Tiananmen Papers*, but that is another subject, one that the Melbourne-based scholar Adam Driver has pursued in his research.

10 Lo, 'The *Ching-shan Diary*', op. cit., p. 104.

11 See Yun Yuding, Jingshan, *et al.*, *Guangxu huangdi waizhuan, Jingshan riji* (An informal biography of the Guangxu emperor, Jingshan diary), Chongqing: Chongqing chuban she, 1998, published in the series *Qingmo baishi jingxuan congshu* (Selected informal histories from the late Qing). In fact, the fake diary was accepted by communist writers cum-historians like Deng Liqun in the 1940s, so the present 'recuperation' of the work in China has a history of its own. See Lo, 'The *Ching-shan Diary*', p. 112, n. 71.

12 Barmé, 'Private Practice, Public Performance: The Cultural Revelations of Dr Li', *The China Journal*, no. 35 (January 1996), p. 126.

13 Chang and Halliday, *Mao: The Untold Story*, p. 546.

14 As Voltaire wrote of the 'despot': 'Now, the emperors of Turkey, Morocco, Hindustan and China were called despots by us; and we attach to this title the idea of a ferocious madman who heeds only his own whims'. Quoted in Alain Grosrichard, *The Sultan's Court: European Fantasies of the East*, translated by Liz Heron, London: Verso, 1998, p. 32. My thanks to Adam Driver for bringing this work to my attention.

15 An audio-visual clip of this sequence from the film can be found at http://www.team america.com

16 Founded 1928. Website: http://www.opusdei.org/

17 Probably the best-known exposés have been an account by Mao's erstwhile doctor (Li Zhisui), and the apparent inside story on the attempted coup by Mao's then designated successor (Lin Biao) and his flight and death in 1971 (Yao Ming-le 1983).

8 Mao and *The Da Vinci Code*

1 http://www.randomhouse.co.uk/catalog/book.htm?command=Search&db= main. txt&eqisbndata=0224071262

2 P. 19. As Nathan patiently explains in his review, the CCP was founded in 1921, although a couple of communist groups had been established the previous year. Spiro Agnew was Nixon's Vice President when the talks described on p. 604 took place.

9 Mao

1 Philip Short, *Mao: A Life*, London: Hodder and Stoughton, 1999; Ross Terrill, *Mao: A Bibliography*, revised and expanded edition, Stanford: Stanford University Press, 1999; Jonathan Spence, *Mao*, London: Phoenix, 2000; Lee Feigon, *Mao: A Reinterpretation*, Chicago: Ivan R. Dee, 2002; Delia Davin, *Mao Zedong*, Phoenix Mill: Sutton Publishing Limited, 1997; Shaun Breslin, *Mao*, London: Addison Wesley Longman, 1998; Michael J. Lynch, *Mao*, London: Routledge, 2004.

2 Mao Zedong, *Maozhu weikangao, 'sixiang wansui' beiji ji qita* (Unofficially published works of Mao Zedong, additional volumes of 'Long Live Mao Zedong's Thought' and other secret speeches of Mao), vol. 11B, Oakton, VI: Center for Chinese Research Materials, 1990, p. 80.

3 Mao Zedong, *Maozhu weikangao*, volume 13, p. 131.

4 Zhang Zhenglong, *Xuebai xuehong* (Snow is white but blood is red), Hong Kong: Dadi chuban she, 1991, pp. 441ff.

5 Hong Kong: Zhonghua ernü chuban she, 2000. A postscript said that one author had participated in the investigation of the Lin Liguo case (p. 507) but in any case, the book belongs to a genre the Chinese call 'wild history' (*yeshi*) or, at best, rapportage liter-ature, because it blends facts and fiction.

6 *Wo yu hongjun* (The Red Army and I), Hong Kong: Nanfeng chuban she, 1954.
7 *Wode huiyi* (My memoirs), 3 vols, Hong Kong: Mingbao yuekan chuban she, 1974.
8 'The Blooming Poppy under the Red Sun: The Yan'an Way and the Opium Trade,' in Tony Saich and Hans van de Ven, *New Perspectives on the Chinese Communist Revolution*, Armonk, NY: M. E. Sharpe, 1995.
9 *Hong taiyang shi zenyang shengqilai de* (How did the sun rise over Yan'an? A history of the Rectification Movement), Hong Kong: Zhongwen Daxue chuban she, 2000.
10 David E. Apter and Tony Saich, *Revolutionary Discourse in Mao's Republic*, Cambridge, MA: Harvard University Press, 1994.
11 Jung Chang with Jon Halliday, *Mme Sun Yat-Sen*, Harmondsworth, Middlesex: Penguin Books, 1986; Jung Chang, *Sun Yixian furen* (Mme Sun Yat-sen), Beijing: Zhongguo heping chuban she, 1988.
12 Guo Chen, *Teshu liandui* (A special company), Beijing: Nongcun duwu chuban she, 1985, pp. 198–9.
13 *Mao Zedong wenji* (The selected works of Mao Zedong) volume 7, Beijing: Renmin chuban she, 1999, p. 106.
14 *Mao Zedong wulüe* (The military strategy of Mao Zedong), Taipei: Huiming wenhua shiye youxian gongsi, 2002.
15 Mao Zedong, *Maozhu weikangao*, volume 11B, p. 68. Mao Zedong, *Jianguo yilai Mao Zedong wengao* (Manuscripts of Mao Zedong since the founding of the state), volume 7, Beijing: Zhongyang wenxian chuban she, 1992, p. 201.
16 Stuart R. Schram, ed., *Mao's Road to Power: Revolutionary Writings, 1912–1949*, vol. 1, Armonk: M. E. Sharpe, 1992, pp. xxxii–xli.
17 Schram, op. cit., pp. 204–7.
18 Schram, op. cit., pp. 277–8.
19 Harrison Salisbury, *The Long March: The Untold Story*, New York: Harper and Row, 1985, pp. 68–71, 120.
20 Yin Jiamin, *Hongqiang jianzheng lu* (Witness to the red wall), Beijing: Dangdai Zhongguo chuban she, 2004, vol. 3, pp. 1201–02. See also Salisbury, *Long March*, p. 120.
21 Mianhuai Mao Zedong editorial group, *Mianhuai Mao Zedong* (Cherish the memory of Mao Zedong), Beijing: Zhongyang wenxian chuban she, 1993, volume 2, p. 204.
22 Guo Chen, *Teshu liandui*, pp. 72–3.
23 *Renmin ribao* (People's Daily), September 25, 1996, in http://big5.china.com.cn/chinese/zhuanti/cz/681674.htm.

10 Jung Chang and Jon Halliday, *Mao: The Unknown Story*

1 Zhonggong zhongyang wenxian yanjiu shi, Zhonggong Hunan shengwei, *Mao Zedong zaoqi wengao* bianjizu, eds, *Mao Zedong zaoqi wengao, 1912.6–1920.11* (Early manuscripts of Mao Zedong, June 1912–November 1920), Changsha: Hunan chuban she, 1990, pp. 146–8.
2 Ibid., pp. 203–4.

11 *Mao: The Unknown Story*

1 Marc Gellman and Tom Hartman (2002), writing in the *Reader's Digest*, are even more inventive. They place Mao not only together with Hitler, Stalin, and Pol Pot but with Osama bin Laden.

12 A critique of Jung Chang and Jon Halliday, *Mao: The Unknown Story*

1 See the article at http://blog.chinesenewsnet.com/?p=3467, or the entire interview video at http://www.berm.co.nz/cgi-bin/video/play.cgi?lz1JaUtTdSM.

2 Available at: http://www2.chinesenewsnet.com/gb/MainNews/Opinion/2005_11_30_20_33_19_572.html.
3 Available at: http://news.creaders.net/china/newsViewer.php?language=gb2312&id=652625.

13 Mao lives

1 In Chinese translation, under the anodyne title *Record of a Journey to the West*, the book also made Mao a hero to many of his countrymen who had hitherto been ignorant even of his existence.
2 To be sure, some did get the story right, and from as early as the 1950s. They included, among others, the Hungarian Jesuit Ladislao La Dany, publisher of the authoritative Hong Kong weekly *China News Analysis*; Raymond J. de Jaegher, author of *The Enemy Within: An Eyewitness Account of the Communist Conquest of China* (1952); the German political scientist Juergen Domes, who was able to arrive at a figure of 10 million victims of Mao's 1959–61 famine in *Internal Politics of China, 1949–72* (1973); Edward Rice, former American consul general in Hong Kong and author of *Mao's Way* (1971); Ivan and Miriam London and their collaborator Ta-ling Lee, who in *The Revenge of Heaven: The Autobiography of a Red Guard* (1972) first brought solid documentation of the Cultural Revolution to an indifferent West; and Jean Pasqualini, son of a Corsican father and a Chinese mother, who after release from years in Chinese prison camps wrote *Prisoner of Mao* (1973) with the American journalist Rudolph Chelminski.
3 In a case of measure for measure, the doctors who diagnosed Mao with Lou Gehrig's disease in the mid-70s agreed not to inform him of it – lest, knowing his days were numbered, he unleash some final purge.
4 One example that can stand for many is a series of essays by Joseph W. Esherick about the Nationalist attempt in the civil war to capture the communist leadership through a pincer campaign against Yan'an. Chang and Halliday state flatly that the Nationalist commander was a secret communist who botched the operation on purpose. They make no reference to Esherick, who happens to be favourably disposed to Mao and the Chinese communists but whose careful research does not support this conclusion.
5 'Eichmann: The Simplicity of Evil', *Commentary*, July–August 2005.

Index

agriculture 68, 100, 150, 156, *see also* famine
Allardice, Lisa 1, 90, 91, 96
arms industry 66, 100, 157
arms trade 59, 66, 71, 100, 114, 144, 150, 167, 169, 174

Barmé, Geremie R. 3, 6, 9, 64, 73–83, 132
Benton, Gregor 3, 43–54, 57, 131
Bolshevism 7, 16

capitalism 57, 70, 111–12, 132, 157–8, 179
centralism 7, 69
Chan, Alfred 4, 99–108, 132
character assassination 2, 22, 28, 32, 64–5, 92, 117, 124, 128, 129, 136, 178
Cheek, Timothy 4, 55–63, 131
Chen Duxiu 7, 44, 124, 181
Chen Yung-fa 4, 102, 111–18, 161
Chiang Kai-shek 1, 8, 17, 18, 21, 23, 25–6, 28, 31, 33, 34, 35–6, 39, 46, 54, 56, 59, 65, 99, 101, 113, 115, 126, 127, 138, 139–40, 143, 144, 145, 149, 166, 169, 178, 180, 181, 182, 183, 185
Comintern 18, 24, 32, 34, 35, 43, 44, 50, 169, 170, 181
Confucianism 44, 76, 102
conjecture 87, 89, 96, 115
conspiracy 6, 48, 69–70, 87–96, 127, 171, 173, 181
corruption 64, 71, 72, 160
Cuba 27, 67
Cultural Revolution 3, 4, 8, 16, 19, 23, 26, 27, 31, 33, 34, 38, 55, 58, 62, 65, 70, 71, 73, 74–7, 80, 91, 93, 112, 114, 127, 154–8, 166, 167, 169, 176, 177
culture 7, 32, 34, 70, 71, 75, 76, 80, 119, 129, 157

Dadu Bridge 17, 23, 46, 47, 126, 136, 140–2, 183
Dalai Lama 3, 120
Davin, Delia 4, 15–20, 69, 90, 93, 95, 126
deaths of Chinese 9–11, 16, 20, 33, 81, 91, 99, 102, 105, 113, 116, 125, 126, 137–8, 147, 148–9, 151–5, 158, 170, 174
democracy 7, 69, 127, 129, 132, 166–7, 182
Deng Xiaoping 4, 9, 19, 22, 55, 69, 70, 73, 74, 96, 111, 112, 114, 117, 127, 149, 150, 158, 159, 173, 185
development: military 17–18, 39, 59, 66, 68, 82, 100, 114, 117, 150, 151, 167; socio-economic 8, 57, 66, 67, 97, 100–102, 135
Dittmer, Lowell 4, 64–72

economic isolation 18
Eisenhower, Dwight 66, 151
evidence: accurate 25, 96, 107, 152, 167, 170, 172; evaluation of 20, 31, 43, 56, 61, 95, 114–15, 178, 180, 185, 121–3; ignored 6, 10, 17, 43, 45, 47, 49, 51, 53, 55, 57, 58, 61, 63, 89, 93, 95–6, 100, 101, 102, 121, 125, 130, 139–40, 172, 177, 178, 180; interpretation of 3, 17, 26, 29, 68–9, 89, 90, 96, 105, 126, 132, 136–60, 178–80; interview 3, 15, 21, 22–4, 25, 30, 31, 36, 37, 46, 57, 58, 61, 64–5, 69, 77, 81, 94–5, 96, 97, 99, 112, 120–1, 126, 128, 130, 135, 136, 140, 165, 171, 176, 183, 184; lack of 6, 18, 45, 51, 53, 87, 122–5, 129, 137–61, 123–4, 139–40, 149; memoirs 3, 15, 16, 22, 24, 26, 27, 35–7, 53, 59–60, 64, 93, 96, 99, 101, 121, 130, 143; misquoted 26–7, 36, 44–5, 53, 58, 61, 100, 106–7, 122, 125, 126, 128, 136, 180;

evidence (*continued*)
    unreferenced 6, 22, 61, 94, 124–5, 180;
    unreliable 18, 19, 21–6, 28, 37–8, 45,
    46, 51, 57–60, 89, 90, 94, 95, 96, 97,
    101, 102, 124, 130–1, 180

famine 8, 10, 16, 20, 28, 31, 33, 34, 62, 68,
    71, 100, 102, 113, 114, 130, 150, 151–3,
    156, 158, 170, 172

Gang of Four 38, 74, 82
Gao Gang 68, 159
Gao, Mobo 4, 119–34
Gong Chu 101, 121
Goodman, David S. G. 4, 5, 60, 87–98
grain requisitions 16, 34, 56, 100, 152
Great Leap Forward 4, 8, 9–11, 16, 31, 34,
    62, 68, 71, 91, 102, 114, 126, 150, 151,
    156, 166, 169, 173, 176
Guomindang (Nationalist Party) 1, 24, 43,
    51, 53, 55, 56, 102, 107, 111, 112, 140,
    141, 185

Han Suyin 26, 176
historical methodology 3, 4, 6, 8, 10, 36,
    65, 88–9, 90, 93, 105, 119, 125, 127–8,
    131, 177
Hitler, Adolf 1, 10–11, 34, 72, 75, 88, 111,
    119, 126–7, 129, 135, 136, 145, 148,
    158–9, 165, 167, 172
Holocaust 11, 165, 173
Hong Kong 36, 59
Hu Jintao 71, 73, 74, 111, 173
Hu Zongnan 2, 51, 53, 56, 115, 130, 147
Hundred Flowers 34, 68, 100, 166, 169
Hutton 1, 120

India 10, 21, 27, 51, 67, 158
individualism 7, 44, 103, 116

Japan 7, 8, 18, 25, 26, 28, 33, 34–6, 38,
    46, 48, 49–53, 55, 56, 58, 61, 68, 91, 96,
    100, 101, 105, 112–14, 120, 127, 143–5,
    146, 153, 166, 169, 183–4
Jiang Jingguo 17, 115
Jiang Qing 38, 70, 75–6, 80, 130
Jiang Zemin 71, 73, 74, 149, 173
Jiangxi Soviet 21, 25, 33, 34, 45, 46, 93,
    94, 101, 113, 115, 121–5, 137, 139
Jin Xiaoding 4, 128, 135–61

Kakutani, Michiko 1, 119, 125
Kang Sheng 56, 61, 113, 169

Khrushchev, Nikita 27, 65, 66–7, 70, 157,
    165, 171, 173
Kim Il-sung 28, 66, 83, 113, 114,
Kissinger, Henry 15, 81, 105, 170
Korea 8, 17, 18, 24, 26, 28, 34, 36, 64,
    65–6, 69, 82, 99, 105, 113, 114, 127,
    148–9, 151, 158, 166, 170, 178, 184
Kristof, Nicholas 1, 8, 90
Kuai Dafu 21, 79, 155, 156
Kuomintang *see* Guomindang

land reform 8, 121, 149, 178
landlords 8, 17, 32, 44, 121, 166
Li Dazhao 7, 181
Li Na 77, 130
Li Zhisui 6, 21, 37, 79, 93, 171
life expectancy 8–9, 20, 71
Lin Biao 19, 23, 28, 37, 38, 70, 101, 105,
    113, 127, 159
Lin Chun 1, 4
Liu Shaoqi 3, 4, 19, 22, 23, 28, 37, 55, 56,
    68, 69, 70, 93, 95, 96, 117, 120, 127,
    130, 144, 155, 156, 157, 159, 180,
    188
Long March 7, 17, 21, 23, 25, 30–1, 34,
    45–6, 51, 90–1, 93, 94, 100, 102, 106–7,
    115, 120, 126, 138, 139, 140, 142, 166,
    168, 171, 180, 182–3
Luding Bridge *see* Dadu Bridge

McLynn, Frank 5, 126
Manchuria 34, 36, 56, 68, 124, 127,
    147
Mao Anying 17, 23
Mao Zedong: family 17, 21, 22, 33, 37, 38,
    77, 82, 107, 112–13, 117, 120–1, 124,
    126, 129–30, 170; legacy 8, 16, 19–20,
    31, 57, 71, 73, 74, 135, 167, 173–5, 185;
    policies 9, 10, 16, 19, 30, 34, 58, 60, 68,
    69, 114, 155; use of terror 1, 18, 43, 54,
    56, 62, 72, 82, 99, 101, 105, 108, 113,
    116, 117–18, 138, 152; as tyrant 1, 6, 9,
    18, 19, 22, 28, 32–4, 43, 56–7, 65, 70,
    71, 74, 79, 81, 93, 99, 119, 168, 170,
    177–8
martyrs 7, 47, 137–8
Mongolia: Outer, 46, 59; Inner 154
Montefiore, Simon Sebag 1, 119
morality 32, 44, 92, 103–4, 113, 115–16,
    117
Moscow 7, 25–6, 27, 35, 43, 44, 48, 50–1,
    54, 59, 60, 66–7, 124, 125, 139, 144,
    157, 165, 168, 169, 170

Nathan, Andrew J. 4, 21–29, 90, 94, 119, 126, 131, 136, 180, 183, 184
Nehru 27, 67
Nixon, Richard 81, 105, 169
nuclear weapons 17–18, 27, 28, 33, 66–7, 101, 151

opium: addiction 47, 148; production 16, 54, 56, 96, 101, 113, 119, 147–8

Paulsen, Friedrich 16, 32, 44, 92, 103, 115, 178–9
Peng Dehuai 17, 27, 34, 39, 45, 47, 68, 69, 70, 105, 117, 127, 152, 159
Peng Zhen 27, 55, 70

Rectification Campaign 55, 56, 58, 61, 102, 113, 126, 146–7
Red Army 7, 25, 27, 30, 45, 47, 94–5, 107, 115, 121, 124, 126, 127, 138, 139–43
Red Guards 76, 112, 127, 156, 176
Russia 17–18, 22, 27–8, 32, 36, 37, 44, 45, 50–4, 56, 59, 68, 70, 73, 74, 80, 111–15, 117, 124, 127, 132, 139, 145, 153, 155, 156, 157–8, 159, 166, 167, 169, 170, 172, 181; agents 18, 26, 28, 35, 50–1, 53, 56, 102, 105, 139–40, 159, 181; archives 15, 21, 24, 31, 58, 59, 61, 65, 91, 99, 112, 140, 177; military power 34, 35, 58–9, 60, 65–7, 71, 124, 144, 151, 174

Schram, Stuart 4, 8, 60, 103, 176, 178, 179
Shao Lizi 48, 51–2, 115
Short, Philip 21, 62, 93, 128
Sino-Japanese War 7, 144, 146, 153, 178, 183
Snow, Edgar 2, 30, 122, 165–6, 178, 183
Song Qingling (Mme Sun Yat-sen) 18, 28, 102, 139, 181
sources *see* evidence
Soviet Union *see* Russia
Spence, Jonathan 4, 30–9, 90, 136
Stalin, Josef 1, 7, 25–6, 34–5, 36, 48, 50, 51, 52–3, 55, 56–7, 59, 60, 65–6, 68, 74, 78, 88, 92, 99, 105, 111–12, 113, 114, 119, 124, 126–7, 144, 147, 150, 159, 165, 167, 169, 173, 174, 184
Sun Yat-sen 182
superpowers 22, 56, 66, 81, 82, 100–1, 131, 150–1, 155–6, 158

Taiwan 27, 35, 36, 65, 66, 105, 111, 115, 147, 149, 166, 170, 171, 185
Teiwes, Frederick 57, 60, 61, 95, 120–1, 125, 177
Tito 65, 66
Trotskyism 3, 7, 124, 147
Tsang, Steve 4, 43–54, 57, 125, 131, 183
Tucheng battle 25, 102

United Nations 26, 105, 150
United States of America 2, 18, 26–7, 28, 31, 36, 39, 56, 64, 65, 66, 67, 81, 113, 117, 130, 150, 159, 166, 167, 170, 174, 184

Vietnam 67, 101, 105, 158, 166, 170, 184

Waldron, Arthur 4, 90, 165–75
Wang Guangmei 3, 19, 23, 37, 69, 120, 180
Wang Jiaxiang 60, 106
Wang Ming 23, 34, 56, 60, 114, 126, 159
Wang Shiwei 58, 61, 126, 147
Wasserstrom, Jeffrey 5, 90, 177
Wei Lihuang 56, 115, 147
Whampoa Academy 26, 35–6, 52
Wild Swans 1, 9, 15, 18, 24, 31, 56, 90, 91, 96, 97, 99, 112, 120, 127, 152, 160, 167, 176–8, 183
Willmott, Bill 4, 9, 176–86
women 4, 6, 7–8, 18, 38, 44, 56, 62, 107, 113, 115, 167, 170, 176, 180

Xi'an Incident 26–6, 48, 59, 113, 183

Yan'an 2, 16, 21, 22, 23, 31, 33, 49, 51, 53, 56, 58, 59, 60–1, 68, 96, 102, 112, 126, 146–8, 169, 170, 178, 182
Yang Kaihui 22, 112–13, 124
Yang Shangkun 21, 156

Zhang Guotao 34, 58–9, 101, 126, 169, 180, 182–3
Zhang Xueliang 48, 127
Zhang Zhizhong 26, 35–6, 37, 51, 52–3, 54, 115
Zhou Enlai 6, 19, 22, 25–6, 28, 34–6, 49, 68, 69, 70, 71, 81, 82, 102, 106, 114, 117, 121, 126–7, 145, 155, 156, 159, 170, 181
Zhu De 34, 106, 127, 144

*9 7 8 0 4 1 5 4 9 3 3 0 7 *

An environmentally friendly book printed and bound in England by www.printondemand-worldwide.com

PEFC Certified

This product is
from sustainably
managed forests
and controlled
sources

www.pefc.org

PEFC/16-33-415

This book is made of chain-of-custody materials; FSC materials for the cover and PEFC materials for the text pages.

#0194 - 090516 - C0 - 234/156/11 - PB - 9780415493307